GCSE BIOLOGY

LONGMAN REVISE GUIDES

SERIES EDITORS:
Geoff Black and Stuart Wall

TITLES AVAILABLE:
Biology
Business Studies
Chemistry
English
English Literature
Mathematics
Physics
World History

FORTHCOMING:
Art and Design
British and European History
Commerce
Computing
CDT:
    Design and Realisation
    Design and Technology
Economics
French
Geography
German
Home Economics
Office Studies

LONGMAN
REVISE
GUIDES

GCSE
BIOLOGY

Martin Barker

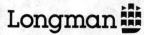

Longman

Longman Group UK Limited,
Longman House, Burnt Mill, Harlow,
Essex CM20 2JE, England
and Associated Companies throughout the world.

First published 1988

British Library Cataloguing in Publication Data

Barker, Martin
  Biology. — (Longman GCSE revise guides).
  1. Biology — Study and teaching (Secondary) —
  England 2. General Certificate of Secondary
  Education — Study guides
  I. Title
  574'.076 QH320.G7

ISBN 0-582-01577-4

Illustrated by Rebecca Bower, Brian Davis and Sarah Jane Sale.

Set in 9/12pt Century Book Roman

Printed and bound in Great Britain at
The University Printing House, Oxford.

C O N T E N T S

EDITORS' PREFACE

Longman Revise Guides are written by experienced examiners and teachers, and aim to give you the best possible foundation for success in examinations and other modes of assessment. Much has been said in recent years about declining standards and disappointing examination results. While this may be somewhat exaggerated, examiners are well aware that the performance of many candidates falls well short of their potential. The books encourage thorough study and a full understanding of the concepts involved and should be seen as course companions and study guides to be used throughout the year. Examiners are in no doubt that a structured approach in preparing for examinations and in presenting coursework can, together with hard work and diligent application, substantially improve performance.

The largely self-contained nature of each chapter gives the book a useful degree of flexibility. After starting with Chapters 1 and 2, all other chapters can be read selectively, in any order appropriate to the stage you have reached in your course. We believe that this book, and the series as a whole, will help you establish a solid platform of basic knowledge and examination technique on which to build.

Geoff Black & Stuart Wall

AUTHOR'S PREFACE

The emphasis throughout this book is on understanding biology as an integrated subject with many unifying themes. These are clearly identified within the text, and liberal use is made of cross-references so that the reader can pursue some of the implications of a given topic. Although the chapters and their contents are arranged in a fairly logical way, the order in which they are studied is not critical as each unit is quite self-contained. I especially want to thank Stuart Wall and Geoff Black for editorial advice, and also Guy and Julia Garfit and Mary Lince for their skilful conversion of my manuscript into something rather more elegant and meaningful.

I am most grateful for the expert and caring work done by Rebecca Bower and Brian Davis on many of the illustrations, and also for the dedicated removal of my typographic errors by Melanie Westwood.

I am particularly indebted to Des Wright for providing invaluable wisdom and biological insight during the preparation of this book. I dedicate this book to all my wonderful pupils, friends and family.

ACKNOWLEDGEMENTS

I gratefully acknowledge the permission granted by the following examining boards to print some of their specimen questions:
London and East Anglian Group (LEAG)
Midland Examining Group (MEG)
Northern Examining Association (NEA)
Northern Ireland Schools Examinations Council (NISEC)
Southern Examining Group (SEG)
University of Cambridge Local Examinations Syndicate (IGCSE)
Welsh Joint Education Committee (WJEC)
The photograph in Figure 4.17 is reproduced by permission of Philip Harris Biological Ltd., Figure 7.15 is from *GCSE Biology* by D.G. Mackean, after C.M. Jackson (John Murray), Figure 9.2 is reproduced by courtesy of the British Museum (Natural History). The photographs in Figure 9.4 were provided by Mr. John Haywood, Oxford University, Figure 9.6 is produced with permission from the journal *Heredity* (Longman), Figure 9.8 is based on a map which appeared originally in the *Scientific American*. Figure 10.3 is reproduced from *Life Story* by F.M. Sullivan (Oliver and Boyd), Figure 10.20 is taken from *Human Biology and Health* by Dorothy Baldwin (Longman), Figure 17.9 is from an examination question from The Associated Examining Board and Figure 17.14 is based on an illustration which appeared originally in *Human Populations* by David Hay. It is reproduced by permission of Penguin Books Limited.
Answers to any examination questions are my own and I accept full responsibility for them.

INTRODUCTION TO GCSE BIOLOGY

AIMS
ASSESSMENT
OBJECTIVES
CORE CONTENT
ASSESSMENT
TECHNIQUES
GRADE DESCRIPTIONS

GETTING STARTED

GCSE Biology has, like all GCSE subjects, evolved from the previous GCE 'O' level and CSE courses. However, both the **content** and the **methods of assessment** in GCSE are quite distinctive. Assessment means being 'graded' by performance in course work and examinations. One important feature of GCSE is the uniformity of standards which exists between the examining boards. This is the result of the commonly agreed **National Criteria**. One consequence of the National Criteria is that, within each subject, there is a similar approach to syllabuses and assessment methods between different examining boards. Differences in emphasis or even content *do* occur between examining boards (see Ch.3). However, the examining boards are required to state fairly specifically in their syllabuses what will be required of candidates.

G C S E   B I O L O G Y

The National Criteria for Biology are the basis by which biology syllabuses are designed and their assessment organised. The main components of the criteria are **aims**, **assessment objectives**, **core content**, **assessment techniques** and **grade descriptions**.

1 > AIMS

Biology courses are intended to be a worthwhile experience in their own right. Courses are also intended to be a preparation for subsequent activities, whether in employment or in further and higher education courses requiring an understanding of biology. The aims of all biology syllabuses include the development of an awareness and an interest in organisms and their relationships with each other and with humans. Biology is an *experimental* subject, and students are expected to be able to learn and use **practical skills**.

2 > ASSESSMENT OBJECTIVES

Only those educational aims that are *measurable* can be assessed. It is hoped, for example, that students will develop a 'respect for all life' but, whilst this is very important in biology, it cannot easily be assessed! There are two main types of ability being tested in GCSE Biology; each theme is worth approximately 50 per cent of the total marks.

Knowledge and understanding

Students should be familiar with the important ideas in biology, including the personal, social, economic and technological applications of the subject. The student should have an understanding of key words (terminology) in the subject.

Skills and processes

Students should be able to make observations and to draw appropriate conclusions based on the available information; this may be presented in various forms, or it may emerge from experimental work. Students are required to design, conduct and evaluate experiments. Experimental work and observational skill are allocated at least 20 per cent of the total marks in all syllabuses.

3 > CORE CONTENT

The core content, present in all biology syllabuses, is divided into four main themes. These are summarised in Fig.1.1, together with the *approximate* allocations of marks; more precise allocations of marks for each examining board are given within their particular syllabus. The chapters within this book which cover each theme are also identified in Fig.1.1 below.

Assessment objectives (themes)	Approximate mark allocation (out of total marks)	Chapters covering each theme in this book
Diversity of organisms	5–10 per cent	Ch. 5
Relationships between organisms and their environment	25–40 per cent	Ch. 16, Ch. 17
Organisation and maintenance of the individual		Ch. 4, Ch. 10–15
Development of organisms and the continuity of life	15–25 per cent	Ch. 6–9

4 > ASSESSMENT TECHNIQUES

The emphasis of assessment, both in coursework and in examinations, is on what the student *can do* rather than what the student *cannot do*. GCSE is taken by candidates of a wide range of ability, and the assessment techniques allow for this. For instance, students may take a common paper as well as additional papers designed for a narrower range of ability. Decisions about the particular combination of examination papers taken by individual candidates are normally made by their teacher. A summary of the methods of assessment for each of the examining boards is given in Fig.1.2 below. Note that different terms are used to describe methods of assessment by the various examining boards. In most cases (except IGCSE), candidates are assessed by **common written papers** as well as **practical work** (though IGCSE also provides written papers for candidates unable to have coursework assessed). Boards offer **alternative** or **additional** written papers for candidates, according to their ability. **Extension (extended) papers** are offered by all boards for those candidates expected to achieve a grade (see below) in the range A–E. **Core papers** are offered by some boards for candidates likely to obtain a grade in the range C–G. The actual composition of each paper varies, too. Written papers include **multiple-choice**, **short answer** and **essay** questions (see Ch.2).

Examining board	Less able students — Core — written		All students — Common — written	All students — Common — practical	More able students — Extended — written	
IGCSE	*P1* 45min 40%	*P2* 1h 40%		20%	*P2* 1h 40%	*P3* 1h 40%
LEAG		*P2* 1.5h 30%	*P1* 2h 50%	*P4* 20%	*P3* 1.5h 30%	
MEG		*P2* 1h 50%	*P1* 2h 30%	*P4* 20%	*P3* 2h 50%	
NEA		*P2:P* 1.5h 35%	*P1* 2h 35%	*Experimental Skills* 30%	*P2:Q* 1.5h 35%	
NISEC			*P1* 1h 40% (20%) *P2* 1.25h 40% (20%)	*Coursework* 20%	*P3* 1.25h 40%	
SEG			*P1* 2h 80% (20%)	*Practical Skills* 20%	*P3* 1.5h 30%	
WJEC		*P1* 2h 80%		*Coursework* 20%	*P2* 2.5h 80%	

Methods of assessment in GCSE Biology (for each of the written papers, the time (h) and mark (%) allocation are given).

Key: *P1* = Paper 1, *P2* = Paper 2, *P3* = Paper 3, *P4* = Paper 4

5 ▷   GRADE

Grade descriptions are provided for teachers to help them predict as accurately as possible the likely performance of any particular student in GCSE. The eventual grade awarded will reflect an *overall ability*, although each student is likely to have certain strengths and weaknesses within the subject. GCSE grades are awarded on a seven-point scale A–G; G is ungraded and is given to candidates who fail to reach a minimum standard in the GCSE. The GCSE grades can be compared with the grades previously awarded in GCE 'O' level and CSE:

GCSE grades						
A	B	C	D	E	F	G
A	B	C/1	2	3	4	5
GCE 'O' grades		**CSE grades**				

EXAMINATION AND ASSESSMENT TECHNIQUES

COURSEWORK
EXAMINATION
PREPARATION
EXAMINATION
STRATEGY

GETTING STARTED

A student's eventual grade in GCSE in biology may not properly reflect his or her ability in the subject. The only qualities of a student which can be assessed are those which become apparent in **coursework** and **examinations**. Performance in *all* areas of assessment can be increased, sometimes very dramatically, by improving **techniques**. This is part of the whole process of studying biology at GCSE. An understanding of the subject itself is of course essential, and in any case is likely to make the subject more interesting. However there are a number of ways in which you can improve your preparation for, and presentation of, units of course work and examination.

EXAMINATION & ASSESSMENT TECHNIQUES

Coursework is an important requirement of GCSE syllabuses; it is allocated 20 per cent (for NEA it is 30 per cent) of the total marks available. Coursework is a good opportunity for students who find examinations difficult because it emphasises practical skills, and also because it can be conducted in much more relaxed circumstances. Practical assessments are normally carried out during lessons, though the actual exercises to be assessed are specified by some examining boards. The practical assessments are generally carried out during the second part of the course; for many schools this will be in the fourth and fifth terms of a six-term course. Student will be assessed *individually* even when working in pairs or larger groups. Depending on the board, students are assessed for **practical ability** in a selection from six or seven *distinct skills*, for example:

➤ the ability to follow written or diagrammatic instructions
➤ the ability to handle apparatus and materials
➤ the ability to observe and measure accurately
➤ the ability to record and communicate results (verbally or in writing)
➤ the ability to formulate a hypothesis, i.e., to suggest a valid reason for something happening
➤ the ability to design an experiment to test a hypothesis
➤ the ability to carry out safe working procedures.

Each of these abilities is assessed at three or four levels, for example at high (H), intermediate (I) and low (L) levels. It is likely that not all of the sort of practical skills listed above will be tested within any particular exercise and of course each will probably be tested more than once, on six or more occasions. Practical assessments should not cause any anxiety if a calm, organised and methodical approach is used. Practical exercises are suggested at the end of each of the Chapters 4–17 in this book.

2 EXAMINATION PREPARATION

Preparation for the examination should occur throughout the course, not just immediately before the examination itself. **Revision** can begin after each topic is completed, whilst the ideas are still fresh; further revision can then be carried out towards the end of the course. Revision means reinforcing and developing an *existing* understanding; if a topic is only partially understood, revision is an opportunity to overcome difficulties. Individuals really need to revise in the way that suits them. Here are some suggestions:

Reviewing. Re-reading and perhaps expanding class notes helps to 'fix' ideas in a long-term memory.

Researching. Reading from more than one source may provide an additional insight. Incomplete or unclear notes can be improved as part of this process.

Testing. Understanding and recall can be tested in various ways, for instance by using past examination questions. Again, notes can be updated if the questions reveal any lack of understanding.

Summarising. Topics can be summarised, using textbooks and class notes. The summary can be written as very concise notes or key words, or given as diagrams, for example flow diagrams. The process is a very good way of discovering problems in understanding; it is difficult to summarise an idea that is not fully understood. The summary will also be useful in the later stages of revision.

Organising. The timing of revision can be fairly critical, for instance to avoid leaving too much revision until immediately before the examination. Also, earlier revision often helps an understanding of topics which come up later in the course. A realistic revision programme should be planned and kept to.

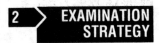

Candidates should be certain where and when the examinations are to take place, what is needed for the examination and also how the question paper is organised. The instructions to candidates (the **rubric**) should be read carefully at the start of the examination. There are several *types* of questions appearing in different papers and set by different examination boards. The student should be familiar with each type of question likely to be encountered in the examination, and should develop an appropriate technique for answering them. The most common types of question set in GCSE Biology papers are described below:

COMPULSORY QUESTIONS

Many GCSE papers have some (or all) of their questions as compulsory questions; these should be attempted, even if the student feels a little uncertain about some aspects of the answer. Many boards are now including **multiple-choice** (multiple response) questions; these should always be attempted, but the choice needs to be made carefully; only one choice should be made unless the instructions indicate otherwise. Even if the single answer is not immediately obvious to you, you should be able to eliminate the more unlikely possibilities so that only a few possible answers remain.

OPTIONAL QUESTIONS

These should be carefully read *before* making a decision on those you are going to attempt. They can usually be done in any order; it is best to answer those you feel will gain you most marks first in case there is a lack of time later. Also starting with what you feel is a good answer will boost your confidence for the rest of the paper.

The **time allowed** for the paper should be used effectively; the amount of time you allocate to each question should correspond with the number of marks available. In many cases answers are written next to the question, and the **space available** will give you a good indication of what length your answer should be, and therefore the time you should spend on it. You can roughly calculate, before the examination, the **marks per minute**. If 100 marks are available in a two hour (120 minute) paper, then you have roughly 1 mark for each 1.2 minutes. A five mark question should then take around six minutes. You must try to avoid exceeding this 'time allocation' for each question.

STRUCTURED QUESTIONS

These occur quite frequently in GCSE Biology examinations. They consist of a series of linked questions, on a common theme. Each sub-question [e.g., (a), (b), (i), (ii) etc.] is usually worth relatively few marks, but the total marks available for the complete question may be quite high. You should work methodically through the sub- questions, remembering that sub- questions may in some cases be intended to increase in difficulty as you progress through the question.

LONGER ANSWER QUESTIONS

For longer answer questions, the first 50–60 per cent of the marks are the easiest to obtain; after this, it becomes increasingly difficult to obtain further marks. *Essays* are often worth a fairly high proportion of marks, but need to be planned properly. Essays should have an *introduction*, telling the examiner what you are going to do. You should try to *develop* your answer in a logical way, with each paragraph perhaps covering a particular point. Finally you should have a *conclusion* reviewing your findings and emphasising any view or results that emerge.

FINISHING THE EXAMINATION

If you have any time to spare at the end of the examination, use this to attempt any answers that you have left undone. Never leave the examination room early, there is always something you can do to use all the time available to good effect. A selection of different examination questions with answers is presented at the end of each of Chs. 4–17, and a number of practice questions are included in Ch. 18.

CHAPTER

TOPICS
IN
GCSE
BIOLOGY

**ADDRESSES FOR
SYLLABUSES
TOPIC CHECKLIST**

G E T T I N G   S T A R T E D

Syllabuses are important because they outline the **content** of the course and also the **methods of assessment** (see Ch.1) that will be used. The syllabus can be used as a **checklist** to ensure that you have revised thoroughly all those topics upon which questions are asked. You should be familiar with the requirements of the syllabus that you are following *during the course* as well as during intensive revision. You should be able to obtain copies of syllabuses and also examination questions from the UK addresses over the page:

G C S E   S Y L L A B U S E S

Requests for syllabuses should be addressed to the **Publications Dept.** for each of the addresses below. Note that a small charge is made for syllabuses and also for past papers.

LEAG   **London and East Anglian Group**
The Lindens
Lexden Road
Colchester CO3 3RL
(0206 549595)

MEG   **Midland Examining Group**
Syndicate Buildings
1 Hills Road
Cambridge CB1 2EU
(0223 61111)

NEA   **Northern Examining Association**
12 Harter Street
Manchester M1 6HL
(061 228 0084)

NISEC   **Northern Ireland Schools Examinations Council**
42 Beechill Road
Belfast BT8 4RS
(0232 704666)

SEG   **Southern Examining Group**
Stag Hill House
Guildford GU2 5XJ
(0483 506506)

WJEC   **Welsh Joint Education Committee**
245 Western Avenue
Cardiff CF5 2YX
(0222 561231)

IGCSE   **International GCSE**
Syndicate Buildings
1 Hills Road
Cambridge CB1 2EU
(0223 61111)

T O P I C S

Below is a table summarising the topics required by each of the GCSE examining boards. You will need to consult your particular syllabus for a more detailed breakdown of sub-topics within each of these groups:

TABLE OF MAIN TOPICS REQUIRED FOR GCSE BIOLOGY								
Examining Board	LEAG A/B	LEAG C	MEG A	MEG B	NEA	NISEC	SEG	WJEC	IGCSE
Chapter								
4 Essentials of life								
Biologically -important molecules, including enzymes	✓	✓	✓		✓	✓	✓	✓	✓
Variety and structure of cells	✓	✓	✓	✓	✓	✓	✓	✓	✓
Passive movement of substances across cell membranes	✓	✓	✓		✓	✓	✓	✓	✓
Active movement of substances across cell membranes	✓	✓	✓	✓	✓	✓	✓	✓	✓
Cell division; mitosis, meiosis	✓	✓	✓	✓	✓	✓	✓	✓	✓
5 Diversity of life								
The species concept			✓	✓					
Natural classification (*)	✓		✓	✓	✓	✓	✓	✓	✓
Artificial classification, including identification keys	✓	✓	✓		✓	✓	✓	✓	✓
6 Reproduction								
Asexual reproduction	✓	✓	✓	✓	✓	✓	✓	✓	✓
Sexual reproduction: flowering plants	✓	✓	✓	✓	✓	✓	✓	✓	✓
Sexual reproduction: animals, including humans	✓	✓	✓	✓	✓	✓	✓	✓	✓
7 Growth & development								
Growth Measurement, patterns of growth	✓	✓	✓		✓	✓	✓		✓
Factors affecting growth	✓	✓	✓		✓	✓	✓		✓
Plant development, including germination	✓	✓	✓	✓	✓	✓	✓	✓	✓
Animal development, e.g. in insects and humans	✓		✓	✓					
8 Heredity & variation								
Chemical basis of heredity	✓	✓	✓		✓	✓	✓	✓	✓
Inheritance of single factors	✓	✓	✓		✓	✓		✓	✓
Incomplete dominance and co-dominance	✓		✓		✓		✓		
Human genetics: inheritance of sex	✓	✓	✓	✓		✓	✓	✓	
Human genetics: blood groups		✓	✓				✓		✓
Continuous and discontinuous variation	✓	✓	✓	✓	✓	✓	✓	✓	✓
Genetic engineering		✓		✓	✓		✓		
9 Evolution								
Evolution, and examples of natural selection	✓	✓	✓	✓	✓	✓	✓	✓	✓
Evidence for natural selection			✓	✓		✓	✓	✓	
Artificial selection	✓	✓	✓	✓	✓	✓	✓	✓	✓

Examining board	LEAG A/B	LEAG C	MEG A	MEG B	NEA	NISEC	SEG	WJEC	IGCSE
10 Respiration									
Internal aerobic and anaerobic respiration	✓	✓	✓	✓	✓	✓	✓	✓	✓
External respiration: animals, including humans	✓	✓	✓	✓	✓	✓	✓	✓	✓
External respiration: plants	✓	✓	✓		✓	✓	✓	✓	✓
11 Homeostasis									
Temperature control in animals	✓	✓	✓	✓	✓		✓		✓
Excretion in animals	✓	✓	✓	✓	✓	✓	✓	✓	✓
Excretion in plants	✓	✓	✓	✓			✓	✓	
Glucose regulation in animals			✓		✓	✓	✓	✓	✓
12 Transport systems									
Animal transport systems: blood	✓	✓	✓	✓	✓	✓	✓	✓	✓
Animal transport systems: lymph	✓	✓	✓	✓	✓	✓	✓	✓	✓
Plant transport systems	✓	✓	✓	✓	✓	✓	✓	✓	✓
13 Sensitivity & response									
Animal sensitivity: nervous system and sense organs	✓	✓	✓	✓	✓	✓	✓	✓	✓
Animal sensitivity: the brain		✓	✓	✓			✓		✓
Animal sensitivity: endocrine system			✓	✓	✓		✓	✓	✓
Animal sensitivity: behaviour			✓	✓	✓				✓
Plant sensitivity: phototropism	✓	✓	✓	✓	✓	✓			✓
Plant sensitivity: geotropism		✓	✓	✓					✓
14 Movement & support									
Plant support		✓	✓				✓		
Animal movement, including joints		✓	✓	✓	✓	✓	✓	✓	
Animal support, including human skeleton			✓	✓		✓	✓	✓	
15 Nutrition									
Factors affecting photosynthesis	✓	✓	✓	✓	✓	✓		✓	✓
Photosynthesis and respiration	✓	✓	✓	✓	✓	✓	✓	✓	
Plant mineral nutrition	✓	✓	✓	✓	✓	✓	✓		✓
Holozoic nutrition, including human	✓	✓	✓	✓	✓	✓	✓		✓
Saprophytic nutrition	✓	✓	✓	✓	✓		✓	✓	
Parasitic nutrition	✓	✓	✓	✓			✓	✓	
16 Environment: abiotic factors									
Climatic factors	✓	✓	✓	✓			✓		
Edaphic (soil) factors	✓	✓	✓			✓			
Circulation of minerals	✓	✓	✓	✓	✓	✓	✓	✓	✓
17 Environment: biotic factors									
Ecosystems (e.g. deciduous woodland*)	✓	✓	✓		✓	✓		✓	✓
Food chains, webs and cycles; ecological pyramids	✓	✓	✓	✓	✓	✓		✓	✓
Populations, including competition	✓	✓	✓	✓		✓			✓
Human impact, including agriculture, industrialization	✓	✓	✓	✓	✓		✓		✓
Practical methods in ecology	✓	✓	✓	✓	✓	✓	✓	✓	✓

* **LEAG syllabus B specifies pond ecosystem and organisms.**

ESSENTIALS OF LIFE

GETTING STARTED

Living things show considerable **diversity**. This is because they are *adapted* to different ways of life. However, there is also a remarkable degree of **uniformity** amongst organisms. This is apparent in two main respects:

1. All organisms demonstrate **characteristics of life**.
2. All organisms are part of an **organisation of life**.

1 ▶ CHARACTER- ISTICS OF LIFE

It is very difficult to define life. However, it is possible to describe those features which are commonly associated with life:

1. **Movement**. Most organisms are capable of moving all or part of their bodies (Ch.14).

2. **Nutrition**. All organisms are capable of obtaining substances from their environment for growth, maintenance and energy (Ch.15).

3. **Respiration.** Living things need energy, released from the breaking down of certain food molecules inside living cells (Ch.10).

4. **Excretion.** Organisms need to remove the waste products of essential chemical processes which occur within them (Ch.11).

5. **Sensitivity.** All organisms can detect and respond to important changes in their internal or external environment (Ch.13).

6. **Growth.** Organisms increase in size, using materials which have been absorbed from their environment. Growth is often accompanied by an increase in complexity (Ch.7).

7. **Reproduction**. Every type of organism is capable of producing offspring which share many of their characteristics (Ch.6).

❝ Try to memorise these characteristics of life. ❞

You should note that living things show most if not all of these characteristics; non-living things demonstrate few if any of them. Other characteristics of life include the existence of **protoplasm** ('living material') and **cells**, **homoeostasis** (Ch.11) and evolution (Ch.9). **Death** is also, in a sense, a characteristic of life.

2 ▶ ORGANISATION OF LIFE

Life is organised in different ways. For instance there is a **hierarchy** of scale:

Molecules

Biologically-important molecules include small, relatively simple **inorganic molecules** (e.g., water, oxygen, carbon dioxide) and also large, complex **organic molecules** (e.g. carbohydrates, proteins, fats and nucleic acids).

Cells

Cells are the structural and functional units of life. Most organisms consist of one or more distinct cells. Individual cells are subdivided by membranes into smaller units called **organelles**, each performing a particular function. **Multicellular** organisms consist of many cells, often of different types.

Organisms

Within multicellular organisms, cells of a particular type are grouped together in **tissues**, such as xylem (Ch.12) and muscle (Ch.14). **Organs** are composed of different tissues and perform a particular function, e.g., leaf (Ch.15), stomach (Ch.15). Organs operate together as **systems** to perform a range of related and co-ordinated functions e.g., vascular system (Ch.12), the digestive system (Ch.15).

Populations

Populations are groups of organisms of the same type; i.e., they belong to the same species (Ch.5). A species is a group of organisms which are capable of reproducing to form offspring with similar characteristics (Ch.8).

Communities

A community is a group of populations existing together in a common **habitat** (Ch.17). Organisms perform particular functions; they occupy a certain **niche** (Ch.17). Individuals interact with their living and non-living environment (Ch.16), to produce a stable **ecosystem** (Ch.16).

ESSENTIAL PRINCIPLES

The **diversity** (collection of differences) of life is most apparent between individual organisms and groups of organisms (Ch.5). The **uniformity** (collection of similarities) of life is more obvious at the molecular and cellular level of organisation.

An understanding of molecules and cells is an important basis of biology as a whole.

1 > **BIOLOGICALLY IMPORTANT MOLECULES**

Molecules consist of combined **elements** (see Appendix 1). Only about 40 per cent of known elements occur in living things. Elements contained in organisms are of low atomic mass and are readily available in the environment.

The most common elements within living cells are oxygen, carbon and hydrogen (Fig.4.1). These elements tend to be in a combined form with other elements as molecules.

The actual amounts and distribution of biologically important molecules varies between and even within species (see Ch.9). However, certain molecules are common to all forms of life. There are two main types of molecule: inorganic and organic.

ELEMENT	PERCENTAGE OF CELL MASS
Oxygen (O)	60%
Carbon (C)	21%
Hydrogen (H)	11%
Nitrogen (N)	3.5%
Calcium (Ca)	2.5%
Phosphorus (P)	1.2%
Chlorine (Cl)	0.2%
Fluorine (F)	0.15%
Sulphur (S)	0.15%
Potassium (K)	0.1%
Sodium (Na)	0.1%
Magnesium (Mg)	0.07%
Iron (Fe)	0.01%
Trace elements	0.02%

Fig.4.1 **Approximate composition of living cells**

(a) INORGANIC MOLECULES

Inorganic molecules are relatively small and simple. They contain a wide variety of elements. However, inorganic molecules do not contain the element carbon (carbon dioxide is an exception). Examples of inorganic molecules include:

(i) Water

Water is important as a habitat for aquatic organisms. It also has important functions within organisms:

As a **component** of living material (protoplasm). Protoplasm is about 65 per cent water in animals and 80 per cent in plants.

As a **transport medium** within cells and also between cells (Ch.12).

To allow **chemical changes** to take place in solution. Water may also take part directly in some reactions, e.g., photosynthesis (Ch.15).

To **dissolve respiratory gases** in land-living organisms (Ch.10).

To **provide support**, especially in non-woody plants (14).

Water is important in living systems because of its chemical and physical properties (see Appendix 1). The availability of water varies, for instance because of climate (Ch.16) and this can affect the distribution of organisms.

(ii) Oxygen

Oxygen is readily available in most environments (Ch.16) as a gas or in dissolved form. Oxygen is available as a waste product of **photosynthesis** in plants (Ch.15). Oxygen is important in **aerobic respiration** (Ch.10) in many living things.

(iii) Carbon dioxide

Carbon dioxide is a waste product of **respiration** (Ch.10). Carbon dioxide levels in the environment tend to be low, however, because it is used by plants for **photosynthesis** (Ch.15).

(iv) Minerals

Minerals are important as components of organic molecules, for example iron in haemoglobin (Ch.12), magnesium in chlorophyll (Ch.15) and iodine in thyroxin

(Ch.13). Some are combined with each other, e.g., calcium and phosphate in bone (Ch.14). Minerals are obtained by plants from the soil (Ch.12) and by animals from their diet (Ch.15). Inorganic molecules can form charged ions in solution (see Appendix 1).

(b) ORGANIC MOLECULES

Organic molecules tend to be large and complex. Organic molecules contain a narrow range of elements, notably carbon as well as oxygen, hydrogen, nitrogen and sulphur.

Organic molecules fall into four main groups: carbohydrates, proteins, fats and nucleic acids.

(i) Carbohydrates

Carbohydrates contain carbon (C), hydrogen (H) and oxygen (O) in the ratio CH_2O. There are three main groups of carbohydrates (saccharides): **monosaccharides**, **disaccharides**, **polysaccharides**. These are summarised in Fig.4.2.

CARBOHYDRATE GROUP	STRUCTURE	CHEMICAL FORMULA	EXAMPLES	FUNCTION
Monosaccharides (Simple sugars)	Consist of a single chemical group.	$C_6H_{12}O_6$	Glucose Fructose Galactose	Soluble; structural units for making larger carbohydrates.
Disaccharides (more complex sugars)	Consist of two joined monosaccharides.	$C_{12}H_{22}O_{11}$	Maltose	Soluble; similar to monosaccharides; sucrose is 'a transport molecule' (plants).
Polysaccharides (large, complex sugars)	Consist of many joined monosaccharides (i.e., they are polymers).	$(C_{12}H_{22}O_{11})n$	Starch Glycogen Cellulose	Insoluble; used as *food store* in plants (starch) or animals (glycogen); used as *structural material* in plants (cellulose).

Fig.4.2 Summary of common carbohydrates

The structural unit of carbohydrates is the monosaccharide. Carbohydrates can be converted from one form to another, according to the organism's needs. For example, polysaccharides can be broken down during digestion (Ch.15) to disaccharides and then monosaccharides; these can be further broken down during respiration (Ch.10) to release energy. Polysaccharides can be made from simpler carbohydrates for growth (e.g., of cellulose cell walls (Ch.14)) and for storage (e.g., of starch, glycogen). Polysaccharides are insoluble, so do not affect osmosis (Ch.4) directly.

Carbohydrates can, like proteins and fats, be identified using standard tests (see Ch.15). There are separate tests for so-called **reducing sugars** (monosaccharides and maltose) and **non-reducing sugars** (disaccharides other than maltose).

(ii) Proteins

Proteins contain carbon, hydrogen, oxygen, nitrogen and, in some cases, sulphur and phosphorus. The structural unit of proteins is the **amino acid**; these are joined together by **peptide bonds** to form short **peptides**, longer **polypeptides**, or even longer protein molecules.

There are about twenty different amino acids in proteins. The precise way in which they are arranged during **protein synthesis** (Ch.4) is determined by genetic information contained within **chromosomes** (Ch.8). The chain of amino acids is often folded into a three-dimensional shape; this may be even further folded. The precise shape of proteins is often important for their function.

Proteins have a wide range of **functions**:

Structure of cells and tissues. This is more important in animals (50 per cent of dry mass (Ch.7)) than in plants, whose main structural component is carbohydrate (Ch.14).

Movement, by muscle fibres (Ch.14).

Control of chemical processes by enzymes (see below) and hormones (Ch.13).

Prevention of disease, by antibodies (Ch.12).

As **energy providers**, especially in carnivores.

The relative number and type of proteins within organisms is characteristic of a given species, and can be used to show how different species are related (Ch.9).

(iii) Enzymes

Enzymes are biological **catalysts** which increase the rate of a reaction without themselves being changed.

Enzymes are made (by protein synthesis) within cells. **Extracellular enzymes** are secreted (Ch.4) outside the cell where they have their affect; e.g., digestion in the gut cavity (Ch.15). **Intracellular enzymes** are retained within the cell, e.g., respiration within mitochondria (Ch.10).

Enzymes are believed to work by forming a temporary 'complex' with the chemical they are acting upon, the **substrate**, before forming the **product** or products. The way in which this could occur is called the 'lock and key' model, shown in Fig.4.3.

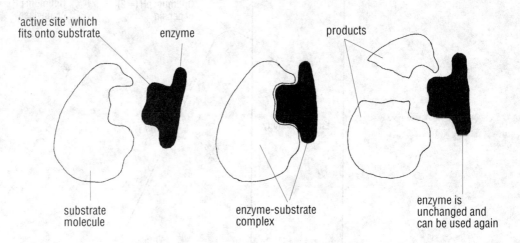

'active site' which fits onto substrate   enzyme   products

substrate molecule   enzyme-substrate complex   enzyme is unchanged and can be used again

Fig.4.3 'Lock and key' model of enzyme action

Fig.4.3 shows a breaking down (*catabolic*) reaction; the 'lock and key' model can also explain building-up (*anabolic*) reactions in which two substrate molecules are combined into a single product.

Enzymes have certain **characteristics** which can be explained in terms of the 'lock and key' model:

(i)   **Enzymes are specific for a particular substrate**:
The active site on the enzyme has to 'fit' the substrate.

(ii) **Enzymes work within a narrow range of temperature** (Fig.4.4):
At high temperatures, enzymes are **denatured**; the shape of the molecule, including the active site, is distorted. At low temperatures, enzyme and substrate molecules are less liable to react together (see Appendix 1).

(iii) **Enzymes work within a narrow range of pH** (Fig.4.5):
Extremes of pH may denature the enzyme; some enzymes are very sensitive to this. Acid or alkaline conditions may affect the other substances involved in the reaction.

Organisms depend on enzymes for many important processes. Organisms therefore maintain favourable reactions by regulating their internal environment. This is the purpose of *homeostasis* (Ch.11).

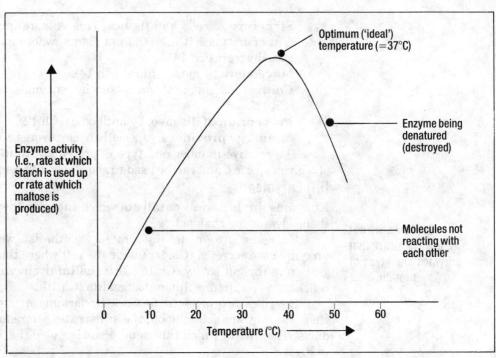

Fig.4.4 Enzymes and temperature

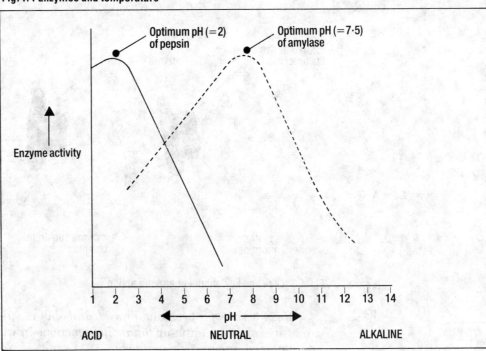

Fig.4.5 Enzymes and pH

iv Lipids

Lipids are *fats* (solids) and *oils* (liquids). They contain carbon, hydrogen and oxygen; the relative amount of oxygen is low, however. A typical fat consists of a *glycerol* unit with three *fatty acids* attached. The fatty acids may be *saturated* (having no double bonds) or *unsaturated* (having double bonds).

Lipids are important for:

forming part of *cell membranes* (Ch.4)

for *energy release*, during respiration (Ch.10).

storing fat until needed, e.g., in seeds (see Ch.7) and in mammals, where it also protects organs and insulates.

v Nucleic acids

Nucleic acids contain carbon, hydrogen, oxygen, nitrogen and phosphorus. The structural units of nucleic acids are **nucleotides**, which consist of a *sugar* (pentose), a *phosphate* and a *base*.

There are two types of nucleic acid:

DNA (deoxyribonucleic acid) is a large, complex molecule, twisted into a 'double helix'.

RNA (ribonucleic acid) is a shorter, single-stranded molecule.

Both DNA and RNA are important in carrying *genetic information* (Ch.8) in all living cells. The information is in the form of a code, determined by the particular sequence of four bases. This code is used in an active cell to direct protein synthesis (Ch.4).

2 ▶ CELLS

Cells are distinct structural and functional units of most living things. Each cell is produced from another cell by **cell division** (see below). Cells inherit genetic information (Ch.8) when they are formed. Cells within a particular organism have the same genetic 'identity', but they may be adapted for different functions. Cells therefore become *specialised* during development (Ch.7); they have a particular structure for their function.

> ❝You will be expected to distinguish between animal and plant cells and comment on their features.❞

(a) GENERALISED CELLS

Cells vary considerably in size, shape and what they contain because they often have different functions. Animal and plant cells have particular characteristics, and these are compared in Fig.4.7. However, most cells have certain structural (as well as functional) features in common. These are shown in Fig 4.6.

Fig.4.6 shows the sort of detail that can be observed using a powerful light microscope (about 1500x magnification).

However, it is possible for much more detail to be seen using an electron microscope (about 500,000x magnification) (see Fig.4.9).

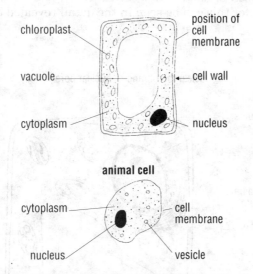

Fig.4.6 Generalized animal and plant cells

FEATURES	PLANT CELLS	ANIMAL CELLS
Relative size	large	small
Relative shape	Regular	Irregular
Cell wall	Present	Absent
Vacuole/ vesicle	Large Permanent vacuole	Small temporary vesicle
Chloroplast	Present in many plant cells	Absent

Fig.4.7 Comparison of plant and animal cells

(b) SPECIALISED CELLS

Multicellular organisms contain many cells. This allows them to grow much larger than is possible for **unicellular organisms** consisting of a single cell. It also allows individual cells to become *specialised* (differentiated) for a particular function. A multicellular organism may contain a wide range of cell types performing many different activities. However, individual cells do not operate in isolation; their activities are coordinated within the organism as a whole. This is sometimes called a 'division of labour'. The degree of specialisation of cells within a multicellular body varies according to the complexity of the organism. For instance, in *Spirogyra* (a simple plant) there is just one type of cell. In *Hydra* (a simple animal) there are seven, whilst in humans there are many different kinds of cell.

Fig.4.8 shows some examples of specialised cells. Each type of cell demonstrates how structure is adapted to function; this is an important idea in biology (see Ch.9).

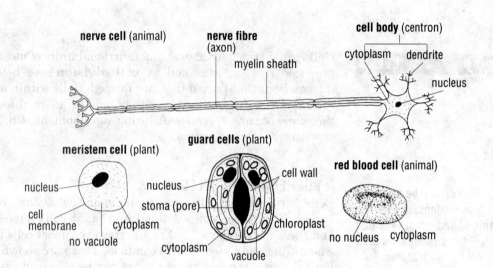

Fig.4.8 Examples of specialised cells

(c) COMPONENTS OF CELLS

The internal structure of a cell is determined by the functions of the cell as a whole. Every cell is essentially a system of membranes which separate different processes within the cell; in other words, cells are internally specialised. The structural evidence for this can be seen in the detail revealed by the electron microscope (Fig.4.9).

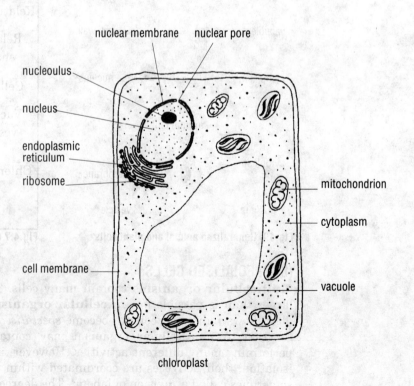

Fig.4.9 Detailed structure of a generalised plant cell

Electron microscopes show organelles more clearly than is possible with a light microscope. **Organelles** are membrane-bound structures performing specialised functions within the cell. A brief description of each of the main components of a cell, including organelles, is given in Fig.4.10.

COMPONENT	DESCRIPTION	FUNCTION
Cell wall *	Non-living structure composed mainly of cellulose (Ch.4); permeable to most molecules.	Maintains regular shape of cell. Supports cell against turgor forces (Ch.4).
Cytoplasm	Semi-fluid medium consisting of water, organelles (except nucleus and vacuole), dissolved substances and undissolved inclusions (including stored food, e.g. starch).	Main site of cell's activities. With the nucleus, Cytoplasm makes up the protoplasm (living material) of the cell.
Cell membrane	Complex structure consisting of phospho-lipids and protein; same structure occurs within organelles.	Maintains structure of the cell (especially in animal cells, which lack a cell wall). Selectively permeable (Ch.4); controls the movement of substances into/out of the cell.
Nucleus	Contains nucleic acids, including DNA which is condensed as chromosomes during cell division (Ch.4). The nucleus is bound by a membrane (except in 'simple' cells such as bacteria.	Directs the cell's activities by making proteins, including enzymes. Contains inherited genetic information (Ch.8) as a genetic code within DNA molecules; the code is carried by RNA through nuclear pores to ribosomes.
Endoplasmic reticulum	Network of membrane-bound spaces spreading throughout the cytoplasm.	Transport system within the cell, e.g. of nutrients and RNA.
Ribosome	Composed of RNA (Ch.4) and protein; attached to endoplasmic reticulation.	Site of protein production; instructions for this are caried by RNA from the nucleus.
Chloroplast *	Complex system of membranes, containing pigments such as chlorophyll (Ch.15).	Site of photosynthesis (ch.15) in green part of plant.
Mitochondrion	Consists of a double membrane; the inner membrane is much folded.	Site of energy release from aerobic respiration (Ch.10). Cells which are very active have many mitochondria.
Vacuole *	Membrane-bound, fluid filled cavity.	Stores useful substances and also some wastes. Allows cell to increase in size by absorbing water (ch.4).

Fig.4.10 Structures and functions of the main cell components. * = present in plant cells only

3 MOVEMENT OF SUBSTANCES ACROSS THE CELL MEMBRANE

Cells are not isolated from their external environment; substances enter or leave cells through their outer surface. The cell membrane has an important function in controlling this movement and so determining the chemical composition of the cell. The relative concentration of substances within a living cell (see Fig.4.1) is often quite different from that of its non-living external environment. The cell's internal environment is maintained by both *passive* and *active* processes:

(i) **Passive processes.** These result from differences in the concentration of substances inside and outside the cell. Dissolved substances move by **diffusion**

(Ch.4) from high to low concentrations. Diffusion of water molecules is called **osmosis** (Ch.4). These passive processes do not require energy from the cell.

Example: oxygen from the environment will tend to diffuse into a cell where the relative concentration is low (Ch.10).

(ii) **Active processes.** Substances can be moved from low to high concentrations; this is the opposite situation to that of diffusion. This process is called **active transport** (Ch.4) and requires energy from the cell.

Example: the uptake of some mineral ions into plant root cells. Large or insoluble substances can enter or leave the cell by processes involving small, membrane-bound **vesicles**.

Example: **phagocytosis** in white blood cells (Ch.12) or **endocytosis** in unicellular organisms such as *Amoeba* (Ch.4).

(a) PASSIVE PROCESSES

Passive processes involve diffusion, including osmosis which is the diffusion of water across a membrane.

(i) Diffusion

Diffusion is the random movement of substances from a region of high to a region of low concentration, down a **concentration gradient.** The rate of movement is determined by how 'steep' the gradient is; diffusion is more rapid where the relative difference in concentrations is large. Diffusion is very important in the movement of substances over short distances between and within cells. However, diffusion is not effective over longer distances (i.e., more than about 1 mm), so larger organisms may require **transport systems** (Ch.12) as well.

(ii) Osmosis

Osmosis is the movement of water molecules from a region of high concentration of water (a 'dilute' solution) to a region of low concentration of water (a 'concentrated' solution), through a **selectively-permeable membrane**.

Osmosis is a type of diffusion involving water molecules. These are small enough to pass through a cell membrane by simple diffusion (Fig.4.11). However, larger molecules such as glucose cannot easily cross a membrane (they require

> **Many students find osmosis difficult to understand, partly because they may not realise that it is simnply a form of diffusion, involving water molecules.**

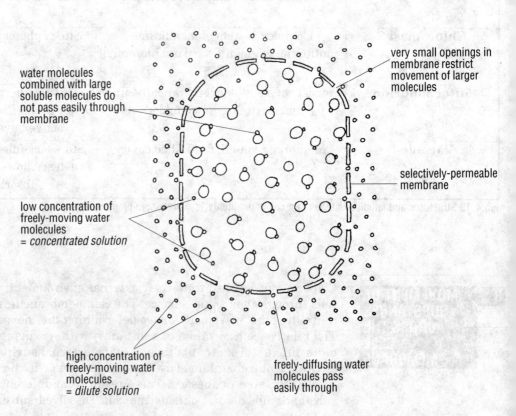

water molecules combined with large soluble molecules do not pass easily through membrane

very small openings in membrane restrict movement of larger molecules

selectively-permeable membrane

low concentration of freely-moving water molecules = *concentrated solution*

high concentration of freely-moving water molecules = *dilute solution*

freely-diffusing water molecules pass easily through

Fig.4.11 The principle of osmosis

active transport (Ch.4)). Large soluble molecules like glucose do not take part in osmosis directly, but they do determine the relative number (= concentration) of freely moving water molecules on either side of the membrane by combining with them.

Relatively more water molecules will tend to move from a dilute solution than from a concentrated solution across a membrane. A living membrane is important in osmosis because it is selectively permeable (partially permeable); osmosis can therefore be regarded as '*restricted diffusion*'. Osmosis will not occur in cells whose membranes are not intact, for instance if the cell is denatured by heat (Ch.4), or plasmolysed (Ch.4).

Osmosis in cells. The concentration of dissolved substances is often higher inside than outside a cell. For this reason, water tends to enter cells by osmosis. Although this is a passive process, it can be controlled in various ways:

(i) the concentration of substances within the cell can be regulated by converting them to an insoluble, osmotically inactive form; e.g., glucose can be stored as starch in plant cells (Ch.4). The amounts of substances inside the cell can be altered by actively transporting them from the cell (Ch.4).

(ii) the concentration of substances immediately outside the cell in a multi-cellular organism can be controlled by various processes in homeostasis (Ch.11); this is particularly evident in animals.

(iii) the pressures resulting from the entry of water by osmosis can be resisted in plant cells by the cell wall. This maintains the cell shape and is important in support (Ch.14).

Osmotic changes in cells. The gain or loss of water from cells can be controlled by individual cells or by the organism as a whole. However this control may not always be possible. One consequence of a variation in water content of cells is a change in their shape. In some cells, for example the guard cells of plant leaves (Ch.12), this may be an important part of their function.

The effect of variations in water content by osmosis on plant and animal cells is shown in Fig.4.12 and Fig.4.13. These variations may have a destructive effect on cells, so they are often avoided in plants and, in particular, animals. Major disruptions to the cell structure such as **plasmolysis** (plant cells), **haemolysis**

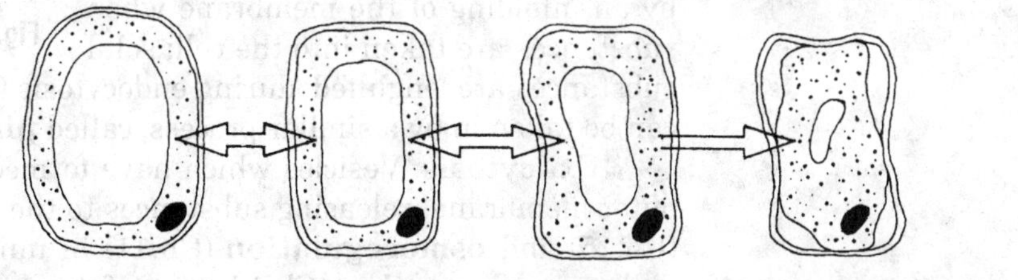

> 66 Plant cells can avoid damage by swelling because, unlike animal cells, they have a cell wall. However, both types of cells can be damaged if too much water is lost. 99

cell in more dilute solution gains water and swells against the cell wall; it becomes *turgid*

cell in same concentration of solution

cell in more concentrated solution loses water and shrinks; it becomes *flaccid*

cytoplasm and cell membrane are pulled from the cell wall; the cell becomes *plasmolysed*

Fig.4.12 Variation of water content in a plant cell

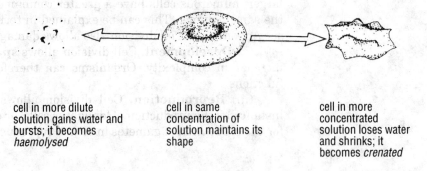

cell in more dilute solution gains water and bursts; it becomes *haemolysed*

cell in same concentration of solution maintains its shape

cell in more concentrated solution loses water and shrinks; it becomes *crenated*

Fig.4.13 Variation of water content in an animal cell

and **crenation** (red blood cells) are often permanent and therefore serious for the organism as a whole.

Experiments to show osmosis in plant and animal tissues are described in the 'coursework' section of this chapter.

(b) ACTIVE PROCESSES

Active processes include active transport and vesicle formation.

(i) Active transport

Active transport is the movement of substances across a cell membrane against a concentration gradient, using energy from respiration. Substances which are in a relatively low concentration on one side of a cell membrane can be moved across the membrane. This process is thought to involve **carrier molecules** within the membrane, and requires energy from **ATP molecules** (Ch.10), produced from respiration. Active transport occurs in cells lining the gut (Ch.15) which take up glucose molecules into the blood which already contains a relatively high concentration of glucose. Glucose is also taken up by cells lining the kidney nephron (Ch.11) during reabsorption.

(ii) Vesicle formation

Vesicles are small fluid-spaces in the cell cytoplasm and are involved in substances entering the cell (endocytosis) or leaving the cell (exocytosis):

Endocytosis. Vesicles are formed by an infolding of the membrane when substances are taken into the cell; solid

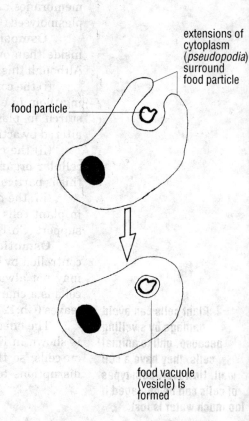

Fig.4.14 Phagocytosis in Amoeba proteus

substances are 'engulfed' during endocytosis (**phagocytosis**) (Fig.4.14), and water can be taken in by a similar process, called **pinocytosis** ('cell drinking').

Exocytosis. Vesicles which have formed in the cytoplasm can fuse with the outer membrane, releasing substances to the outside. This occurs during **egestion** (Ch.15) and **osmoregulation** (Ch.11) in unicellular organisms such as *Amoeba*, and also in **secretion** (Ch.13) of useful substances in many multicellular organisms.

---

4 ❯ CELL DIVISION

Cells increase in size by taking in materials from their environment (Ch.7). There are several ways in which cell division is important:

(i) **Growth and maintenance.** Cell division allows an organism to grow larger; numerous cells have a greater combined surface area than a single cell of the same volume. (This can be explained in terms of **surface area/volume ratio**; see Appendix-1). Cell division also allows damaged tissues to be repaired.

(ii) **Development**. Cell division allows **specialisation** of cells (Ch.7) and an increase in complexity. Organisms can therefore become **adapted** for different functions.

(iii) **Reproduction.** Cell division allows asexual reproduction (Ch.6), for instance by the production of 'daughter cells' or of spores. Cell division is necessary for the production of gametes in sexual reproduction (Ch.6).

(a) THE PROCESS OF CELL DIVISION

In *multicellular* animals most cells retain the capacity to divide. However most plants cells which have formed a cell wall and a vacuole (= **vacuolation**) cannot divide; instead, cell division is limited to unspecialized **meristem** cells (Ch.7). The process of cell division may be initiated when a growing cell reaches a certain critical size. The nucleus undergoes reorganisation, including the formation of **chromosomes** (Ch.8) which then separate. This is followed by a separation of the cytoplasm, each half containing roughly equal quantities of organelles (Ch.4).

There are two main types of cell division, depending on whether the *chromosome number* (Ch.8) in the cell is to be maintained or halved:

(i) Mitosis

Mitosis results in the formation in new body (**somatic**) cells. Mitosis occurs in **asexual reproduction** (Ch.6) in unicellular organisms and **growth** in multi-

> 66 students often confuse mitosis and meiosis. Remember that meiosis only occurs during gamete formation; it is a 'specialised' form of cell division. Mitosis is the 'normal' type of division, occuring in all organisms 99

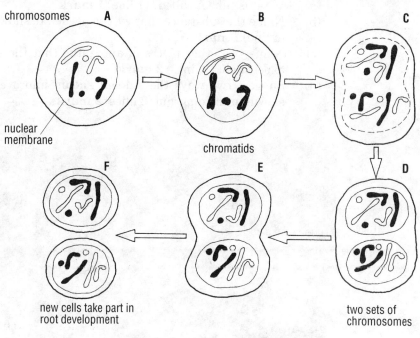

chromosomes

nuclear membrane

chromatids

new cells take part in root development

two sets of chromosomes

Fig.4.15 Mitosis in root tip cells in crocus (Crocus balansae)

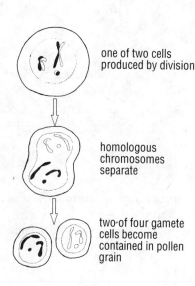

one of two cells produced by division

homologous chromosomes separate

two of four gamete cells become contained in pollen grain

Fig.4.16 Meiosis in young anther of crocus (Crocus balancae)

cellular organisms (Ch.7). The number of chromosomes in the new cell remains the same (i.e., they are **diploid**, 2n). The nuclear membrane breaks down, then each **chromatid** in the chromatid pair separates and moves apart (Fig.4.15). The separated chromatids are now called chromosomes again. Nuclear membranes then reform around the two sets of chromosomes, and the cytoplasm begins to divide. Each cell dividing by mitosis will form two 'daughter' cells.

(ii) Meiosis

Meiosis results in the formation of **sex cells** (**gametes**). Meiosis occurs as part of sexual reproduction (Ch.6). The number of chromosomes is reduced by half (i.e., the gametes are **haploid**, n). This is because pairs of male and female gametes may become combined during **fertilization** (Ch.6). Meiosis is essentially a **reduction division** and consists of mitosis followed by a reduction of the chromosome number; each chromosome of a **homologous pair** (Ch.8) separates (Fig.4.16). Each cell dividing by meiosis will form four 'daughter' cells.

EXAMINATION QUESTIONS

QUESTION 1

A student has been asked to find out how long it takes for starch to be changed to sugar by an enzyme at a temperature of 0°C. The diagram shows the student about to mix known volumes of the enzyme with starch.

(a)   What is tube A called? (1 line) **1 mark**

(b)   Name the substance that will be needed to show that starch has disappeared (1 line) **1 mark**

(c)   Name two other pieces of apparatus that the student should have for this experiment (2 lines) **2 marks**

(d)   Suggest two ways the student should improve the part of the experiment shown in the diagram (2 lines) **2 marks**

Total 6 marks (SEG)

Tube A

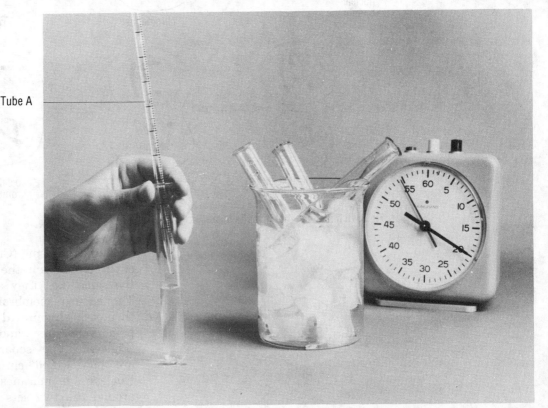

Photo: Philip Harris Biological Ltd.

QUESTION 2

(a)   What is the importance of **meiosis** (reduction division) in the human life cycle? (2 lines) **2 marks**

(b)   Give two ways in which mitosis differs from meiosis (2 lines) **2 marks**

Total 4 marks (SEG)

QUESTION 3

The diagram below shows some features of an animal cell as seen by an electron microscope.

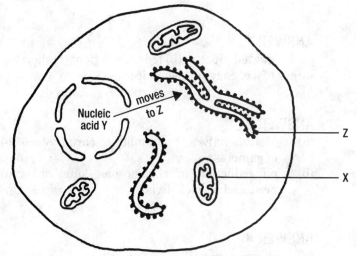

(a)   (i) Name structure X. (1 line) **1 mark**
         (ii) What is the function of structure X? (2 lines) **1 mark**
(b)   (i) Name the nucleic acid labelled Y. (1 line) **1 mark**
         (ii) Name structure Z. (1 line) **1 mark**
         (iii) Explain briefly the relationship between the nucleic acid Y and the function of structure Z. (3 lines) **3 marks**

Total 7 marks (IGCSE)

QUESTION 4

The diagram below is a drawing of a specially prepared, squashed cell from a root tip.

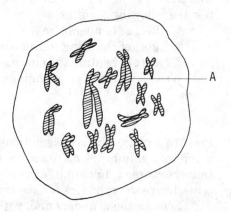

(a)   What is the structure labelled A called? (1 line) **1 mark**
(b)   What is the function of the structure labelled A? (1 line) **1 mark**
(c)   The cell is about to divide by mitosis. How many of these structures would you expect to find in each of the daughter cells after cell division is complete? (1 line) **1 mark**

Total 3 marks (LEAG)

Further practice questions on the topics discussed in this chapter are provided in Chapter 18 (questions 1 and 2).

OUTLINE ANSWERS

ANSWER 1
(a) graduated pipette; (b) iodine solution; (c) thermometer, white tile (d) larger container of ice, enzyme also in ice

ANSWER 2
(a)   Meiosis halves the number of chromosomes (46 to 23) during the formation of gametes
(b)   no reduction in chromosome number occurs in mitosis; two cells are produced at each division in mitosis rather than four as in meiosis.

ANSWER 4
(a)   chromosome;
(b)   carries genetic information;
(c)   14.

COURSE WORK – A STEP FURTHER

1 ❯ ENZYME EXPERIMENTS USING CATALASE

Catalase is an enzyme which is found in the tissues of many organisms. It converts the substrate hydrogen peroxide into water and oxygen. Use 10 cm³ of 3 per cent hydrogen peroxide (CAUTION: avoid contact with skin and eyes) in a 250 cm³ measuring cylinder. Add a small amount of living tissue, such as yeast, liver, potato, blood. There should be a fairly vigorous reaction and a froth should appear.

Use the scale on the measuring cylinder to assess the activity of the enzyme by recording the height reached by the froth. Test the gas with a glowing splint; this should re-light if the gas is oxygen. Design a series of simple experiments to test the following conditions:
1. Effect of temperature
2. Effect of changing the amounts of substrate or enzyme
3. Effect of heating the enzyme
Write a report of your findings.

2 ❯ OSMOSIS IN TISSUES

Prepare a range of sucrose solutions as follows: 5, 10 and 20 per cent. Using a cork borer (e.g. number 4 or 5), cut a cylinder of fresh potato exactly 40 mm long. Immerse three cylinders in each of the sucrose solutions, and also in water (0 per cent). Leave the cylinders for about one hour.

Remove the cylinders and, without mixing them up, re-measure them. Calculate average (mean) length for the cylinders in each of the sucrose concentrations. Summarise your results in a table. Which concentration do you think is the most similar to the concentration within the potato cells? Explain your answer.

3 ❯ OSMOSIS IN CELLS

Carefully mount a small, thin piece of the red epidermis of a rhubarb (*Rheum rhaponicum*) on a microscope slide with a small drop of water. Add a coverslip. Examine a few cells under the high power of a microscope. Identify the major components of the cells (see Fig.4.6). Make a large, clearly labelled diagram.

If possible without removing the slide from the microscope, apply a drop of 5 per cent sucrose solution to one end of the coverslip. Suck the solution under the coverslip by applying a piece of filter paper to the other end. Re-examine the cells; if they have changed in any way after a few minutes, redraw them.

Write brief comments on your findings.

4 > SOURCES OF INFORMATION

For further information on The Essentials of Life, see for example *The Chemistry of Life*, Stephen Rose (Penguin, 1979); *The Cell Concept*, L. Kramer and J. Scott (Macmillan, 1979).

STUDENT'S ANSWER – EXAMINER'S COMMENTS

In an osmosis investigation using potato, six cylinders of potato were cut to a length of EXACTLY 50 mm.

Three of the cylinders were put in water.

Three of the cylinders were put in 30% sugar solution.

After two hours the cylinders were taken out and dried. They were put on 2 mm graph paper to measure their lengths. The outline of each cylinder is drawn on the graph paper below.

Cylinders in WATER	Cylinders in 30% SUGAR SOLUTION
1	
2	
3	

66 Good; these values show accurate observation (and use of a ruler). 99

(a) Find the length of the three cylinders from each of the liquids and record your results in the table below. *(2 marks)*

	Water	30% Sugar Solution
Cylinder 1	54	47
Cylinder 2	52	44
Cylinder 3	54	45

66 These answers have been written the wrong way round; also, one value has been incorrectly calculated. 99

(b) Find the mean length of the cylinders in each liquid after 2 hours.

Mean length of cylinders in water = 44·0

Mean length of cylinders in 30% sugar solutions = 53·3

(2 marks)

(c) At the start the cylinders were all 50 mm long. Why did the cylinders in the 30% sugar solution change in length?

they shrink in the 30% sugar solution

(1 mark)

66 This does not answer the question; the change in length is due to loss of water, by 'reverse osmosis'. 99

(d) After 2 hours the cylinders from the sugar solution would feel different from those that had been in water. What would be the difference in feel?

they would feel soft.

(1 mark)

66 Correct. 99

NEA

(Total 6 marks)

DIVERSITY OF LIFE

GETTING STARTED

There are many different kinds of organisms; this diversity occurs because organisms have become **adapted** (Ch.9) to different ways of living. Each type of organism, called a **species**, has both similarities and differences in comparison with other species.

The species concept. A species is a group of organisms which share many similarities and which consequently can often **interbreed** to produce fertile offspring. There are nearly two million known species. Using a wide variety of features, biologists have classified these species into **groups**, this **process of classification** being called **taxonomy**.

Natural and artificial classification. There are two main approaches to classification; natural and artificial classification.

Natural classification. This is based on **similarities** between organisms. This is done by placing organisms into classification groups and sub-groups. The groups form a sort of hierarchy and are arranged in order of decreasing diversity:
kingdom → phylum/division* → class → order → family → genus → species
(*The word 'division' is often used instead of the word 'phylum' for the plant kingdom.)

Organisms are named according to the groups to which they belong. Each group contains organisms which share certain characteristics. Organisms belonging to the same group may have **evolved** (Ch.9) in a similar way.

Artificial classification. This is based on **differences** between organisms. It is used to distinguish organisms from each other and is a means of identifying a particular individual.

Identification. The process of identification may involve the use of certain features which are usually fairly distinct but are not necessarily the features used in natural classification. One way in which individual organisms are distinguished is by the use of **identification keys**. These consist of a series of paired questions or statements which gradually eliminate all possible identities until only one remains.

Unit of classification. The unit of classification is the **species**. A species may be known by more than one common name, for example the dunnock or hedge sparrow. Therefore to avoid confusion, each species is given an internationally recognised Latin name, its **binomial** name. This is made up of two parts, a *specific* (species) name for example, *modularis* and a *generic* (genus) name, for example, *Prunella*. The binomial name for the hedge sparrow is *Prunella modularis*.

ESSENTIAL PRINCIPLES

Classification is used to sort living organisms into small, comprehensible groups. Classifying living things allows comparisons to be made between them. The way in which organisms are related to each other may be an expression of the way in which they have evolved (Ch.9). Each species is thought to have arisen from a previous species by independent natural selection (Ch.9).

---

1 ▷ THE SPECIES CONCEPT

A **species** consists of a population of individual organisms which share many structural and functional similarities. Organisms within (but not between) species can, if conditions allow, interbreed to produce fertile offspring. There are, however, some *difficulties* in applying the species concept in classifying organisms:

PROBLEMS IN USING THE SPECIES CONCEPT FOR CLASSIFICATION
(i) **Differences within a species may occur for some characteristic**,
     for example, because organisms are at different stages of growth or development (Ch.7), or because of male/female differences (Ch.6). This results in *variation* (Ch.8).
(ii) **Similarities between species may cause confusion**,
     particularly if the species are closely related. This could be a problem in **identification** (see below).
(iii) **Interbreeding may not occur within a species**
     This may be because individuals are isolated, self-fertilized (Ch.6), physically incompatible (for example, some breeds of dog), or because of asexual reproduction Ch.6).
(iv) **Interbreeding between species may result in fertile offspring**.
     The formation of a new **hybrid species** is more common amongst plants than animals (Fig 5.1). Problems in applying the species concept can be overcome by using as many different characteristics as possible. **Taxonomists** (biologists who classify living things) use various features of an organism. These include **morphology** (body form), **anatomy** (body structure), **biochemistry** (body chemistry). All such inheritable characteristics are a direct or indirect expression of the genetic material (Ch.8) that the organism has inherited from its immediate or remote ancestors (Ch.9).

SPECIES 1	SPECIES 2	OFFSPRING
Horse (***Equus equus***)	Donkey (ass) (***Equus hemionus***)	Mule (infertile)
Tiger (***Panthera tigris***)	Lion (***Panthera leo***)	Tigron (infertile)
Cabbage (***Brassica oleracea***)	Radish (***Raphanus sativus***)	Rabbage (***Raphanobrassica***) (fertile)
Cabbage (***Brassica oleracea***)	Turnip (***Brassica rapa***)	Swede (***Brassica napus***) (fertile)

Fig.5.1 Examples of interbreeding

2 > NATURAL CLASSIFICATION

Natural classification is based on *biologically important similarities* of organisms. For example, the arrangement of bones in a bat wing, a dolphin fin and a human arm show many similarities; they are **homologous structures** (Ch.9) because they are thought to have evolved in a similar way.

Natural classification can therefore be used to show the way in which organisms are thought to be related in evolution. This can be shown in diagrams (called **dendrograms**); an example is given in Fig.5.2. In the diagram, species A and B, for example, belong to the same genus and may have evolved in a similar way. Species F has few similarities with any of the species A–E, so may have evolved in a different way. Organisms which are closely related will have many features in common and will consequently tend to belong to the same classification groups. Those organisms with the *greatest possible number of features in common* will belong to the *same species*.

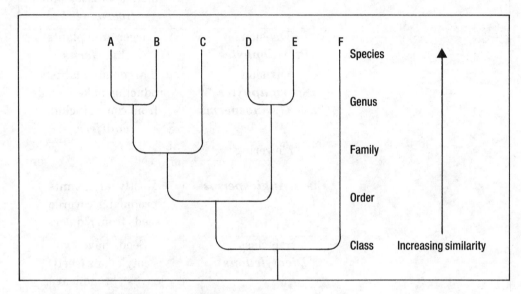

Fig.5.2 Relative similarities between different species

CLASSIFICATION OF THE LIVING WORLD

An outline of the main classification groups, together with examples, is presented in Fig.5.3.

KINGDOM	CLASSIFICATION SUB-GROUPS	DESCRIPTION	EXAMPLES
Monera (0.1%)		Unicellular, contain no distinct nucleus or organelles; includes bacteria (Ch.15).	*Salmonella typhi* (typhoid bacteria)
Protista (1.4%)		Unicellular plant-like protophyta or animal-like protozoa. Nutrition: autotrophic and/or heterotrophic (Ch.15).	*Euglena gracilis* (Euglena) *Amoeba proteus* (Amoeba)
Fungi (3.5%)		Unicellular, or multicellular with strands (hyphae) containing many nuclei. Nutrition: heterotrophic (Ch.15).	*Saccharomyces* (yeasts) *Mucor* ('pin mould')

Plants (16%)		Multicellular: cells have cellulose walls and contain chlorophyll. Nutrition: autotrophic (Ch.15).	
	'Non-flowering'		
	Division: *Algae*	Land and aquatic plants; include seaweeds.	*Fucus* (seaweed)
	Division: *Bryophytes*	Small land plants; include *mosses* and *liverworts*.	*Sphagnum* (moss)
	Division: *Pteridophytes*	Larger land plants; include *ferns*.	*Dryopteris filix-mas* (fern)
	Division: *Spermaphytes* Class: *Gymnosperms*	Large land plants, producing 'naked' seeds from cones; include *conifers*.	*Taxus baccata* (yew)
	'Flowering'		
	Class: *Angiosperms*	Mostly land plants, producing 'covered' seeds from *flowers*.	
	Sub-class: *Dicotyledons*	Seeds have two cotyledons (seed leaves), broad leaves.	*Ranunculus acris* (meadow buttercup)
	Sub-class: *Monocotyledons*	Seeds have one cotyledon (seed leaf), narrow leaves; includes grasses.	*Lolium perenne* (rye-grass)
Animals (79%)		Multicellular organisms; cells have no cell walls or chloroplasts. Nutrition: heterotrophic (Ch.15).	
	'Invertebrates'		
	Phylum: *Coelenterates*	External skeleton, or skeleton; no backbone; soft bodied aquatic animals.	*Aurelia aurita* (jellyfish)
	Phylum: *Platyhelminthes*	Aquatic or land animals flatworms. Many are parasitic (Ch.15).	*Taenia solium* (tapeworm)
	Phylum: *Annelids*:	Aquatic or land animals, ringed worms.	*Lumbricus terrestris* (earthworm)
	Phylum: *Molluscs*	Aquatic or land animals, soft-bodied, sometimes protected by one or two shells.	*Helix aspersa* (common snail)

Phylum: **Arthropods**	Largest animal phylum. Move using jointed limbs. Classes within the phylum include: **insects** (53% of all living species): three pairs of legs, three regions of body (head, thorax, abdomen), often two pairs of wings. **Crustaceans**: many segments to body, many 'appendages' such as legs, antennae. **Arachnids** (spiders): two regions of body, four pairs of legs. **Myriapods**: many segments on long body, many pairs of legs.	**Stenobothrus stigmaticus** (grasshopper) **Oniscus asellus** (woodlouse) **Tegenaria domestica** (house spider) **Lithobius forficatus** (centipede)
'Vertebrates'		
Phylum: **Chordates**	Internal skeleton; have a backbone.	
Class: **Fish**	Aquatic animals, swim using fins. Skin is covered with scales. Produce eggs without shells. 'Cold blooded'.	**Salmo trutta** (trout)
Class: **Reptiles**	Mostly land animals. Move using four limbs. Skin covered with scales. Produce eggs with soft shells. 'Cold blooded'.	**Lacerta vivpara** (Common lizard)
Class: **Amphibia**	Mostly land animals, though reproduce in water. Move using four limbs, no skin covering. Produce eggs without shells. 'Cold blooded'.	**Rana temporaria** (Common frog)
Class: **Birds**	Land animals. Fly using wings; also have two legs. Skin covered with feathers. produce eggs with hard shell. 'Warm blooded'.	**Erithacus rubecula** (robin)

| | | Class: *Mammals* | Mostly live on land. Move using four limbs. Skin usually covered with hair. Produce eggs which develop inside the mother, who feeds young on milk from mammary glands. 'Warm blooded'. | *Oryctolagus cuniculus* (rabbit) |

Fig.5.3 Outline of the main classsification groups (The approximate percentage of all species in each kingdom is given in brackets).

One way in which various organisms could be related to each other is shown in a sort of 'family tree' or **cladogram**. An example of a cladogram which includes the five main kingdoms is shown in Fig.5.4.

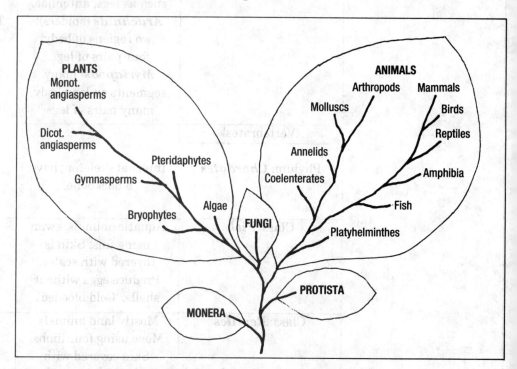

Fig.5.4 Cladogram showing the possible ancestry of the main classification groups.

3 ▸ ARTIFICIAL CLASSIFICATION

Artificial classification is devised for convenience, for example, for identification. It is based on a *limited range of distinguishing characteristics*.

❝Students are sometimes unable to answer fairly basic questions on classification because of an unfamiliarity with the features which distinguish different classification groups.❞

IDENTIFICATION KEYS

It is possible to identify unknown organisms by using a **branching (dichotomous)** or **key diagram** (Fig.5.5) or by *a series of paired questions or descriptions* (Fig.5.6) In each case only one of the two alternatives will apply to the organisms being identified.

The type of branching diagram shown in Fig.5.5 occupies a lot of space and would be difficult to use for identifying many different organisms. For this reason numbered keys are often used instead. An example of a numbered key, based on the branching key in Fig.5.5, is shown in Fig.5.6. The numbers of each of the paired questions in Fig.5.6 correspond to the numbers in the branching diagram (Fig.5.5). In the examples given in Figs.5.5 and 5.6 very few characters are used, and they are relatively easy to apply; the keys have been constructed *specifically* for organisms A to F, and would need to be re-designed if other organisms were included. Keys are constructed for a particular purpose; keys which are for more

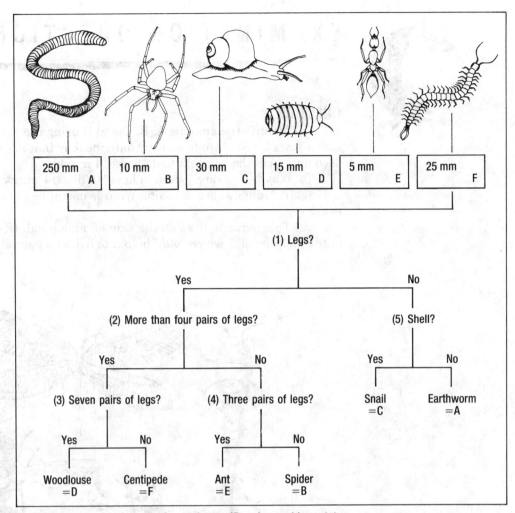

| 250 mm | 10 mm | 30 mm | 15 mm | 5 mm | 25 mm |
| A | B | C | D | E | F |

(1) Legs?

Yes   No

(2) More than four pairs of legs?   **(5) Shell?**

Yes   No   Yes   No

(3) Seven pairs of legs?   **(4) Three pairs of legs?**   Snail   Earthworm
                                              =C   =A

Yes   No   Yes   No

Woodlouse   Centipede   Ant   Spider
=D   =F   =E   =B

Fig.5.5 Branching key for some invertebrates (Drawings not to scale)

1. Legs Present?.................................... Yes:	2	(B,D,E,F)
.... No:	5	(A,C)
2. More than Four pairs of legs?................... Yes:	3	(D,F)
...........................No:	4	(B,E)
3. Seven pairs of legs present?...................Yes:	woodlouse	(D)
...........................No:	centipede	(F)
4. Three pairs of legs present?...................Yes:	ant	(E)
...........................No:	spider	(B)
5. Shell present? .... Yes:	snail	(C)
...........................No:	earthworm	(A)

Fig.5.6 Numbered key for some invertebrates

general use tend to be more complex, for instance in using a wider range of characters.

There are many other ways in which the organisms A to F could be identified. Other convenient characters include *antennae* (organisms B, C, D, E, F but not A), *segmented body* (A, B, D, E, F but not C) *exoskeleton covering all of body* (B, D, E, F but not A and C). Some features, such as *body length*, are not always reliable because of **variation** within the population (Ch.8) owing to age and environmental factors. A key should be based on clearly observable features which do *not* normally vary within the species. Features such as size, colour, habitat and behaviour tend to be less reliable than the *presence* or *absence* of certain body structures or *number* of such body structures. The number of paired questions or statements in a numbered key will normally be *one less* than the number of different organisms being identified. In the key shown in Fig.5.6 for instance, *five* paired questions were used to identify *six* types of invertebrate.

66 **Some students experience difficulties in constructing keys; it does require practice!** 99

EXAMINATION QUESTIONS

QUESTION 1

(a) Identify the animals A, B, C and D using the key. The key can be used for six animals but you are to identify only the four that are shown. Write the letter of each animal in the box next to its name. **4 marks**

(b) Why is size rarely used in keys? (3 lines) **1 mark**

(c) (i) Animal C is a parasite. What is meant by the term **parasite**? (3 lines) **2 marks**

(ii) This parasite lives on the skin of a mammal. Describe **one** feature shown in the diagram of C which *could* help it to live as a parasite. (3 lines) **1 mark**

Total 8 marks (SEG)

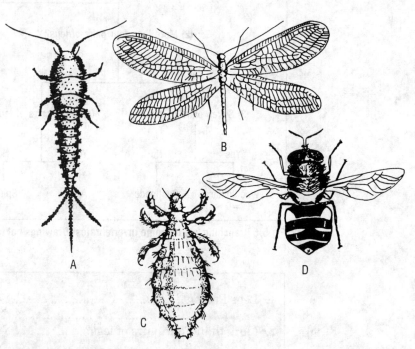

1	Wings present	2
	Wings absent	4
2	Antennae as long as body	*Chrysopa septempunctata* ☐
	Antennae shorter than body	3
3	One pair of wings	*Stratiomyia potamida* ☐
	Two pairs of wings	*Aphis rumicis* ☐
4	Body more than three times longer than wide	*Lepisma saccharina* ☐
	Body not more than three times longer than wide	5
5	Legs longer than body	*Tegenaria domestica* ☐
	Legs shorter than body	*Pediculus humanus* ☐

QUESTION 2

The drawings below show five different arthropods, A, B, C, D and E which are found in woods. The key which follows can be used to identify them.

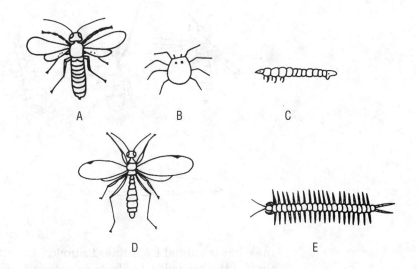

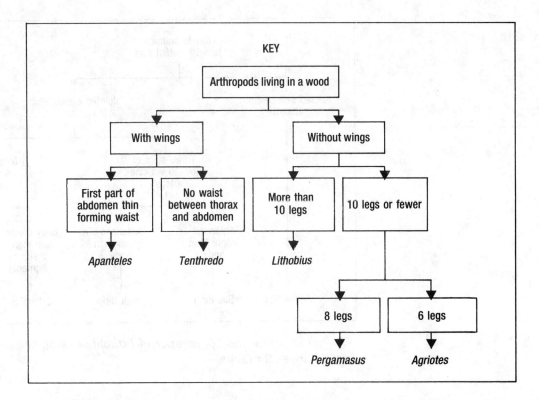

Use the key to identify the arthropods shown in the drawings A to E.
Write the letter of each arthropod next to its name below.

Agriotes..
Apanteles..
Lithobius..
Pergamasus...
Tenthredo...

Total 5 marks (LEAG)

QUESTION 3

The animals drawn below were all found in a pitfall trap set up in a hedge-row. They are not drawn to the same scale.

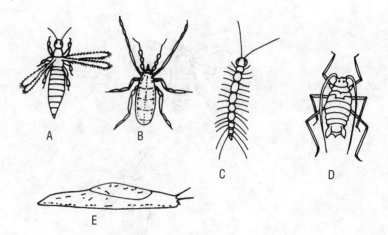

(a) What is animal E? (1 line) **1 mark**

(b) Use the key below to identify animals A and B (2 lines) **2 marks**

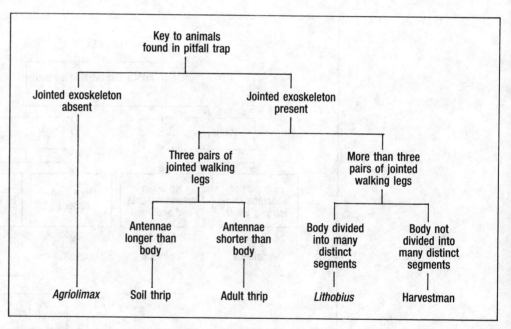

(c) Describe the appearance of *Lithobius* using the information given in the key. (3 lines). **2 marks**

Total 5 marks (LEAG)

QUESTION 4

The drawings below show two insects, A and B, which are found in a wood.

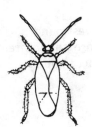

A

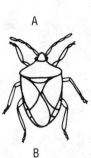

B

(a) Make a drawing of the hind leg of insect A which is twice as large as the drawing above (magnification = x 2) **3 marks**

(b) Complete the table below to show the difference you can see in the drawings between insect A and insect B. **3 marks**

Part of insect	Insect A	Insect B
Antennae		
Legs		
Head		

Total 6 marks (LEAG)

A further practice question on the topics discussed in this chapter is provided in Chapter 18 (question 3).

OUTLINE ANSWERS

ANSWER 1

(a) Antennae as long as body *Chrysopa septempunctata*   B
     One pair of wings *Stratiomyia potamida*   D
     Body more than three times longer than wide *Lepisma saccharina*   A
     Legs shorter than body *Pediculus humanus*   C

(b) Size is a variable feature within the same species for different conditions, for instance age and food availability.

(c) (i) A parasite feeds directly from its living host, with which it is in close relationship.
     (ii) Hooks and bristles on its legs allow it to hold on to the host's skin.

ANSWER 2
C, D, E, B, A, respectively

ANSWER 3
(a)   slug (mollusc)
(b)   A = adult thrip, B = harvestman
(c)   jointed exoskeleton; more than three pairs of jointed walking legs; body divided into many distinct segments.

ANSWER 4
(a)

(b)

Part of insect	Insect A	Insect B
Antennae	Segments are different lengths.	Segments are approximately the same length.
Legs	Covered with hairs/bristles; extra segment.	Not covered with hairs/bristles; no extra segments
Head	Attached to thorax by distinct 'neck'.	Not attached to thorax by distinct 'neck'.

COURSE WORK – A STEP FURTHER

1 ▶ NATURAL CLASSIFICATION

(a) LIVING ORGANISMS
(i) Visit a local zoological or botanical gardens, or wild-life park as a means of investigating the diversity of living things. Individual animals and plants often have their classification displayed next to them. Various publications may be available which provide further information (see below).

(ii) Conduct a survey of a limited number of animals or plants (perhaps 20) in a particular habitat (see Ch.17), such as a square metre of grassland. Count or estimate (see Appendix 3) the number of each type of organism. Identify each type as far as you are able, using keys or guides. Avoid damaging the habitat or the organisms; replace all organisms after your survey is complete. Write a brief summary of your survey.

(b) PRESERVED ORGANISMS
Visit a local natural history museum. The display of plants and animals, including those which are now extinct, is usually arranged according to classification groups.

2 ARTIFICIAL CLASSIFICATION

1. Construct a **branching identification key** (see Fig.5.5) of fairly similar groups of organisms or parts of organisms. Examples include leaves, wild fruits and soil invertebrates. Use only a limited number of different specimens (perhaps eight). Replace all living organisms once you have observed and sketched them. Avoid using variable, indistinct or unreliable features (see Ch.5). Your key should be easy to use by someone who is not familiar with the specimens.

2. Construct a **numerical identification key** (see Fig.5.6), using the branching key you have already constructed. Repeat the exercise with another group of specimens; this time, construct the numerical key directly.

3 SOURCES OF INFORMATION

There are many useful publications on the diversity of life and classification. The following is a selection (those marked* are more advanced):

Diversity Among Living Things, Biological Sciences Curriculum Study (Murray, 1972)

Handbook of Animal Types, Kathleen Cratchley (Longman, 1980)*

Animal Diversity, Diana Kershaw (University Tutorial Press, 1983)*

Classification of the Animal Kingdom, (English Universities Press/The Reader's Digest Association, 1970)

Plant Taxonomy, V. H. Heywood (Institution of Biology/Arnold, 1976)*

Sorting Animals and Plants into Groups, Donald Reid and Philip Booth (Heinemann, 1970)

Classification, Susan Jones and Anne Gray (British Museum (Natural History), 1983)

STUDENT'S ANSWER – EXAMINER'S COMMENTS

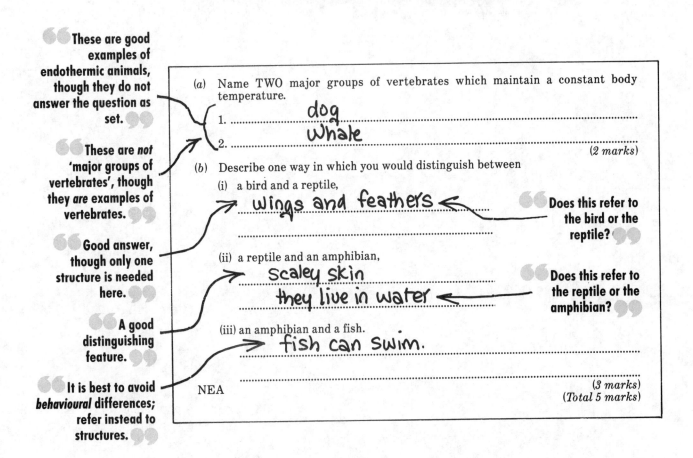

" These are good examples of endothermic animals, though they do not answer the question as set. "

" These are *not* 'major groups of vertebrates', though they *are* examples of vertebrates. "

" Good answer, though only one structure is needed here. "

" A good distinguishing feature. "

" It is best to avoid *behavioural* differences; refer instead to structures. "

(a) Name TWO major groups of vertebrates which maintain a constant body temperature.

1. .... dog ....

2. .... whale ....   *(2 marks)*

(b) Describe one way in which you would distinguish between

(i) a bird and a reptile,

.... wings and feathers ....

" Does this refer to the bird or the reptile? "

(ii) a reptile and an amphibian,

.... scaley skin ....

.... they live in water ....

" Does this refer to the reptile or the amphibian? "

(iii) an amphibian and a fish.

.... fish can swim. ....

NEA   *(3 marks)*
                       (Total 5 marks)

REPRODUCTION

GETTING STARTED

Reproduction is the production of new, independent organisms with similar, though not necessarily identical, characteristics to their parents. Reproduction is one of the *characteristics of life* (see also Ch.4). However, it is needed for the **survival of a species** rather than of individual organisms. We have seen in Ch.4 that a species is a group of similar organisms which may reproduce with each other but not with individuals from other species. An increase in **population** results if the rate of reproduction exceeds the rate of death within a species. In natural conditions populations tend to remain fairly constant; reproduction is therefore an example of **homeostasis** (Ch.11).

Complete **life cycles** of organisms involve growth, development, reproduction and death. These processes are linked and continuous so that a species may continue to exist, even though individuals die. A lifespan is the time required to complete a life cycle and varies between species. Lifespans range from minutes (in bacteria) to several years (in mammals) to centuries (in some trees).

The more complex organisms in general have relatively long periods of growth and development. Life cycles may be interrupted by disease, predation or unfavourable changes in the environment. However, the extinction of a species may be avoided if at least *some* individuals have the opportunity to reproduce.

TYPES OF
REPRODUCTION
ASEXUAL
REPRODUCTION
SEXUAL
REPRODUCTION
SEXUAL
REPRODUCTION IN
FLOWERING
PLANTS
SEXUAL
REPRODUCTION IN
ANIMALS

ESSENTIAL PRINCIPLES

Reproduction can be thought of as the overall purpose of life. Growth and development can be regarded as a preparation for reproduction. Other **characteristics of life** (see Ch.4) such as respiration, nutrition and excretion may keep the individual alive until after its genes have been transferred to the next generation. Indeed, many organisms die soon after they have taken part in reproduction.

There are two main types of reproduction:

(a) **Asexual reproduction** Part of a single 'parent' separates and becomes an independent organism, which is genetically identical to the parent. Asexual reproduction occurs in many plants and in simpler animals.

(b) **Sexual reproduction** Two parents each produce special sex cells, called gametes, which become fused together during fertilization. This process forms an individual which combines characteristics of both parents but is different from each parent. This is important, because it increases variation amongst individuals (Ch.8).

> **This is an important idea in understanding variation and natural selection.**

Many organisms reproduce asexually but most organisms reproduce sexually. Some organisms are capable of both sexual and asexual reproduction depending, for instance, on environmental conditions. In all cases, reproduction involves the transfer of genetic information to the next generation.

Fig.6.1 summarises the main features of asexual and sexual reproduction.

FEATURE	ASEXUAL	SEXUAL
Ocurrence	Simpler, smaller plants and animals.	Complex, larger plants and animals.
Parent(s)	Only one parent involved.	Usually two parents involved.
Specialised structures needed.	Reproductive tissue may include various outgrowths, spores, etc.	Reproductive tissue is specialised for the production (by meiosis) and transfer of gametes.
Inheritance	Offspring are genetically identical to the parent, i.e. they are clones.	Offspring are genetically different from each parent. This increases variation.
Reproductive rate	Relatively fast	Relatively slow.

Fig.6.1 Comparison of asexual and sexual reproduction

Asexual reproduction involves a separation from the parent of cells or tissues, which then become independent. Separation occurs after a period of growth and dependency and is followed by growth (see Ch.7). Offspring from asexual reproduction are genetically identical **clones**. They will only be different from the parent if a **mutation** (Ch.8) during their formation alters their genetic make-up (genotype). However, even in clones the outward appearance (phenotype) can vary because of environmental influences, such as the availability of nutrients.

Clones reduce variability in a population; they do, however, increase genetic certainty. They can also be produced rapidly and without the need for two parents. Asexual reproduction may therefore be an advantage in a fairly constant environment to which the organism is already well adapted. It could also be important if the reproducing organism is isolated from other members of the species, when sexual reproduction would be impossible. However, organisms produced by asexual means also inherit parental characteristics which may reduce the chances of survival in a particular environment. This might lower the ability of an organism to adapt to changing conditions.

The comparative advantages and disadvantages of asexual reproduction vary between species, and also within a particular species' lifespan. Aphids (*Aphis*), for example, reproduce asexually and then sexually during one season.

EXAMPLES OF ASEXUAL REPRODUCTION
(i) Binary fission

Binary fission involves a splitting of a single cell into two. This involves an equal division of the nucleus, followed by organelles and cytoplasm. Binary fission occurs in bacteria, protozoa, e.g. *Amoeba,* and simple algae, e.g. *Pleurococcus*.

The total number of cells in the population can, in theory, increase in an *exponential* way (see Appendix 1) e.g. 1, 2, 4, 8, 16, 32. However, environmental factors (see Chs.16 and 17) limit such growth in number. Individual cells cease to exist when they divide; they do not necessarily die, so perhaps they are immortal!

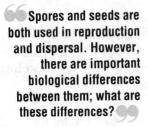

> This exponential increase occurs in growth both of individual organisms and of populations. However, students often misunderstand the sequence; refer to Appendix 1 if you are still unsure.

(ii) Budding

Budding occurs in the unicellular fungi called yeasts (*Saccharomyces*) and also in *Hydra* (animal) and *Bryophyllum* (plant).This involves the formation of a swelling or **bud** which then develops into a complete organism. In yeast, since the buds may not separate when formed, chains of cells result. *Hydra* is a multicellular animal, and buds are formed only from undifferentiated cells.

(iii) Fragmentation

Part of the parent organism breaks away and develops separately. This occurs in *Spirogyra* (plant) and *Planaria* (animal). The multicellular, filamentous algae such as *Spirogyra* produce additional cells by growing extra cross walls (*septation*). A new filament is formed when it breaks away from an existing strand.

(iv) Spore formation

Spores are small particles, consisting of one or more cells, which are covered by a tough outer covering and are resistant to harsh conditions, such as desiccation. Spores are easily dispersed by air currents and germinate in favourable conditions. Large quantities of spores are produced to offset possible losses.

> Spores and seeds are both used in reproduction and dispersal. However, there are important biological differences between them; what are these differences?

Examples of organisms forming spores include bacteria, protozoa, mosses and ferns and also fungi such as *Mucor* (pin mould). Spore formation (**sporulation**) occurs more frequently in plants than animals. In *Mucor*, specialised reproductive structures called **sporangia** are formed. These produce and store spores until they can be released (Fig.6.2).

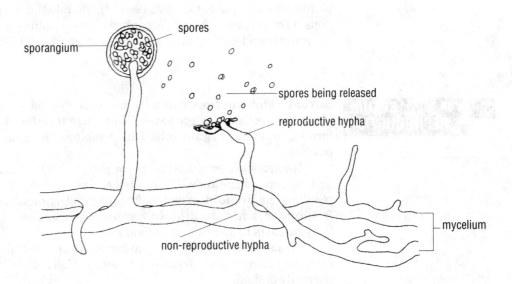

Fig.6.2 Sporulation in Mucor

(v) Vegetative reproduction

Asexual reproduction by vegetative means in flowering plants occurs as an alternative or as an addition to sexual reproduction. Specialised structures arise from the somatic or vegetative (non-sexual) tissues and then become separated as independent young plants. In many cases these are originally parts of perennating organs. These allow herbaceous (non-woody) perennial plants to food to allow growth to be resumed after a period of dormancy.

Examples of vegetative structures include **runners**, e.g. strawberry, (*Fragaria*) (see Fig.6.3), and those with **perennating organs**, such as **tubers**, e.g. potato (*Solanum*); **rhizomes**, e.g. iris, (*Iris*); **bulbs**, e.g. onion, (*Allium*); and **corms**, e.g. Crocus (*Colchium*).

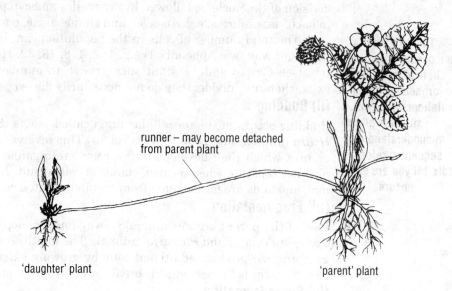

runner – may become detached from parent plant

'daughter' plant   'parent' plant

Fig.6.3 Vegetative propogation in strawberry (Fragaria)

(vi) Artificial propagation

Gardeners may make use of the vegetative reproduction of their plants in order to propagate (or multiply) them. They may take **cuttings** from a plant, which are then rooted in soil. Another method is by **grafting**, in which the cutting, or **scion**, from the donor plant is bound to a **root stock** of the recipient plant.

(vii) Parthenogenesis

Sometimes called 'virgin birth', parthenogenesis can occur in certain animals and plants such as aphids (*Myzus*), bees (*Apis*) and stick insects (*Dixippus*) and dandelions (*Taraxacum*). These organisms can produce many genetically identical offspring from female gametes which develop without fertilization.

3 > SEXUAL REPRODUCTION

Sexual reproduction normally involves two parents, each of which produces special sex cells called **gametes**. These fuse together during fertilization, initially forming a single **zygote** cell. This combines the genetic characteristics of both parents.

Gametes are produced within reproductive tissues by a particular type of cell division, called **meiosis** (Ch.8). Meiosis halves the total number of chromosomes, resulting in **haploid** gametes. The original chromosome number is restored at fertilization, when the **diploid** zygote is formed. The zygote then divides repeatedly by **mitosis** to form a new individual.

Meiosis only occurs in reproductive tissue; cell division in non-reproductive (*somatic* or *vegetative*) tissue is by mitosis. Cells other than gametes are therefore normally diploid.

In simple organisms such as protozoa, algae and fungi (see Fig.6.4), gametes are all very similar. (For convenience they may be given the symbols + and -). In more complex organisms, gametes are structurally and functionally distinct; they are male (♂) or female (♀).

Single-sexed (**dioecious**) organisms produce either male or female gametes; this is very typical in animals.

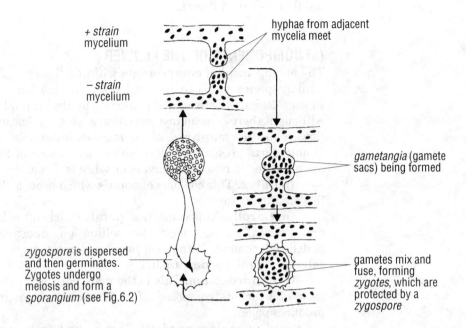

Fig.6.4 Sexual reproduction in the fungus Mucor

Bisexual (**monoecious** or **hermaphrodite**) organisms produce both male and female gametes; this is fairly common in simpler animals and is widespread in the more advanced plants.

The female gamete is often relatively large (it may contain a foodstore), e.g. bird's egg. The male gamete tends to be small and mobile, so it can easily be moved by **vectors** such as wind (e.g. as in the pollen grain). Some male gametes are *motile* and can move themselves (e.g. sperm).

Specialised tissues are needed to produce, store and release gametes for sexual reproduction. The development of these tissues is determined by heredity (Ch.8). Development may be accompanied by more general differences in form between females and males of the same species; this is called **sexual dimorphism**.

EXAMPLES OF SEXUAL REPRODUCTION

Whilst asexual reproduction occurs in many species, **sexual** reproduction occurs in most species at some stage during their life cycle. This is probably because sexual reproduction results in increased **variation** (Ch.8) which is important in adapting to a changing environment.

Simpler *multicellular* organisms such as *Spirogyra* and *Mucor* (Fig.6.4) are capable of sexual, as well as asexual, reproduction. Even *unicellular* organisms such as protozoa and bacteria are thought to be capable of sexual reproduction. Gametes, which may either consist of nuclei or entire cell contents, are fused when two organisms become attached to each other. This process is known as **conjugation**.

4 SEXUAL REPRODUCTION IN FLOWERING PLANTS

Advanced plants typically show more cell specialisation than is seen in simple organisms. For example, they have vascular tissue (see Ch.12) and also have more elaborate reproductive structures. The most advanced plants may produce **seeds** from flowers or cones. Less advanced plants such as mosses and ferns do not produce distinct seeds, and their life cycles involve spore-producing as well as seed-producing stages.

The **flower** is the reproductive organ of sexual reproduction in the flowering plants. The flower is a modified shoot, with modified leaves mounted on a **receptacle** and attached to the rest of the plant by a flower stalk, or **pedicel**. The numbers and arrangements of flowers (**inflorescences**) on a single plant vary considerably. Composite flowers like dandelion (*Taraxacum*) are made of individual flowers called **florets**.

(a) COMPONENTS OF THE FLOWER
The arrangement of **components** within a flower is often characteristic for a particular species and can be used for identification and classification (see Ch.6). Flower design is determined primarily by the method of **pollination** (see below). Although there are many variations, certain features frequently occur. Most flowers are **hermaphrodite** (or **monoecious**), that is they have both male and female parts present. Flowers commonly consist of four main components which are arranged in concentric layers or **whorls**. From the outside these whorls are:

(i) **Calyx.** This consists of **sepals** which protect the flower in bud and in some flowers attract insects.

(ii) **Corolla.** This consists of **petals** which, often being conspicuously coloured and scented, attract insects for pollination; **nectaries** (sugar sacs) may be an added inducement. Petals are fused in some flowers. The collective name for the calyx and corolla is **perianth**.

(iii) **Androecium.** This is the male part of the flower consisting of **stamens**, each of which is composed of a **filament** supporting an **anther**. The anther produces pollen.

(iv) **Gynaecium** or **pistil**. This is the female part of the flower consisting of **carpels**. Each carpel is made up of a swollen **ovary** and an extended **style** which terminates in a **stigma** that receives pollen.

These components are shown in their relative positions in a generalised flower (Fig.6.5). This flower is not, however, to be seen as representative of flower structures in general because they are modified in so many different ways.

If you are familiar with the names and functions of the main parts of a flower, you will more easily gain a greater understanding of *particular* examples of flowers.

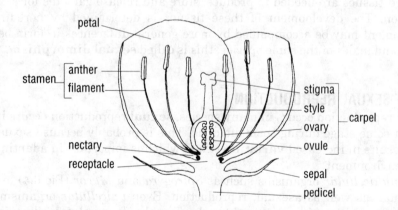

Fig.6.5 Structure of a generalised flower (vertical section)

(b) POLLINATION
Pollination is the transfer of pollen from an anther to a stigma. Pollen can be transferred *between* plants, by **cross pollination**, or *within* plants, by **self pollination**. Cross pollination involves different plants (**outbreeding**), so it increases genetic variability (Ch.8). Self-pollination involves the same plant (**inbreeding**), and variability is therefore reduced. For this reason plants often avoid self pollination and encourage cross pollination, the mechanisms involved sometimes being very elaborate. Some of the main methods are presented in Fig.6.6. You should note, however, that self pollination may take place in hermaphrodite plants if cross pollination does not occur; e.g. in isolated plants. Some species (e.g. groundsel (*Senecio*)) are self pollinated.

MECHANISM	DESCRIPTION	EXAMPLES
Unisexual (dioecious) plants.	Separate male and female plants.	holly (*Ilex*) willow (*Salix*)
Unisexual (dioecious) flowers	Separate male nad female flowers on same bisexual plant.	oak (*Quercus*) hazel (*Corylus*)

Protogyny	Female parts mature before the male parts in a bisexual flower.	bluebell (*Endynmion*) plantain (*Plantago*)
Protandry	Male parts mature before the female parts in a bisexual flower.	white deadnettle (*Lamium*) dandelion(*Taraxacum*)
Self-incompatibility	Pollen grain from the plant does not successfully produce a pollen tube	sweet pea (*Lathyrus*) clover (*Trifolium*)
Heterostyly	Male and female structures are positioned differently in different insect-pollinated flowers.	primrose (*Primula*)

Fig.6.6 Mechanisms of avoiding self-pollination

Methods of Pollination

The *actual transfer* of pollen during cross pollination is achieved in various ways. The two main methods are **insect pollination** and **wind pollination**, and flowers tend to be adapted to one or the other. This is reflected by structural differences summarised in Fig.6.9.

Insect Pollination is common amongst herbaceous plants. Insects and insect-pollinated plants provide benefits for each other. The life cycles and the distribution of insects and the plants they pollinate correspond very closely. Each is adapted to the other. This is an example of **co-evolution** (Ch.9).

Insects are a convenient vector (carrier) of pollen since they are small, numerous and highly mobile. Some plants are pollinated by various insects and have a fairly open plan, e.g. buttercup (*Ranunculus*). Other plants are pollinated mainly by a particular type of insect, for instance with a certain length of proboscis (tongue). Such plants are fairly closed, with fused petals, e.g. white deadnettle (*Lamium album*) (Fig.6.7).

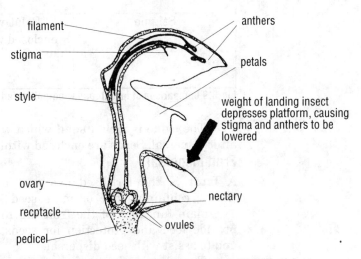

Fig.6.7 Insect-pollinated flower: white deadnettle (Lamium album) (half-flower)

The white deadnettle flower incorporates all of the characteristic features of insect-pollinated plants. These features are summarised in Fig.6.9.

Wind Pollination is common amongst trees and grasses. Wind is a convenient vector (carrier) because it is relatively independent of seasons. An example of a wind-pollinated flower is meadow grass (*Poa* spp) (Fig.6.8). The main characteristics of wind-pollinated flowers are given in Fig.6.9.

Clearly insects can pollinate wind-pollinated flowers, too. Some terrestrial (land) plants are pollinated by other animals such as mammals (bats, possums) or birds. Aquatic plants such as Canadian pondweed (*Elodea canadensis*) are pollinated by water. Flowers can also be pollinated artificially, in **artificial selection.**

(c) FERTILIZATION

When pollination is successfully completed, the pollen grains germinate to produce a **pollen tube**. This carries a **tube nucleus**, and also two **male nuclei** which fuse with **female nuclei** within the ovule (Fig.6.10). In a **double fertilization**, an **embryo** zygote and an **endosperm** (food) zygote are formed.

> **Remember that pollination and fertilization are not the same; pollination occurs before fertilization, and fertilization may not take place at all!**

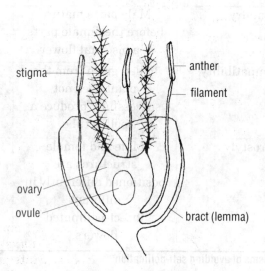

Fig.6.8 Wind-pollinated flower: meadow grass (Poa spp.) (half-flower)

FEATURE	INSECT-POLLINATED	WIND-POLLINATED
Petals	Large, conspicuous, brightly coloured.	Small or absent.
Nectar	May be present	Absent
Scent	May be present	Absent
Anthers	Small, enclosed within flower	Large, hanging outside flower
Filament	Short, rigid	Long, flexible
Pollen grains	Sticky, rough and relatively large. Adhere to insect body	Smooth, light and relatively small. Produced in large quantities, to offset losses.
Stigma	Relatively small; enclosed within flower	Feathery, large surface area exposed on outside of flower to collect pollen.

Fig.6.9 Comparison of insect- and wind-pollinated flowers

The ovule is now a **seed** which will, if conditions are favourable, germinate after dispersal. Seeds are enclosed within **fruits** which are important in dispersal.

Fruit dispersal

A **fruit** is the fertilised ovary of a flower, containing one or more seeds. The main functions of the fruit are to provide food and protection for seeds, and to assist with seed dispersal.

The development of a fruit is accompanied by certain changes in the flower. The ovary wall, now called the **pericarp**, may swell considerably; to protect, nourish and, eventually, disperse the seeds enclosed within it. In 'false fruits', e.g. the apple (*Malus*) the

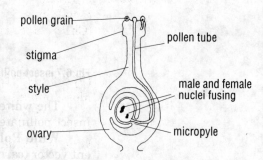

Fig.6.10 Fertilization in a generalised carpel

swollen receptacle performs a similar function.

Other floral parts, for instance the sepals, petals and androecium, may wither away. The stigma and style of each carpel may also degenerate, though in some flowers they are involved in dispersal.

Dispersal is important because:

Seeds which grow near the parent plant may **compete** for similar resources such as water, mineral ions and light (Ch.17).

It helps **avoid overcrowding** which increases the chance of the spread of disease.

It provides an opportunity to **colonise** new areas.

There are two main types of fruit, *fleshy* (succulent) or *dry*. Some examples of each of these, together with their methods of dispersal, are presented below:

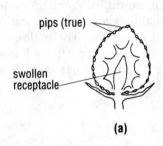

(a)

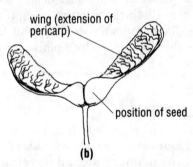

(b)

Fig.6.11 (a) Fleshy fruit: strawberry (Fragaria) (vertical section) (b) Dry fruit: sycamore (Acer)

Students often confuse pollination and seed dispersal because both involve wind or animal vectors

Fleshy fruits. These are often brightly coloured, scented and nutritious. Once the fruit has been eaten, dispersal involves seeds being either spat out or ejested, unharmed, with faeces. Examples of 'true' fruits include plum (*Prunus*) and blackberry (*Rubus*). 'False' fruits include apple (*Malus*) and strawberry (*Fragaria*) (Fig.6.11 (a)).

Dry fruits. These have more varied means of dispersal:

Splitting (dehiscent) fruits spring open, sometimes quite violently, as they dry out, throwing seeds away from the parent plant. Examples include pea (*Pisum*), violet (*Viola*), lupin (*Lupinus*).

Wind-borne fruits have adaptations to delay a fall to the ground. These include wings, e.g. in sycamore (*Acer*) (Fig.6.11 (b)) and ash (*Fraxinus*) and 'parachutes', e.g. in dandelion (*Taraxacum*) and willow (*Salix*). In some species, small, light seeds are thrown from the plant as it sways in the wind. Examples of this 'censer' mechanism include poppy (*Papaver*) and foxglove (*Digitalis*).

Nuts are carried by birds and mammals to hiding places and then, in some cases, forgotten. Examples are oak (*Quercus*) and hazel (*Corylus*).

Buoyant fruits of plants living in or near water are dispersed by water currents. Such plants include water lily (*Nymphaea*) and coconut (*Cocos*).

5 ▷ SEXUAL REPRODUCTION IN ANIMALS

Almost all animals **reproduce sexually**. The **hermaphrodite** (bisexual) condition, common in advanced plants, tends to occur in simpler animals. Examples include hydra (*Hydra*), earthworm (*Lumbricus*) and snail (*Helix*). However, cross-fertilization (outbreeding) (Ch.8) between two parents tends to occur. Self-fertilization (inbreeding) may be necessary in an isolated animal, such as the endoparasite (Ch.15) tapeworm (*Taenia*).

(a) SITE OF FERTILIZATION

Most animals, especially the vertebrates (Ch.5), are unisexual, being either male or female. A major variation within this group is whether the **site of fertilization** is *external* or *internal*. This will tend to affect both the number and size of the gametes produced.

(i) External fertilization

Fertilization is **external** in animals which live, or perhaps just reproduce, in water. Many invertebrates, fish, amphibians (but not aquatic mammals) use this method. Males and females release their numerous gametes together into the water. The chances of successful fertilization are increased in some fish by using shallow water 'spawning grounds'. This may involve long migrations during the breeding season. Examples include trout (*Salmo trutta*). In the trout, females scrape a depression in gravel to protect the eggs. Fertilization in stickleback (*Gasterosteus*) and the trout is made more likely by an elaborate courtship ritual and (in stickleback) by parental care. Young trout ('alevins') are nourished for a while by yolk sacs.

(ii) Internal fertilization

The transfer of gametes is more difficult out of water. **Internal** fertilization is therefore an adaptation to a land existence and occurs in terrestrial animals such as insects, reptiles, birds and mammals. The male and female need to come into close contact for fertilization to take place; this is known as **copulation**. In internal fertilization, it is more likely, compared with external fertilization, that gametes will meet.

(b) SITE OF DEVELOPMENT

Another way in which reproduction can vary between different animal groups is in whether the **site of development** of a fertilised egg (zygote) is *external* or *internal*, or even both.

In most animals development takes place **externally** (**oviparous** development); the embryo is protected and nourished by its own food supply within an egg. This tends to be a very distinct structure in reptiles and birds. In most *mammals* (the exceptions are the marsupials; development takes place **internally**. The embryo is supported within the female by a placenta (**viviparous** development).

(a) SEXUAL DEVELOPMENT

Individual humans are either male or female, and this is determined by the inheritance of **sex chromosomes** (Ch.8). Individuals of each sex are, however, similar in many respects until the **primary sexual development** of the **gonads**, which are the sites of gamete production. Gonads also produce **hormones** (Ch.13) which stimulate the development of **secondary sexual characteristics**.

The bodies of children undergo extensive changes which prepare them for the possibilities of reproduction as **adults**. The period of transition of children into adults is called **adolescence**, and the onset of primary sexual development is called **puberty**. This is accompanied by the development of secondary sexual characteristics. Some of the physical changes which take place include:

Male: development of muscles, widening of shoulders, deepening of the voice, development of coarser hair on body surface, especially on face, under arms and in the pubic region.

Female: development of subcutaneous fat, development of breasts, widening of hips, slight deepening of the voice, development of hair under arms and in the pubic region.

In both males and females there is a general growth of body tissues, although this does not occur at the same rate throughout the body (this is called **allometric growth**, see Ch.7). The effect of secondary sexual development is, in effect, to advertise maturity to possible sexual partners. In females, development is also a preparation for pregnancy and birth if fertilization occurs. In general, the process of puberty begins earlier in females than in males (Ch.7), though there is much variation between individuals.

The function of the male and female reproductive systems includes the production of gametes and hormones. In males, there is a means of transferring gametes into the female. In females, provision is made for the possible development of one or more fertilized eggs (zygotes).

(i) Male reproductive system.

The male reproductive system is shown in Fig.6.12. The male gamete is the **sperm** (Fig.6.14a) and the gamete-producing structures (gonads) are the **testes**. Each testis consists of about 500 metres of sperm tubules which produce and store sperm. Between the tubules are cells which produce **testosterone**, the male sex hormone (Ch.13).

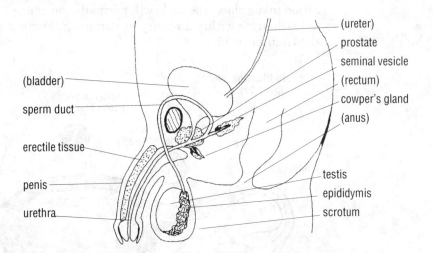

Fig.6.12 Human male reproductive system (section - side view)

(ii) Female reproductive system.

The female reproductive system is shown in Fig.6.13. The system is more

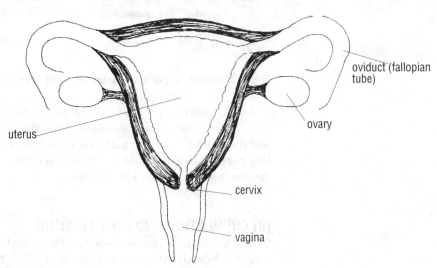

Fig.6.13 Human female reproductive system (section - front view)

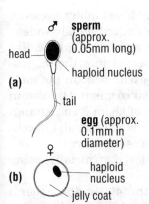

Fig.6.14 Male ((a), sperm) and female ((b), egg) gametes

complex than that of the male because, apart from the production of gametes and sex hormones, it may be the site of development if fertilization occurs.

The female gamete is the **egg** (*ovum*) (Fig.6.14b). Eggs (*ova*) are produced in the two **ovaries**, which are the female gonads. Each ovary is also responsible for producing various hormones including **oestrogen**, the female sex hormone (Ch.13).

(iii) Female menstrual (oestrous) cycle

Females produce eggs as part of a regular **menstrual** or **oestrous cycle**, often of about 28 days. About 400 eggs are released between puberty (around twelve years) and **menopause** (around forty-five). This periodic and limited release of gametes is unlike the situation in males, who normally produce gametes continuously (millions per day) and over a longer period (from about age 12 to 70 years).

The menstrual cycle involves two important events:

(a) **Menstruation** ('period') at days 1–5. This is the shedding of the lining of the uterus (endometrium), which had previously been thickened to receive a possible fertilised egg.

(b) **Ovulation** (egg release) at days 13–15. A single egg is usually released from alternate ovaries during each cycle.

Both these processes can be interrupted by fertilization and **implantation**, and ovulation can be interrupted by the contraceptive pill (see below). If no fertilization takes place, the cycle will normally continue.

Changes within an ovary at various intervals during the menstrual cycle are shown in Fig.6.15.

> **Remember, menstruation and ovulation are quite distinct processes, though one follows the other in a cycle.**

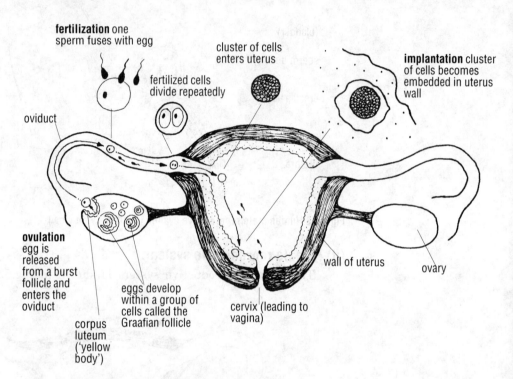

Fig.6.15 Summary of ovulation, fertilization and implantation

The relative amounts of the hormones including oestrogen and progesterone vary during the cycle. Oestrogen from the ovary tissue has various effects, including the thickening of the uterus lining following menstruation. Progesterone from the **corpus luteum** maintains the thickened lining; a drop in progesterone levels causes menstruation to take place.

(b) COPULATION AND FERTILIZATION

Copulation is a process which brings male and female gametes (Fig.6.14) into contact. **Fertilization** (conception) is when they fuse and their chromosomes are combined, forming a diploid zygote.

The **penis** of a sexually excited male becomes erect as blood under pressure fills the spongy **erectile tissue.** The **vagina** of a sexually excited female widens and becomes lubricated by the secretion of mucus. During copulation (also called mating, sexual intercourse, coition) the erect penis is inserted into the vagina. Movements of the penis may result in increasing physical excitement in the male and the female and can lead to a peak of excitement, called **orgasm**. Orgasm in the male is a reflex process which results in the ejaculation of about 5 cm^3 **semen** by rhythmic contractions of the vas deferens. Orgasm in the female results in contractions of the vagina and uterus, which draws sperm towards the uterus.

The transfer of sperm (**insemination**) can also be achieved artificially, using a syringe.

Only a small proportion (i.e. several hundreds) of the 400 million sperm deposited at the cervix actually reach the site of fertilization in the oviduct. One sperm only is allowed successfully to penetrate any egg present in the oviduct.

This must be within thirty-six hours of ovulation. The sperm will lose its tail, and the haploid nuclei of the sperm and egg will form the diploid zygote of a new life.

Twins

There are two ways in which twins (and other multiple births such as triplets etc.) are formed:

(a) **Identical twins.** An egg is fertilized as normal with a single sperm and the resulting zygote divides into two cells. However, the cells do not remain together; instead, they separate and continue independent development. Identical twins have the same genotype (Ch.8) so will for example, be of the same sex. Identical twins have been useful in studying inheritance (Ch.8).

(b) **Non-identical (fraternal) twins.** Two eggs are released at the same time, by one or both ovaries. Both eggs are fertilized separately by different sperm. Non-identical twins have the same genetic relationship as brothers or sisters; they need not be of the same sex.

(c) PREGNANCY AND DEVELOPMENT

Pregnancy (*gestation*) is the interval between the conception and birth of an individual. This normally takes 40 weeks (9 months) in humans.

Development involves both the growth and organisation of tissues (Ch.7); this prepares an **embryo** or **foetus** for a relatively independent existence as a **baby**. It may take four days for the cilia on the inside of the oviduct to waft the zygote down to the uterus, during this time the zygote divides repeatedly by **mitosis** (Ch.4). The resulting embryo of about 128 cells becomes embedded (**implanted**) in the thickened lining of the uterus, which supplies essential nutrients. The uterus lining is maintained by secretions from the uterus of progesterone, which prevents menstruation and ovulation during pregnancy. This early development is shown in Fig.6.15.

The growing embryo gradually begins (at about 8 weeks) to show distinct human features and is now called a **foetus**. The foetus and the mother jointly form a **placenta** (from about 12 weeks). This allows materials to be exchanged between the blood of the foetus and mother; substances diffuse across a very small gap between foetal and maternal capillaries (Fig.6.16). The surface area available for diffusion is increased by the presence of **villi**. However, their blood never actually mixes. This is important because the blood may be incompatible (Ch.8), and there are differences in pressure between the two systems.

The foetus is connected to the placenta by an **umbilical cord** and is supported and protected in an **amniotic sac** containing **amniotic fluid**, which acts as a shock-absorber.

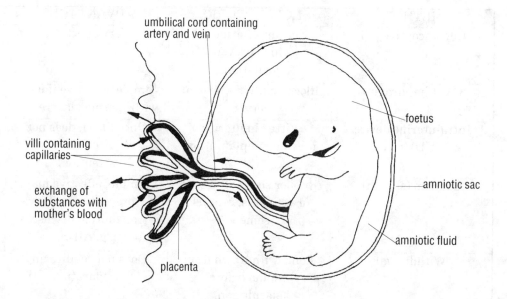

Fig.6.16 Exchange of substances at the placenta

(d) BIRTH

Birth (**parturition**) is the transition of a dependent, 'parasitic' foetus into a relatively independent baby. Processes such as gaseous exchange, nutrition and excretion which have been undertaken by the placenta need to be taken over by specialised organs.

Birth normally commences after about 40 weeks with the baby in a head-down position; less usually the baby may be born feet first (**breech birth**). The baby is expelled by rhythmic involuntary contractions of the uterus, which increase in intensity and frequency during **labour**.

The cervix, vagina and even the hips expand to allow the baby through. The separate bones of the baby's skull, which are not yet fused, allow the head to be compressed. Amniotic fluid is released as the baby is born, and the placenta (**afterbirth**) is delivered shortly afterwards. The umbilical cord is then tied.

The sudden temperature drop at birth causes a **reflex response** (Ch.13) in the baby, which begins to breathe. This involves an inflation of the lungs as the pulmonary circulation (Ch.12) comes into use.

(e) PARENTAL CARE

Mammals in general, and humans in particular, show a considerable degree of **parental care**. This corresponds with the long period of development of these complex animals.

Babies are normally **breast-fed** (*suckled*) from about 24 hours after birth. Initially babies receive **colostrum**, which is easier to digest than milk and also contains **antibodies** (Ch.12). The **mammary glands** develop during pregnancy to produce milk; this is a characteristic feature of most mammals (Ch.5). The production of milk is stimulated by the suckling action; this is another example of a reflex response. Human milk contains the correct balance of nutrients (Ch.15), delivered at a suitable temperature. Babies are gradually **weaned** onto solid food.

(f) CONTRACEPTION

Sexual partners may want to remove the possibility of conception (fertilization) from sexual intercourse. This is called **contraception** (birth control, family planning).It is achieved by preventing the egg and sperm from meeting. There are various ways in which this can be done; these are summarised in Fig.6.17. Contraception is one means of limiting an increase in human populations (Ch.17).

METHOD	HOW IT WORKS	ADVANTAGES	DISADVANTAGES
Contraceptive pill	Contains hormones which prevent ovulation.	Very effective.	Possible side effects; possible to forget.
Cap (diaphragm)	Blocks path of sperm at cervix.	Simple, effective if used with spermicidal cream.	May be incorrectly fitted.
Intra-uterine device (IUD) (coil)	Fitted in uterus; prevents implantation.	Once fitted, does not require frequent attention.	May cause pain or heavy bleeding.
Condom (sheath)	Rubber sleeve, fits over erect penis; retains semen.	Simple, effective may prevent sexually transmitted diseases e.g. AIDS.	May be damaged; may not be carefully removed.
Withdrawal	Penis withdrawn from vagina before ejaculation.	Does not require any preparation.	Semen may be released before ejaculation.

Rhythm method (safe period)	Intercourse avoided during 'high risk' time around ovulation.	Relatively 'natural'; acceptable to Roman Catholic church.	Menstrual cycles may be irregular.
Sterilization	Male: sperm ducts surgically cut (vasectomy). Female: oviducts surgically cut.	Totally effective.	Permanent, irreversible.

Fig.6.17 Summary of some common methods of contraception (presented in decreasing order of percentage use in the UK)

EXAMINATION QUESTIONS

QUESTION 1
Fig.6.18 shows a liverwort.
(a) Liverworts, like the one shown, often grow in damp areas, for example the banks of streams just above the fast moving water. Several kinds of liverwort produce structures called gemmae which are dispersed and then will grow into new plants.
(i)   What does the word 'dispersal' mean? (1 line) **1 mark**
(ii) Give two reasons why dispersal is important. (4 lines) **2 marks**
(iii) Suggest how the gemmae may be dispersed. (2 lines) **1 mark**
(b) Fig.6.19 shows the fruits of a lime tree (drawn actual size).
(i)   Suggest how the fruit may be dispersed from the parent plant. (2 lines) **1 mark**
(ii) How does structure A help in this process? (2 lines) **1 mark**

Total 6 marks (LEAG)

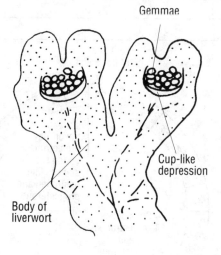

Fig.6.18

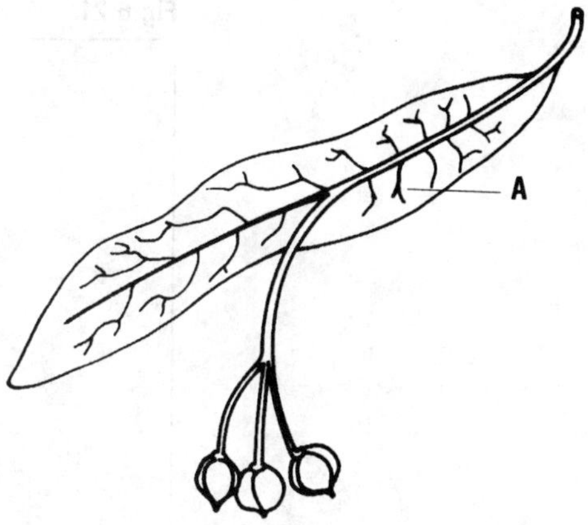

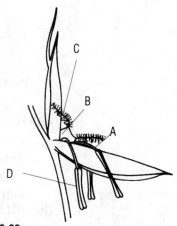

Fig.6.19

QUESTION 2
Fig.6.20 shows the parts of a mature, wind-pollinated flower.

(a) Name the parts indicated by the letters in Fig.6.20. (4 lines) **2 marks**
(b) Name two structural features, shown in Fig.6.20 that indicate that the flower is adapted for wind pollination. (2 lines) **2 marks**

Fig.6.20

(c) Explain how the two features that you have chosen in your answer to part (b) assist the wind pollination mechanism. (6 lines) **2 marks**

Total 6 marks (IGCSE)

QUESTION 3

Oestrogen and progesterone are two female sex hormones. Fig.6.21 shows some of the events in a 28-day menstrual cycle: the width of the outer band indicates the relative quantity of sex hormones in the blood.

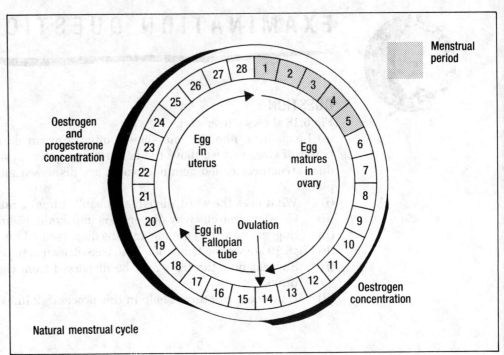

Fig.6.21

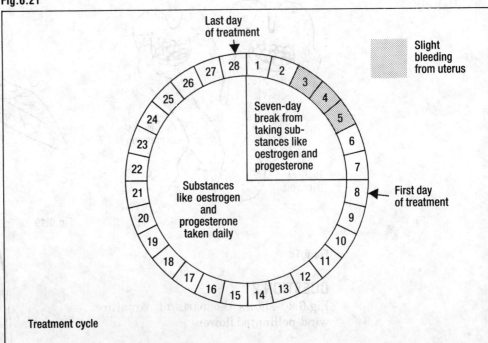

Fig 6.22

(a)   (i) On which three days of this cycle would fertilisation of the egg be most likely? **1 mark**

        (ii) If sperms can live in the female reproductive organs for up to eight days, on which days could insemination lead to fertilization? **1 mark**

(b)   How does the concentration of sex hormones appear to control events in the menstrual cycle? **3 marks**

(c)   Substances like oestrogen and progesterone are now factory-made and are sometimes used to regulate a menstrual cycle. Fig.6.22 shows one form of this treatment (though the relative quantities of sex hormone in the blood are not shown).
Compare events in the natural 28-day menstrual cycle and the 28-day treatment cycle and describe similarities and differences between them. Suggest reasons for the differences wherever you can. **10 marks**

Total 15 marks (SEG)

QUESTION 4
(a) Fig.6.23 shows the human female reproductive organs.

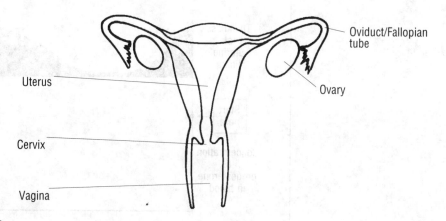

Fig.6.23

Read the following passage and with the help of the diagram answer the questions below.

A woman with blocked oviducts/Fallopian tubes cannot have a baby in the normal way but can now have a 'test-tube baby'. A doctor, using a fine tube through the body wall, sucks up several eggs from the ovary, puts them in a dish and mixes sperm with them. The eggs are then kept for a few days before they are put into the woman's uterus via the cervix.
(i)   Describe what can normally happen in the oviduct/Fallopian tube. (3 lines) **3 marks**
(ii)   Why does the doctor get the eggs from the ovary through the body wall and not through the vagina and uterus? (2 lines) **1 mark**
(iii) Why must sperm be mixed with the eggs before they are put back in the woman? (1 line) **1 mark**
(iv)   Why do you think the eggs are kept for a few days before they are put back into the woman? (2 lines) **1 mark**
(v)   Why are the eggs put into the uterus? (2 lines) **2 marks**
(vi)   Why do you think they are called 'test tube babies'? (3 lines) **2 marks**
(b) The diagram below shows the circulation of blood to and from the embryo inside a pregnant woman.

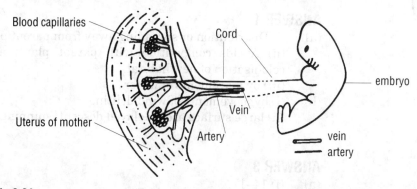

Fig.6.24

    (i)   What is the name of the cord? (1 line) **1 mark**
    (ii)   Name the part where the cord is attached to the uterus. (1 line) **1 mark**
    (iii) Draw an arrow on the diagram to show the direction in which the blood flows in the arteries in the cord. **1 mark**
    (iv) How does the embryo get the food and oxygen it needs? (1 line) **1 mark**
    (v)   Name one waste substance the embryo produces (1 line) **1 mark**
(c) Describe how the baby is born. (6 lines) **5 marks**

                                     Total 20 marks (LEAG)

QUESTION 5

(a) The simplified graph shows some of the features of a normal menstrual cycle.

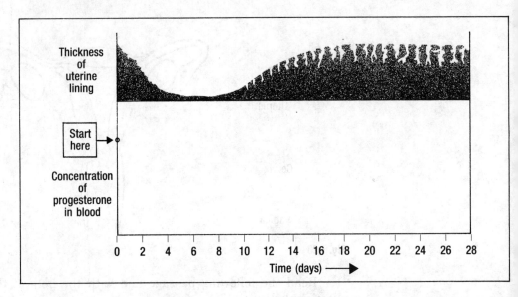

      Complete this graph by drawing a line to represent the concentration of progesterone between day 0 and day 28. Start your line at the place shown. **3 marks**

(b) The uterine lining helps to form the placenta.
    (i)   Briefly explain the importance of the placenta in providing the developing baby with food. (2 lines) **2 marks**
    (ii)   In a placenta the blood of the mother and embryo do not mix. Briefly give two reasons why this is important for the survival of the embryo. (4 lines) **2 marks**

                                    Total 7 marks (SEG)

      Further practice questions on the topics discussed in this chapter are provided in Chapter 18.

OUTLINE ANSWERS

ANSWER 1

(a)   (i) Distribution or spreading away from parent plant
        (ii) Avoids competition with parent plant; avoids overcrowding; allows colonisation of new habitat.
        (iii) by movements of water
(b)   (i) by movements of wind/drifting
        (ii) large surface area; delayed descent/ spinning, rotating descent

ANSWER 3

(a)   (i) 14–17
        (ii) 7–17

(b)   Menstrual period begins (day 1) when progesterone and oestrogen levels drop; ovulation occurs (day 14) when oestrogen level drops; development of uterus lining corresponds with increase in oestrogen and progesterone.

(c)   Similarities: both twenty-eight day cycles; development of uterus lining and also menstruation occurs in both cycles; same hormones involved in both cycles. Differences: amount and duration of bleeding reduced in treatment cycle; no ovulation, no egg in treatment cycle; uterus lining not as fully developed in treatment cycle; no ovulation because oestrogen levels have not dropped; hormones renewed regularly.

ANSWER 4

(a)   (i) Eggs are moved down the tube (by cilia in tube lining); sperm swim up the tube; fertilization may occur if an egg and a sperm meet. (ii) Because the tube is blocked/ ovary easier to reach. (iii) To allow fertilization to take place. (iv) To increase the chances of fertilization/to allow zygote to grow in size (by cell division). (v) Implanted zygote is given suitable conditions, including food supply (eventually from placenta). (vi) Because fertilization occurs in a laboratory, (though not actually in a test tube!).

(b)   (i) Umbilical cord

          (ii) placenta

          (iii) away from the embryo

          (iv) diffusion of substances from mother's blood through the placenta

          (v) urea

(c)   Cervix opens; involuntary contractions of muscles of uterus, voluntary contractions of abdominal muscles; baby pushed out by series of contractions, which increase in frequency and intensity; hips, vagina widen, baby's head turned and slightly compressed.

ANSWER 5

(a)

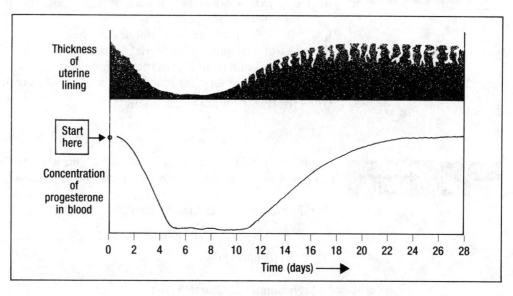

(b)   (i) Food which is needed for growth (amino acids and fatty acids) and for energy provision diffuses across placenta from mother's blood; the placenta provides a large surface area (villi) and close indirect contact between mother's and baby's blood systems.

          (ii) Incompatible blood groups; harmful substances, e.g. toxins, drugs, microbes etc. not allowed across; mother's blood pressure too high.

COURSEWORK – A STEP FURTHER

1 › ASEXUAL REPRODUCTION

Using a suitable growth medium (e.g. exposed dampened bread) allow mould to grow. Record the time taken for (i) the first signs of mould to appear, (ii) the first spore-producing structures (sporangia) to appear. Examine the mould carefully using a lens or, if possible, a microscope. Find evidence of asexual (and sexual) reproduction.

2 › SEXUAL REPRODUCTION IN PLANTS: FLOWERS

Using a sharp knife, cut a vertical section of a suitable flower (e.g. buttercup (*Ranunculus*), rose (*Rosa*) or tulip (*Tulipa*)). Draw a large, well-labelled diagram of the half-flower (see Fig.6.5)

3 › SEXUAL REPRODUCTION IN PLANTS: FRUITS

(a)　Investigate the distribution and numbers of a wind-borne fruits such as sycamore (*Acer*) or ash (*Fraxinus*) in relation to nearby 'parent' trees of the same type. Make a map showing your results.

(b)　Investigate the descent rate of different sizes and types of wind-borne fruits. Note down your observations.

(c)　Collect several different types of fruit. Make large, clearly labelled diagrams of them and suggest how they might be dispersed.

4 › SEXUAL REPRODUCTION IN ANIMALS

Research the following aspects of sexual reproduction in various animal groups, including fish (e.g. trout, *Salmo*), reptiles, (e.g. adder, *Vipera*) amphibia (e.g. frog, *Rana*), bird (e.g. thrush, *Turdus*) and mammals (e.g. humans):

(a)　approximate number of each type of gametes (male and female) produced (one, few, many, very many)

(b)　site of fertilization (internal or external)

(c)　site of development (internal or external)

(d)　amount of parental care (none, some, much)

　　Make a summary, for instance in a table, of your findings. Make general comments on your summary.

5 › SOURCES OF INFORMATION

The following addresses may be useful if you want to find out more about human reproduction, including family planning and child development.

Family Planning Information Service
27-35 Mortimer Street
London W1N 7RJ
Tel. 01 636 7866

National Childbirth Trust
9 Queensborough Terrace
London W2 3TB
Tel. 01-221-3833

STUDENT'S ANSWER – EXAMINER'S COMMENTS

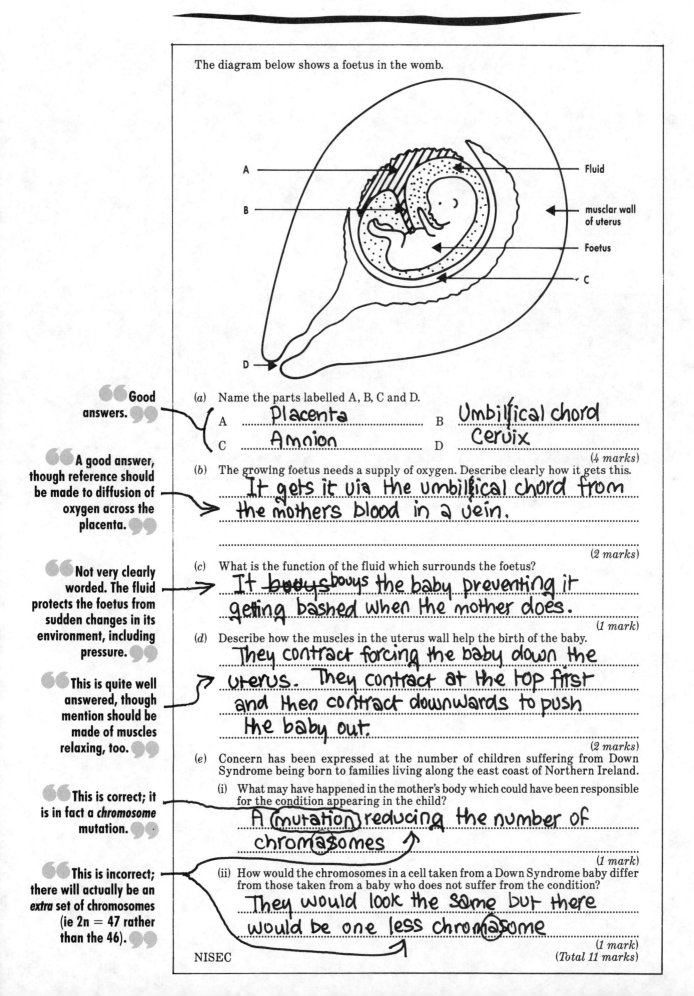

The diagram below shows a foetus in the womb.

A ——————

B ——————

Fluid

musclar wall of uterus

Foetus

C

D

"Good answers."

(a) Name the parts labelled A, B, C and D.

A   Placenta   B   Umbilfical chord

C   Amnion   D   Cervix

(4 marks)

"A good answer, though reference should be made to diffusion of oxygen across the placenta."

(b) The growing foetus needs a supply of oxygen. Describe clearly how it gets this.

It gets it via the umbilfical chord from the mothers blood in a vein.

(2 marks)

"Not very clearly worded. The fluid protects the foetus from sudden changes in its environment, including pressure."

(c) What is the function of the fluid which surrounds the foetus?

It ~~bouys~~ bouys the baby preventing it getting bashed when the mother does.

(1 mark)

"This is quite well answered, though mention should be made of muscles relaxing, too."

(d) Describe how the muscles in the uterus wall help the birth of the baby.

They contract forcing the baby down the uterus. They contract at the top first and then contract downwards to push the baby out.

(2 marks)

(e) Concern has been expressed at the number of children suffering from Down Syndrome being born to families living along the east coast of Northern Ireland.

"This is correct; it is in fact a *chromosome* mutation."

(i) What may have happened in the mother's body which could have been responsible for the condition appearing in the child?

A (mutation) reducing the number of chromasomes

(1 mark)

"This is incorrect; there will actually be an *extra* set of chromosomes (ie 2n = 47 rather than the 46)."

(ii) How would the chromosomes in a cell taken from a Down Syndrome baby differ from those taken from a baby who does not suffer from the condition?

They would look the same but there would be one less chromasome

(1 mark)

NISEC

(Total 11 marks)

GROWTH

AND

DEVELOPMENT

GROWTH
PATTERNS OF GROWTH
FACTORS AFFECTING
GROWTH
DEVELOPMENT

GETTING STARTED

Growth and development are part of an individual's life span beginning, and in many cases ending, with reproduction. Growth and development can be regarded as preparation for reproduction and, eventually, death.

Once formed by reproduction, new individuals undergo a period of **growth**, during which materials and energy from the environment are absorbed and become incorporated into living matter. This may be accompanied by **cell division (mitosis)**, each new cell having a similar genetic identity. The overall effect of growth is usually an increase in size and mass of the organism. Advantages of this include the opportunity for **development**, and a chance to dominate the immediate environment more effectively.

Growth may be continuous during the individual's life span (especially in plants) or mainly confined to the early part of life (more common in animals). Growth in plants tends to be restricted to specialist tissues, resulting in a *branching* form. Growth in animals occurs throughout the body, and typically maintains a *compact* form.

Development is an increase in complexity of an organism, and often occurs at the same time as growth. Development involves the **specialisation (differentiation)** of cells, which become adapted for a particular function within the organism. **Tissues** are groups of similar cells which perform a certain function. **Organs** are composed of different tissues, and are usually capable of performing a range of functions. Different organs and tissues are linked together as **systems**.

The overall effect of development is to produce a versatile, adaptable organism which can more effectively exploit its environment. Development often involves the production of specialised tissues and organs for reproduction (see Ch.6) Growth is a quantitative (measurable) process, whilst development is largely a qualitative (non-measurable) process.

ESSENTIAL PRINCIPLES

1 ▷ GROWTH

(a) DEFINITION

A permanent increase in the size of an organism, caused by the formation of new protoplasm. A 'permanent increase in size' is achieved by the synthesis of the protoplasm (cytoplasm and nucleus) of cells, which enlarge and may divide (see Ch.4). The synthesis of new protoplasm involves chemical reactions which use the raw materials and energy obtained from nutrition. These raw materials are either assembled into structural and storage components, or broken down during respiration to provide energy. Growth occurs when the overall rate of *anabolic* ('building up') reactions exceeds the rate of *catabolic* ('breaking down') reactions (Fig.7.1). Anabolic and catabolic reactions are part of an organism's **metabolism**.

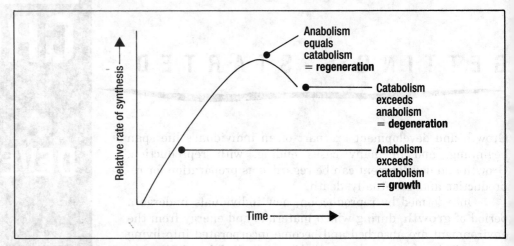

Fig.7.1 Growth as a building process

(b) MEASUREMENT OF GROWTH

The main variables which are used to measure growth of individuals, or populations of small organisms, are length, volume, fresh mass and dry mass. Each method offers both advantages and disadvantages.

(i) Length changes

Measurements are made of all or part of an organism (Fig.7.2).

Example: tail length of a mouse (*Mus domestica*).

This method is relatively easy to use. However, changes in the length of all or (especially) part of an organism may not reflect overall growth patterns. Some parts of a body may grow at a different rate from others; this is called **allometric** growth.

> 66 **GCSE Biology examinations require students to be able to interpret graphs such as these. You may be given data and asked to draw your own graph (see Appendix 2).** 99

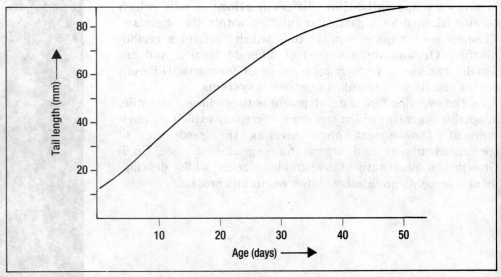

Fig.7.2 Growth in tail length of a mouse (Mus domestica)

(ii) Volume changes

Example: volume of pea (*Pisum sativum*) seeds (Fig.7.3).

Volume can be found (for plant material) by water displacement, or by calculations using length or surface area. Volume changes may give a more accurate impression of the size of small organisms than length, and can be used for populations, e.g. of many small seeds. However, the method is impractical or inaccurate for larger, non-submersible organisms.

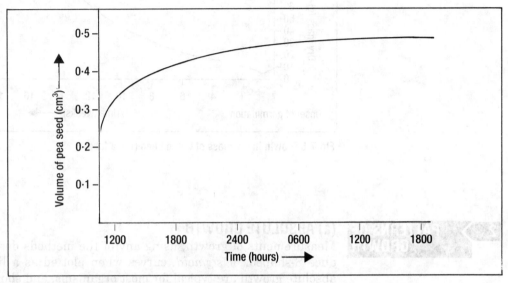

Fig.7.3 Growth in volume of pea (Pisum sativum) seeds

(iii) Fresh mass

Example: mass of rat (*Rattus norvegicus*) (Fig.7.4).

Fresh mass is easy to determine for many organisms. The disadvantage of using fresh mass is that it may reflect the uptake or loss of fluids including water, or solid gain (food) or loss (faeces). This may be reversible and may not directly involve the incorporation of new protoplasm. In plants, much 'growth' is caused by the uptake of water and the formation of expanded cells by **vacuolation**.

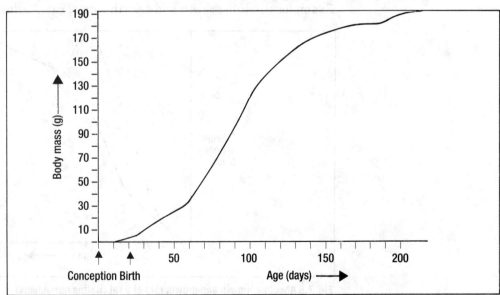

Fig.7.4 Growth in body mass of a rat (Rattus norvegicus)

(iv) Dry mass

Example: dry mass of an annual flowering plant, broad bean (*Vicia faba*) (Fig.7.5).

Dry mass is found by heating organisms (at about 110°C) until no further loss in mass occurs; this process removes water from tissues, and gives a more reliable indication of the amounts of protoplasm (and also stored material). The plants need to be given constant conditions from day to day. The difficulty with this method is that it involves the destruction of organisms; random samples are taken (at a particular time of day) from a growing population of uniform age. A further drawback of this technique is the time needed to prepare material for weighing.

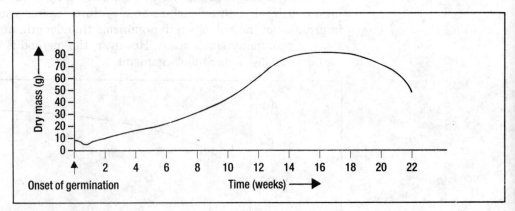

Fig.7.5 Growth in dry mass of broad bean (Vicia faba)

2 > PATTERNS OF GROWTH

(a) ABSOLUTE GROWTH

Measurements of growth, using any of the methods described above, tend to produce S-shaped, or *sigmoid*, curves when plotted as a line graph. Such curves of absolute growth are typical for most organisms, and shows that the period of most rapid growth occurs during an intermediate stage of the individual's life span. The sigmoid curve is also characteristic of the growth of populations (see Ch.17).

(b) GROWTH RATE

Variations in growth rate can also be shown by plotting separate increases (increments) of a particular growth value against time. This usually produces a bell-shaped curve. Growth rate can also be related to overall size of the organism by using a percentage growth rate.

Example: absolute growth and growth rate of rat (*Rattus norvegicus*) (Fig.7.6).

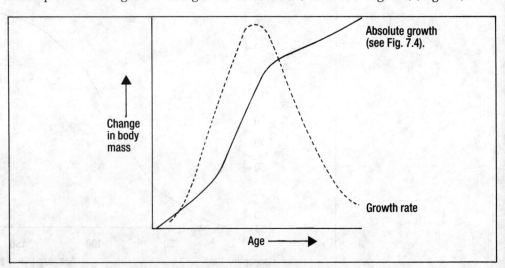

Fig.7.6 Absolute growth and growth rate of a rat (Rattus norvegicus)

The fact that absolute growth and growth rates show similar and characteristic patterns in many organisms suggests that growth processes are influenced by *common* factors.

FACTORS AFFECTING GROWTH

The two main factors influencing growth are heredity (an 'internal' factor) and the environment (an 'external' factor).

(a) EFFECTS OF HEREDITY

Genetic factors (see Ch.8) determine the growth rate and the limits of growth. Growth may be controlled by a relatively small number of genes which therefore produce a small range of alternative growth patterns.

Example: tall and dwarf varieties of pea (*Pisum sativum*) plants (Fig.7.7).

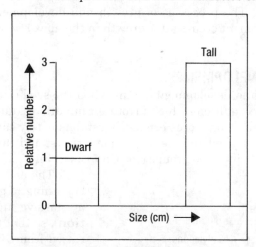

Fig.7.7 Number and size of tall and dwarf varieties of pea plant (Pisum sativum)

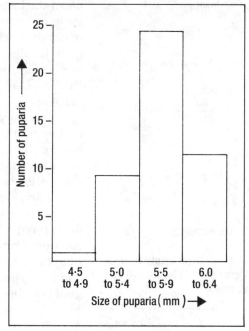

Fig.7.8 Number and size of pupa of housefly (Musca domestica)

This is an example of **discontinuous variation** since normally there are no intermediate forms.

Growth is more commonly controlled by several genes, a large range of growth patterns is possible. In a population, intermediate forms occur and in fact are likely to be more common than extreme forms; this is called a **normal distribution** (see Appendix 2).

Example: Size of pupa of housefly (*Musca domestica*) (Fig.7.8)

This is an example of continuous variation since intermediate forms can occur; Fig.7.8 shows a frequency histogram (Appendix 2). Alleles (genes) exert their effects by controlling the production of proteins such as **hormones** (Ch.12) and **enzymes** (Ch.4) which have long-term and short-term effects respectively on metabolism, which in turn affects growth and development. The potential for growth is determined by the organism's **genotype** (Ch.8) but the actual growth (the **phenotype**) is decided by the interaction of various environmental factors.

(b) EFFECTS OF ENVIRONMENT
(i) Nutrients

The availability of nutrients, including water, influences growth because they provide the raw materials for the synthesis of protoplasm. Nutrients are also needed for the production of extracellular substances, e.g. cellulose and lignin in plants, chitin and bone in animals.

(ii) Temperature

Growth tends to occur more rapidly with increased temperature, within certain limits and provided other factors are favourable. Temperature influences the rate of metabolic reactions, including the synthesis of new protoplasm, and also the rate of respiration, which provides energy for synthesis. Endothermic animals (see Ch.10) are less directly dependent on favourable temperatures than ectothermic animals.

(iii) Light

Light is essential for photosynthesis in green plants (see Ch.15).This process provides energy and materials for the plants' own metabolism and also for other organisms (consumers and decomposers) which are directly or indirectly dependent on green plants (producers) in food chains. Light affects the development of chlorophyll and also the size and shape of stems and leaves. Light is directly important in some mammals, including humans, for the formation of vitamin D, which indirectly affects the development of bones.

4 > DEVELOPMENT

Development involves coordinated processes of **specialisation** and **redistribution** of tissues. This produces a progressive change in shape and form (**morphology**) of the individual.

In animals, including humans, most development actually occurs *before* much growth occurs. The processes of growth and development overlap much more in plants; development occurs after growth in the apex regions.

(a) PLANT DEVELOPMENT

Plant growth and development begins when the seed containing the embryo plant is subjected to conditions which favour germination. Materials for growth are provided initially by food stores originally established by the parent plant (see Ch.6). Food is stored in seeds in one of two main ways, and this is even used to classify flowering plants into two groups (see Ch.5) as in Fig.7.9.

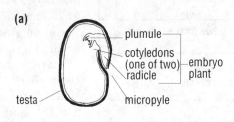

(a)

plumule
cotyledons
(one of two) — embryo
radicle   plant
testa
micropyle

(b)

cotyledon
(one only)
endosperm
coleoptile
fused
testa
and   plumule
pericarp   embryo
radicle   plant
coleorhiza

Fig.7.9 Classification of seeds (a) Dicotyledonous seed: broad bean (Vicia Faba) (b) Monocotyledonous seed: maize (Zea mays)

The end of seed dormancy and the beginning of germination is marked by a massive uptake of water (**hydration**), so that the proportion of water is raised from 10 per cent to about 90 per cent of fresh mass. Water triggers *hydrolytic* enzymes (Ch.4) which break down the large molecules of stored food, such as starch, into smaller, mobile, molecules which can take part in growth and energy release. Soluble molecules also have a role in the further uptake of water by **osmosis** (Ch.4).

During germination there will be an increase in fresh mass due to water uptake, but an overall decrease in dry mass because some food is used up in respiration (see Fig.7.10).

Early development in many plants occurs below ground, so is dependent on food stored within the seed. The cotyledons may remain below ground (= **hypogeal** germination) or may emerge and take part in photosynthesis (= **epigeal** germination) (see Fig.7.11).

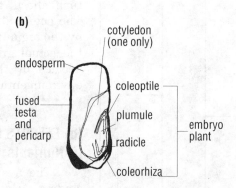

Fruit and
leaf loss

Rapid
growth
Death

Seed
germinating
and losing
weight   No
growth

Dry weight

Slow
growth

Time

Fig.7.10 Change in dry mass during germination

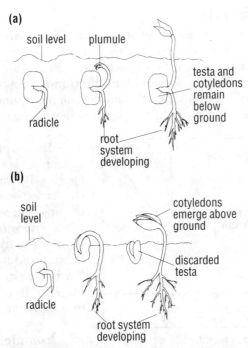

Fig.7.11 (a) hypogeal germination (e.g. broad bean - (Vicia faba) (b) epigeal germination (e.g. French bean)

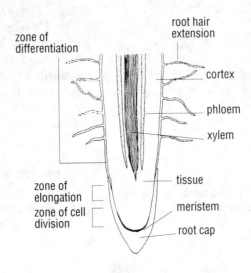

Fig.7.12

Growth and development in plants is confined mainly to regions near the stem and root tips, around the circumference of stems and roots, and in lateral buds. Cell numbers are increased by rapid cell division (mitosis, see Ch.4) in the **meristematic** tissues of these regions. Once produced, a cell will then increase in size by forming a cell wall and vacuole (= **vacuolation**). This occurs in **zones of elongation** and is a very economic type of growth because it does not involve the synthesis of much new protoplasm (see Fig.7.12).

Cells may then **differentiate** into **specialised** tissue, e.g. xylem, phloem, cortex. This is called **primary growth** and occurs in herbaceous (non-woody) plants. Further **secondary growth** occurs in woody plants (trees and shrubs), which form extra woody tissue from a type of meristem called **cambium**. This provides additional support (see Ch.13), allowing plants to grow to a much larger size.

The production of new tissues and organs such as leaves, flowers, fruits and food stores may correspond with seasonal changes in the plant's environment, especially in temperate regions (see Ch.17). This growth and development is accompanied by a general increase in dry mass (see Fig.7.5). In general, growth and development in plants are continuous processes occurring throughout the plant's life, but confined to particular regions within the plant. The coordination of these processes is controlled by various **plant hormones**, which affect both cell division and growth (see Ch.12). The result is a branching form, providing a large surface area for the exchange of substances with, and the absorption of light from the environment.

(b) ANIMAL DEVELOPMENT

Growth and development in some animals (particularly the endotherms, see Ch.11) is often completed in the earlier part of their life whilst for others it may be a continuous and potentially unlimited process. Although, unlike in plants, growth takes place *throughout* an animal's body this does not necessarily occur at a constant rate. Growth and development can occur unevenly, producing changing bodily proportions; this is called **allometric growth** and is characteristic of mammals. A more uniform pattern, called **isometric growth**, occurs in most other animals (and in plants); there is a progressive increase in size and mass which is not accompanied by much change in overall shape.

Different patterns of growth and development in animals can be demonstrated in insects and in humans.

(i) Insect development

Insects have a hard, inelastic **exoskeleton** (Ch.14) which they periodically moult to allow growth. The pattern of growth as shown by both length and mass increases is characteristically 'stepped' (see Fig.7.13) They may also undergo dramatic changes in form, known as **metamorphosis**, during their life span. Metamorphosis is, like all growth and development, under hormonal control (see Ch.13). There are two fairly distinct types of development in insects:

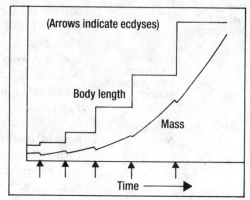

Fig.7.13 Discontinuous growth pattern of an insect (arrows indicate ecdyses)

Incomplete metamorphosis occurs in about 10 per cent of all insect species. It is a gradual process whereby the larval stages (nymphs or instars) become increasingly similar to the adult (**imago**) with each moult (**ecdysis**). The nymph may share the same habitat and food as the adult, e.g. cockroach, *Periplaneta americana* (see Fig.7.14(a)) or occupy different **niches** (p..), e.g. dragonfly, *Aeschna juncea*.

Complete metamorphosis occurs in about 90 per cent of insect species. In this more advanced form of development the larval stages are very different from the adult (e.g. housefly, *Musca domestica*; cabbage white butterfly, *Pieris brassicae*, see Fig.7.14(b)).

The significance of metamorphosis is that it allows larvae and adults to exist to exist in different habitats (e.g. aquatic and terrestrial) and on different diets (e.g. herbivorous and carnivorous); this reduces competition within the species (Ch.17).

(ii) Human development

A human is first formed as a single cell at conception (see Ch.6) and then rapidly grows by cell division. Most of the

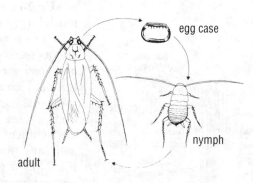

Fig7.14(a) Life-cycle of the locust, Locusta sp., showing incomplete metamorphosis

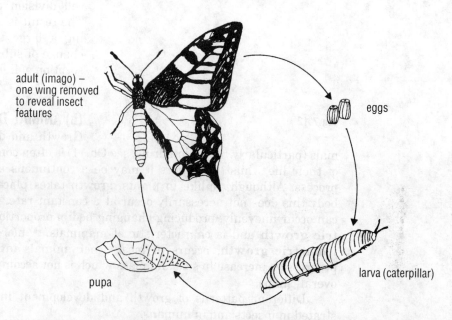

Fig.7.14 (b) Life-cycle of the large white butterfly Pieris brassicae showing complete metamorphosis

cell division occurs before birth, the fertilized egg dividing 44 times, to produce 2×10^{12} cells. A further four cell divisions produces the 6×10^{13} cells which make up an adult! The average number of cell divisions for any cell is therefore about 45.

Further growth occurs in size rather than in number of cells. This can be part of a compensatory growth response (= hypertrophy) when tissues such as muscle, bone and blood have additional demands imposed upon them.

Development mostly takes place during the early stages of growth, and there is an increase in diversity of cell type so that at birth an individual will have most of the required 1000 different types of cell present, arranged in a characteristically human form.

Growth rate is not constant in humans; the maximum rate occurs between conception and two years after birth. There is another, smaller increase during adolescence which begins earlier in girls, although the rate is generally more rapid in boys, who tend to attain a greater maximum average height. Growth and development cause a steadily increasing difference between males and females, as **secondary sexual characteristics** (see Ch.13) appear. This represents a preparation for adulthood, including reproduction.

The uneven (allometric) growth in humans produces changes in the relative proportions of the body (see Fig.7.15); this reflects the changing emphasis on different functions during an individual's life.

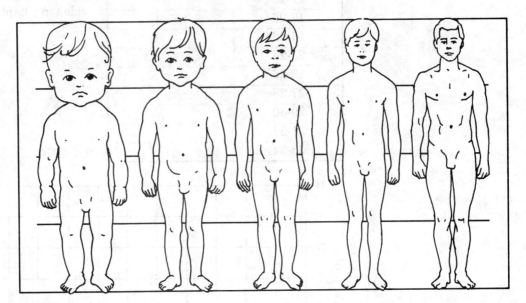

Fig.7.15

(c) DEATH

All multicellular organisms complete their life span by a period of ageing (**senescence**) and death, unless their life is interrupted prematurely, for instance by predation or disease. The length of life span (**longevity**) tends to be characteristic for different species; aquatic organisms tend to live longer than 'comparable' terrestrial organisms. The purpose of ageing and death seems to be to 'make way' for new generations of the species, which might be better adapted (see Ch.9). Biologists are not, however, agreed on the mechanisms of ageing and death.

EXAMINATION QUESTION

A group of pupils collected pond snails from the school pond. The shells were measured accurately and the results are shown in Fig.7.16.

(a) Use the data to complete the following table. **3 marks**

Sizes of snails (mm)										
5	14	17	9	21	19	25	27	33	34	30
18	6	7	16	11	22	23	23	26	29	31
8	19	9	18	15	13	17	29	22	27	25
12	16	10	11	21	24	25	28	19	21	24
19	25	20	23	23	28	20	20	10	15	23
21	28	22	26	21	27	30	18	7	8	20
26	24	26	31	30	24	32	22	24	10	17

Size of snail shell (mm)	Number of snail shells this size
5-6	
7-8	
9-10	
11-12	
13-14	
15-16	
17-18	
19-20	
21-22	
23-24	
25-26	
27-28	
29-30	
31-32	
33-34	

(b) Use the results obtained in the table to plot a bar graph of the number of snails against shell size. **3 marks**

(c) Suggest *one* explanation for the results shown in your bar graph. (2 lines) **1 mark**

Total 7 marks (LEAG)

Further practice questions on the topics discussed in this chapter are provided in Chapter 18 (questions 4 and 5).

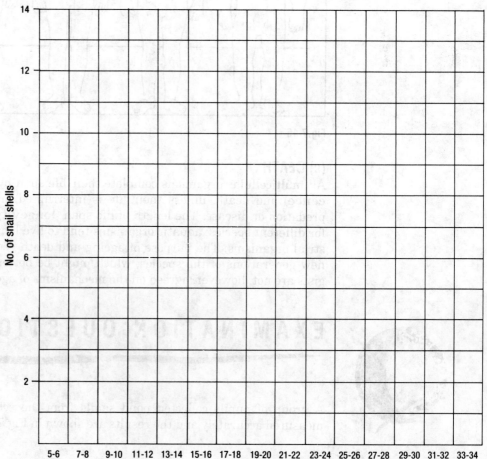

OUTLINE ANSWER

This question is based on experimental and theoretical aspects of variation in size.
(a)   Work through the data systematically, one size group at a time. Count using the tally method, crossing out values that you have counted. Calculate totals for each size group when you have finished.
(b)   The bar graph (frequency histogram) must be accurate.
(c)   Possible reasons for variation are:
         snails at different stages of growth;
         different species included in sample;
         snails from different habitats within the pond.
Note that measurements were accurate, so discount experimental error.

COURSE WORK – A STEP FURTHER

EXPERIMENTAL DESIGN

(See Appendices 2 and 3) You should
(a)   design and, if time and materials permit,
(b)   perform one or more experiments to demonstrate growth.
Suitable projects are:
         Survey of heights within a particular class/year group.
         Effect of different light intensities on dry mass (or stem length) of a green plant species, e.g. cress seedlings.
         Study of discontinuous growth, e.g. fresh mass of locust, from first instar.

FORMULATING A HYPOTHESIS

This should involve a single factor which varies in two distinct situations.
         For example: 'Suggest a hypothesis to explain differences in leaf sizes between nettle plants growing in shady and sunny environments' (see Ch.16).

FURTHER IN-FORMATION

SUPERLATIVES
Extreme examples of the size and longevity of various types of organisms can be found in various publications, for example:
         'Guiness Book of Records' (Guiness Superlatives)
         'Everyman's Factfinder' (Dent and Sons)
         'Reader's Digest Book of Facts' (Reader's Digest)

GOVERNMENT STATISTICS
Average trends in human height, longevity etc. are published at regular intervals.

STUDENT'S ANSWER – EXAMINER'S COMMENTS

The following table relates to the feeding and growth of stick insects through a series of growth or nymphal stages. All the figures are averages for six insects and each lasted approximately the same time.

		Growth stage (or nymphal stage)						
		1	2	3	4	5	6	
Cumulative dry mass (mg) by the end of each stage with respect to:	Privet leaves consumed	30	2	80	105	160	380	500
	Food assimilated	22	34	56	73	105	224	258
	Food respired	17	26.5	46	58	83	179	213
	Faeces produced	8	16	24	32	55	156	242
	The stick insect	5	7.5	10	15	22	45	45

(a) (i) Like many other insects, stick insects moult at the end of each nymphal stage. Describe briefly what happens when an insect moults and explain why moulting is an essential feature of its growth.

> **66** An excellent answer, very concisely put. **99**

When an insect moults its exoskeleton has become too small. It splits allowing the insect to wriggle out. A new bigger cuticle then hardens. As the exoskeleton does not stretch this prosess is necessary for growth.

(3 marks)

(ii) State two other characteristics of insects as a group.

> **66** Correct. **99**
>
> **66** Not unique to the insects. Body divided into head, thorax and abdomen is a better feature. **99**

Two other characteristics are (3 prs of legs) and (compound eyes).

(2 marks)

(b) Values for food assimilated and food respired have been calculated from the other data provided. Briefly explain the method of calculation for both of these using the figures for the first growth stage.

> **66** This is inaccurate; faeces are *egested*, not excreted. **99**
>
> **66** Excellent answer; clearly-worded. **99**

Food assimilated is the total amount consumed minus the amount (excreted): 30-8 = 22. Food respired is the amount of food assimilated minus the insects mass: 22-5 = 17

(4 marks)

(c) Compare average insect dry masses at the end of growth stages 1, 4 and 6. What do they indicate about the rate of growth in the later nymphal stages compared with the earlier? Assume each growth period takes the same time.

> **66** It is a good idea to refer directly to data like this. **99**
>
> **66** Although the answer is basically correct, it is not very clearly stated. **99**

These masses (5, 15, 45) indicate that the rate of growth is 9 times as fast in the later stages than in the early ones.

(4 marks)

(d) (i) Name the trophic levels occupied by privet and stick insect.

> **66** Correct answer (question (d) refers to ecological principles – see Ch.17). **99**

Privet = producer
Stick insect = primary consumer.

(2 marks)

(ii) For the adult stage calculate the value of

$$\frac{\text{Dry mass of stick insect}}{\text{Total dry mass of leaves consumed}} \times \frac{100}{1} \%$$

Correct, with the calculation shown.

$$\frac{45}{500} \times \frac{100}{1} = 9\%$$

(2 marks)

(iii) Assume that a similar value would be arrived at for animals reared for food and use it to explain the biological reasoning behind the following quotation: 'To help the world's food supply people, especiallly in the Developed World, should eat more plant and less animal produce'.

Using a similar value as to the one above it would be more economical and less wasteful to eat plant produce as about nine times as much energy goes into obtaining animal produce than you actually get ~~or profit~~ from the animal produce. By eating more plant that amount of energy which was used for the animal would go to us directly and so more would be obtainable.

This answer is reasonable, though it should refer more directly to *energy flow*, through trophic levels.

NISEC

(4 marks)
(Total 21 marks)

HEREDITY
AND
VARIATION

**HEREDITY
PATTERNS OF
    INHERITANCE
HUMAN GENETICS
VARIATION**

GETTING STARTED

Heredity. Organisms often share certain characteristics with their parents. These characteristics are determined by genetic information transferred during reproduction (Ch.6). Individuals produced by sexual reproduction tend to be more varied than those produced by asexual reproduction. This is because sexual reproduction usually involves the combination of genetic information from two rather than one parent. Genetic information is carried within the nucleus of cells within thread like **chromosomes**. Particular sections of each chromosome, called **genes**, determine certain characteristics within the organism. Characteristics are controlled by one gene, or by several genes operating together.

Variation. There is both considerable variation and uniformity amongst living things. The way in which individual organisms are similar or different to each other is determined by the genetic information they contain (their **genotypes**) and also the effect of the environment in which they live. During an organism's growth and development (Ch.7) there is an interaction between the genotype and its environment. The outcome of this interaction is the **phenotype**, which is the set of characteristics which make up the organism.

The genotype is what the organism *could* become. The phenotype is what the organism *does* become as a result of its genotype and its environment acting together.

Even in organisms of the same **species**, the phenotype can be quite varied for certain characteristics. There are two types of variation, continuous and discontinuous. **Continuous variation** tends to occur when characteristics are determined by several genes, or because growth and development are readily affected by the environment. **Discontinuous variation** tends to occur when characteristics are determined by one gene, or when the environment does not directly affect that particular characteristic.

ESSENTIAL PRINCIPLES

1 > HEREDITY

(a) THE CHEMICAL BASIS OF HEREDITY

Characteristics of organisms are determined by the proteins they contain. This is because proteins are used for structure and (as enzymes and hormones) for control (Ch.4). The genetic information inherited by each cell decides which proteins are produced, and can therefore control growth and development (Ch.7).

Genetic information is held as a chemical code within large nucleic acid molecules (Ch.4) such as DNA (**deoxyribonucleic acid**) and RNA (**ribonucleic acid**). DNA molecules are packaged, as tight coils around proteins (**histones**), in units called **chromosomes**.

Chromosomes are more distinct during cell division (Ch.4). At other times, when the cell is active in making proteins, DNA is extended rather than compact so distinct chromosomes are not apparent.

Proteins are assembled (*synthesised*) from available amino acids (Ch.4) in the cytoplasm of cells. The precise sequence of amino acids is determined by a genetic code within DNA molecules. DNA never leaves the nucleus; the genetic message is carried from the nucleus by messenger RNA (mRNA).

Specific regions along chromosomes, called **genes**, are often responsible for making a particular protein. This is called the 'one-gene-one-protein' theory.

(b) THE INHERITANCE OF GENES

The usual number of chromosomes contained within each cell tends to be characteristic for each species. Some examples of this are given in Fig.8.1. These normal, or **diploid**, numbers occur in all body (**somatic**) cells but not in gametes (Ch.6).

All chromosomes within any individual are precise copies of the original chromosomes inherited inherited from the parents. In sexually reproducing organisms chromosomes, contained in the gametes (Ch.6), are contributed by each parent.

Gametes contain half the normal chromosome number, i.e. they are **haploid**. When they combine during **fertilization** the normal diploid number is restored. Fertilization tends to be called 'crossing' in genetics; individuals are crossed with other organisms. Hermaphrodite organisms (p..) can be self-fertilized, or 'selfed'.

A diploid cell contains two complete sets of chromosomes, consisting of pairs of similar, or **homologous**, chromosomes. A haploid cell has only one set of chromosomes, one from each homologous pair. Each pair of chromosomes carries pairs of alleles. **Alleles** are alternative forms of genes occupying a similar position (locus) on homologous chromosomes.

These pairs of alleles may control the same characteristic, e.g. fur colour in mice (*Mus domestica*), height in peas (*Pisum sativum*). However, each allele may be expressed in different ways; for example black or brown fur colour in mice (Fig.8.2), and tallness or shortness in peas. These are examples of **single**

Species	Chromosome Number
PLANT	
Maize (*Zea mays*)	10
Pea (*Pisum sativum*)	7
Onion (*Allium spp.*)	16
	6
ANIMAL	
Fruit-fly (*Drosophila spp.*)	6 or 12
Human (*Homo sapiens*)	46
Frog (*Rana pipiens*)	26
Goldfish	100

Fig.8.1 Diploid chromosome numbers in various species

> *try to avoid confusing the words gene and allele; they have distinct meanings. Alleles are really just types of genes*

factor inheritance, in which a particular gene (or pair of alleles) determines a single characteristic.

(c) SINGLE FACTOR INHERITANCE

Studies of inheritance are made simpler by using examples involving characteristics determined by a single pair of alleles.

During sexual reproduction each parent contributes gametes, each of which contains a haploid set of chromosomes. At fertilization, homologous chromosomes pair up so that similar genes from each chromosome are positioned next to each other. Each allele is therefore contributed by one of the parents.

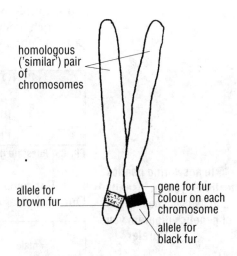

Fig.8.2 Alleles for fur colour in mice (Mus domestica)

In simpler patterns of inheritance, there are various predictable ways in which parental alleles can be passed on to offspring. How these alleles are actually expressed depends on an interaction between them; different alleles may be dominant or recessive:

dominant alleles will always be expressed if at least one is present;

recessive alleles will normally only be expressed if a corresponding dominant allele is not also present.

One possible way in which fur colour is inherited in mice is shown in Fig.8.3.

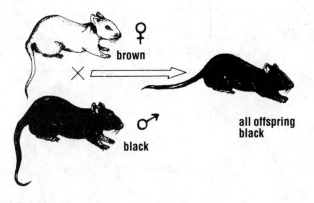

Fig.8.3 Inheritance of fur colour in mice (Mus domestica)

In the example given in Fig.8.3, the allele for black fur is clearly dominant because it is expressed in all the offspring. The allele for brown fur is obviously recessive, because it is not expressed in the offspring.

The inheritance of different alleles can be shown by symbols, often determined by the dominant allele. The appropriate symbols in this example are 'B' = dominant (black) and 'b' = recessive (brown). Organisms are normally diploid, so for a particular gene both alleles are shown. Three possible combinations are possible in each case; the different types of combinations are:

homozygous dominant, i.e. pair of identical dominant alleles;

homozygous recessive, i.e. pair of identical recessive alleles;

heterozygous, i.e. pair of different alleles, one dominant and one recessive.

The various allele combinations form part of the individual's **genotype, or genetic content. The** phenotype is the genetic (and environmental) expression.

> there are several words in genetics which may be unfamiliar. However, once their meanings are understood they can be used to give very precise answers to genetics questions

An example of genotype and phenotype is given in Fig.8.4. You can see that, for any such gene consisting of dominant and recessive alleles, there will be two possible phenotypes, determined by three possible genotypes.

GENOTYPE	PHENOTYPE	DESCRIPTION
BB	Black	Homozygous dominant
Bb	Black	Heterozyous
bb	Brown	Homozygous recessive

Fig.8.4 Possible genotypes and phenotypes for fur colour in mice (Mus domestica)

In answering gentics questions, you are usually free to use whichever type of genetics diagram you prefer

Patterns of inheritance can best be studied by using **genetics diagrams**. One such diagram is shown in Fig.8.5; this is based on the diagram in Fig.8.3.

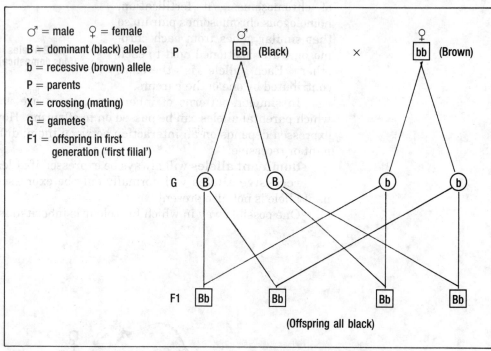

Fig.8.5 First (F1) generation inheritance of fur colour in mice (Mus domestica)

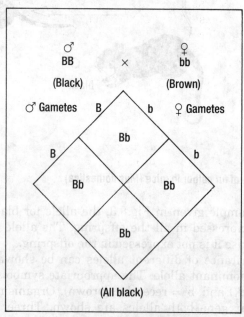

Fig.8.6 First (F1) generation inheritance of fur colour in mice (Mus domestica): Punnett Square

Another type of diagram (the **Punnett square**) showing this inheritance is shown in Fig.8.6. The alleles contributed by the male are usually shown on the left of the diagram.

Diagrams such as Figs.8.5 and 8.6 show all possible gamete combinations; it is assumed that male and female gametes fuse in a random way.

When offspring from the first (F1) generation are sexually mature, they can pass on their genes to their offspring, the second (F2) generation. One possible cross is shown in Fig.8.7.

When two parents which are homozygous for the same allele are crossed, all the offspring will normally have the same genotype as the parents. Such parents are said to **true breeding** (or **pure breeding**).

When two parents which are homozygous for different alleles (see Fig.8.5) or are heterozygous (see Fig.8.7) are crossed, the offspring will not necessarily have the same genotype as the parents. Parents which are homozygous for different alleles produce **hybrid** offspring; this process is called **hybridisation**.

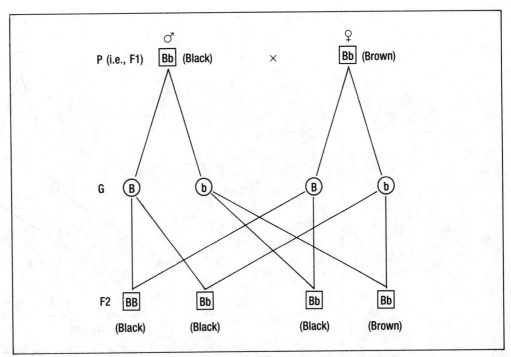

Fig.8.7 Second (F2) generation inheritance of fur colour in mice (Mus domestica)

<table>
<tr><td>**2**</td><td>**PATTERNS OF INHERITANCE**</td></tr>
</table>

The earliest systematic study of genetics was conducted by Gregor Mendel (1822–1884). Mendel used the garden pea (*Pisum sativum*) which has a hermaphrodite flower and is normally self-pollinated (Ch.6). For this reason the plants were usually true breeding before they were artificially cross-pollinated.

Mendel carefully observed patterns of inheritance in the phenotypes of many crosses. One classic example of his work is briefly presented here. (Modern terminology is given in brackets):

(i) When tall or dwarf pea plants were self-pollinated ('selfed') repeatedly, no variation in height occurred in the offspring. Conclusion: each parent was true-breeding (homozygous).

(ii) When tall and dwarf were cross-pollinated ('crossed', or hybridised), the offspring from the first generation were all tall. Conclusion: the 'germinal unit' (allele) for tallness was dominant. The germinal unit for dwarfness was recessive.

(iii) Hybrid (heterozygous) offspring from the first generation (F1) were either self-pollinated, or else cross-pollinated with each other. The offspring in the next (F2) generation were tall and dwarf in the ratio 3:1. (This is known as the **monohybrid ratio**). Conclusion: a pair of contrasting characteristics (alleles) are carried separately within individual gametes = **segregation of germinal units**. This example is shown as a genetics diagram in Fig.8.8.

> **can you suggest what the advantage might be to a pea plant being tall rather than dwarf**

The monohybrid (3:1) ratio shown in Fig.8.8 is characteristic of a cross involving two heterozygous (e.g. *Tt*) parents, or a selfing of one heterozygous hermaphrodite individual. You should note that the 3:1 ratio assumes random fertilization of gametes and is only approximate in a small number of samples. (See Appendix 3 on experimental design for more guidance on this). In Mendel's original experiment, he obtained 787 tall (i.e. about 200 cm high) and 277 dwarf (i.e. about 30 cm high) plants; this ratio is actually 2.84:1.

(a) BACKCROSSING

The genotype of an individual which is homozygous for a recessive allele will be obvious from its phenotype. For example, the genotype of a dwarf pea plant can only be *tt*. However, the genotype of a tall plant could be homozygous dominant (e.g. *TT*) or heterozygous (e.g. *Tt*); there are two genotypes for one phenotype.

It is not possible to see genes directly, even using a very powerful microscope. To determine whether an individual with a dominant phenotype is homozygous or

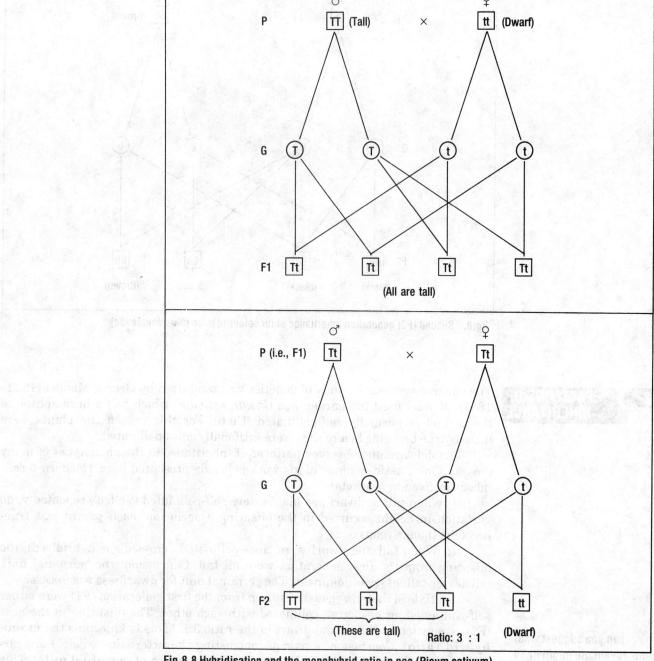

Fig.8.8 Hybridisation and the monohybrid ratio in pea (Pisum sativum)

heterozygous, it is necessary to perform a **backcross** (or '**test cross**'). This involves a homozygous recessive individual, whose genotype is therefore known.

There are two possible outcomes to a backcross; these are shown in Fig.8.9.

(a) *All offspring are tall*; this is characteristic of a cross involving a homozygous dominant individual (see Fig.8.8).

(b) *Half of the offspring are tall*, the other half are dwarf; this is characteristic of a cross involving a heterozygous individual.

(b) INCOMPLETE DOMINANCE

Heterozygous (hybrid) individuals sometimes show a third, possibly intermediate, 'blended' phenotype. One way in which this occurs is for the recessive allele to be only partially 'masked' by the dominant allele in the heterozygous condition. This is known as **incomplete dominance** and an example of this is sickle-cell anaemia, (see Ch.9). New symbols often need to be invented for genetics diagrams showing incomplete dominance. This also applies for co-dominance.

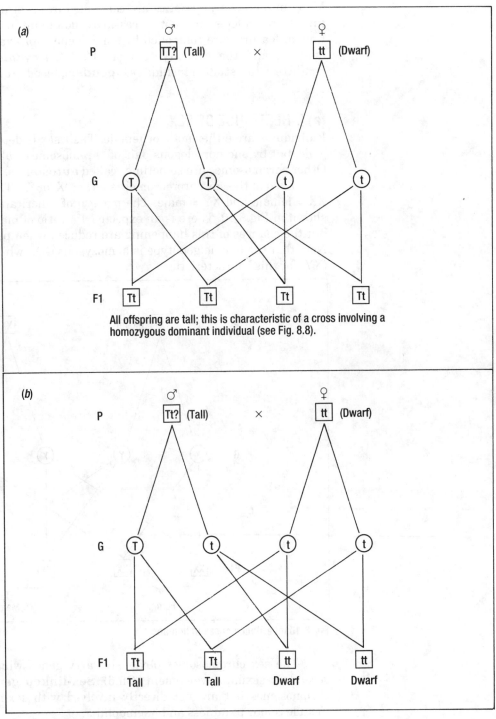

Fig.8.9 Backcross in the pea (Pisum sativum)

(c) CO-DOMINANCE

Genes may have alternative alleles which are neither dominant nor recessive to each other. This is called **co-dominance** and, like incomplete dominance, results in a third phenotype. An example of this is blood groups in humans (see below).

The principles of genetics established by Mendel and others are mostly based on work with fairly simple organisms. Examples of such organisms include pea (*Pisum sativum*), mouse (*Mus domestica*), maize (*Zea mays*) and fruit fly (*Drosophila melanogaster*). These species have relatively few chromosomes or genes, their generation time is short and breeding experiments present perhaps fewer ethical problems.

An understanding of human genetics is derived mostly from studies of patterns of inheritance in closely related individuals, for instance within families.

Many human characteristics are controlled by several genes (**polygenic inheritance**) and alleles are not necessarily dominant or recessive. However, some human features are controlled by single genes, for example tongue- rolling ability (see p..) and the capacity to taste PTC (*phenylthiocarbamide*). Other human characteristics studied include sex (**gender**), blood groups, haemophilia.

(a) INHERITANCE OF SEX

Individuals are either male or female. Their sex is determined, not by a particular gene, but by one homologous pair of chromosomes, called the **sex chromosomes**. Other chromosomes are sometimes called **autosomes**.

Each of the sex chromosomes is either 'X' or 'Y'. The alternative genotypes are XX = female and XY = male. The pattern of inheritance of sex in chromosomes is shown in Fig.8.10. There is an expected 1:1 ratio of males:females in the offspring, but the chances of this happening are reduced when parents have fewer offspring. Note that the female genotype is homozygous (XX) whilst the male is heterozygous (XY) for this characteristic.

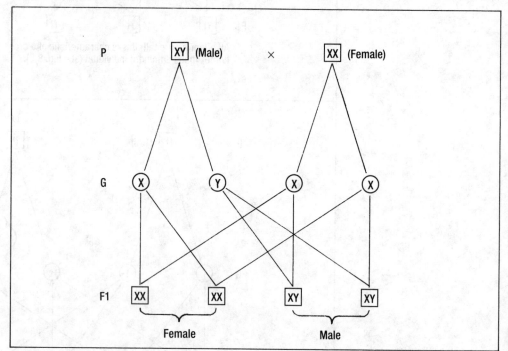

Fig.8.10 Inheritance of sex in humans

The sex chromosomes obviously carry genes which determine primary and secondary sexual development (Ch.6). **Sex-linked genes** are carried on the sex chromosomes but are not directly involved with sexual development. Examples include colour blindness and haemophilia.

(b) HUMAN BLOOD GROUPS

The composition of blood (Ch.12) includes red cells. These have an inherited chemical 'identity' and this is the basis for blood groups. The identifying protein on the surface of certain types of red blood cells is called an **antigen**. There are three alleles determining the presence or absence of these antigens:

     allele A – causes antigen A to be formed
     allele B – causes antigen B to be formed
     allele O – causes no antigen to be formed

Alleles A and B are co-dominant with each other. Allele O is recessive to both alleles A and B. Inheritance of these alleles occurs in a Mendelian way. Fig.8.11 summarises possible genotypes with corresponding phenotypes. The relative number of these phenotypes in the population varies throughout the world. The proportion of each type in the UK is shown.

PHENOTYPE (BLOOD GROUP)	GENOTYPE	OCCURRENCE IN UK POPULATION (%)
A dominant	AA or AO	40
B dominant	BB or BO	10
AB co-dominant	AB	3
O recessive	OO	47

Fig.8.11 Co-dominance in humans: blood groups

Blood plasma may contain special sorts of **antibodies** (Ch.12).These antibodies are called **agglutinogens** because they cause 'foreign' blood to coagulate or agglutinate. The antibodies are produced in response to 'foreign' antigens, i.e. A or B, or both. There are two types of antibody, anti-A and anti-B. One or both of these are produced by individuals with blood groups A, B or O.

In blood transfusions, care has to be taken to ensure that blood from the **donor** is compatible (matched) with that of the **recipient**. If not, **coagulation** (**agglutination**) may occur. This is summarised in Fig.8.12. Note that blood group AB is a universal recipient, whilst blood group O is a universal donor.

BLOOD GROUP	ANTIGEN PRESENT ON RED CELLS	ANTIBODY IN PLASMA	BLOD GROUPS WHICH CAN BE RECEIVED	BLOOD GROUPS WHICH CAN RECEIVE
A	A	anti-B	A and O	A and AB
B	B	anti-A	B and O	B and AB
AB	A and B	none	any	AB
O	none	anti-A and anti-B	O	any

Fig.8.12 Compatibilty in human blood groups

Variations between individuals are caused by the separate or combined effects of internal (genetic) and external (environment) factors. Characteristics determined by genes are inherited, but the way in which these are expressed in the phenotype is determined by:

(i) the interaction of alleles and genes in the genotype, for instance dominant and recessive alleles, polygenic inheritance, and

(ii) the interaction of the genotype with the environment.

<table>
<tr><td>4 ▷ VARIATION</td></tr>
</table>

Discontinuous and continuous variation

Discontinuous variation occurs when the characteristic is determined by a single gene, or when there is little interaction of the genotype with the environment. The result of discontinuous variation will be a limited number of alternative phenotypes, with no intermediate forms. Examples of this include blood groups in humans (Fig.8.13) and plant height in pea (see Fig.7.7, Ch.7). Note that the dominant allele for tallness in pea offers a selective advantage (p.) to the plant, and will tend to occur with greater frequency amongst the phenotypes.

Continuous variation occurs when the characteristic is determined when the genotype interacts with itself (i.e. involving several alternative genes) or with its environment. Examples include

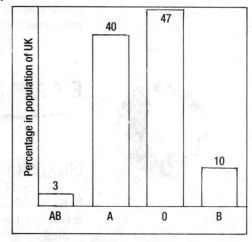

Fig.8.13 Discontinuous variation in humans: blood groups

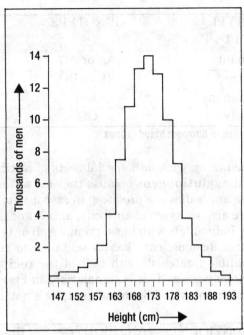

Fig.8.14 Continuous variation in humans: height

human height (Fig.8.14) and human mass. Note that human height is less variable than human mass in genetically similar individuals. Human height is probably more strongly controlled by genotype than is mass. This can be shown especially in studies of identical twins (Ch.6) which have grown up in separate environments.

(d) INHERITED AND ACQUIRED CHARACTERISTICS

Inherited characteristics are determined by the genotype, although the way in which this is expressed may be modified by the environment. Inherited characteristics are significant because they arise through evolution (Ch.9) and may ensure that offspring are 'preadapted' to their environment. Some characteristics cannot be expressed in an alternative way without being lethal; variation will not occur in such characteristics.

Acquired characteristics arise from the effects of the environment and do not result in a change in the genotype. Variation caused in this way is adaptive; it is a means of modifying the organism in response to a changing environment. Examples include increased human fitness through exercise, and tanning of the skin.

Changes to the genotype

There are three main ways in which a genotype may be changed in an inheritable way:

(i) **Meiosis.** During the production of gametes by meiosis (Ch.4) separating chromosomes may acquire different alleles. Errors in meiosis may, for instance, cause an additional pair of chromosomes to be inherited, resulting in Down's syndrome (Ch.17).

(ii) **Fertilization**. During sexual reproduction (Ch.6), new combinations of homologous chromosomes will result.

(iii) **Mutation**. Permanent changes in the number or composition of chromosomes of gametes may result from certain types of radiation and chemicals.

Genetic engineering

Particular sections of DNA can be isolated from one organism and then be inserted into a piece of DNA within another organism. For example, a gene determining the production of the hormone insulin (Ch.13) can be 'spliced' into the DNA of bacteria or yeast cells, which then produce the hormone; this can then be used by diabetics.

EXAMINATION QUESTIONS

QUESTION 1

Fig.8.15 shows the offspring of crosses between pure bred Aberdeen Angus bulls, which are black, and pure bred Redpoll cows, which are red. The ratio of the colours of the offspring of the first generation is also shown. Coat colour is controlled by a single gene which has two forms (alleles): one for black and one for red coat.

(a)   What letters are suitable to represent the two forms (alleles) of the gene?

black coat..

red coat ....

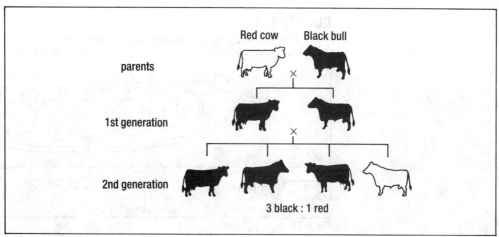

Fig.8.15

1 mark

(b)   (i) Draw a circle around each animal in the diagram which is definitely homozygous for the gene for coat colour. **1 mark**

(ii) Draw a square around each animal in the diagram which is definitely heterozygous for the gene for coat colour. **1 mark**

(c)   Explain why some of the animals in the diagram could be either homozygous or heterozygous for the gene for coat colour. (4 lines) **2 marks**

Total 5 marks (LEAG)

QUESTION 2

(a)   (i) State all the possible genotypes of the four blood group phenotypes shown in the table.

Blood group	Genotypes
A	....
B	....
AB	....
O	....

4 marks

(ii) Which alleles (forms of the gene) are dominant? (1 line) **1 mark**

(iii) Which alleles (forms of the gene) show incomplete dominance (co-dominance)? (1 line) **1 mark**

Explain your answer. (2 lines) **1 mark**

(b)   (i) Complete the following diagram to show the possible offspring of the marriage between a man of blood group O and a woman of blood group AB.

Parents	Man (group O)	Woman (group AB)		
genotypes	....			
gametes	....	....	....	....
F1 genotypes	....	....	....	....
F1 phenotypes	....	....	....	....

4 marks

(ii) What is the probability of the first child of the marriage having

1   blood group O?...

2   blood group B?...

3   blood group AB? ....

4   blood group A?...

4 marks

Total 15 marks (IGCSE)

QUESTION 3

The drawing below shows a ripe pea pod.

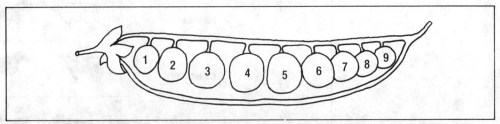

Seed number	1	2	3	4	5	6	7	8	9
Mass (g)	0.7	0.8	1.2	1.4	1.6	0.8	0.7	0.5	0.4

Fig.8.17

The seeds were removed and weighed individually. The results of the weighings are given in Fig.8.17.

(a)   What is the average (mean) mass of the seeds? Explain how you arrived at your answer. (3 lines) **2 marks**

(b)   How would you test the hypothesis that the smaller pea seeds grow into smaller plants? (6 lines) **4 marks**

(c)   What cause (other than genetic) might account for the difference in size of the peas in the pod? (1 line) **1 mark**

Total 7 marks (LEAG)

OUTLINE ANSWERS

ANSWER 1

(a)   Suitable symbols would be:
       B (= black) and b (= red)

(b)   (i)   Circle both parents and red bull in F2.
       (ii)   Square around both F1 animals.

(c)   Homozygous dominant (black) and heterozygous have the same phenotype.

ANSWER 3

(a)   0.9 g; i.e. 81 (total mass) - 9 (number of seeds)

(b)   Measure height (or mass) of seeds given same (ideal) conditions; allow enough time for growth potential to be reached.

(c)   Different time of fertilization (e.g. due to different germination times of pollen tubes) or overcrowding within pod.

COURSE WORK – A STEP FURTHER

1 ▶ CHROMOSOME SQUASH   Study the chromosomes in onion (*Allium cepa*) by squashing young root tips and staining with acetic orcein stain [You will need to ask your teacher to provide the necessary apparatus for this]. Using a microscope, draw and label a diagram of chromosomes taking part in mitosis.

2 ▶ RANDOM SELECTION OF GENES   Obtain at least 100 plastic beads (or similar); half of these (i.e. 50) should be one colour, the rest another colour. These beads represent alternative alleles. Decide which colour is dominant and which recessive.

Put the beads into a suitable container then, without looking, choose any two beads; these represent the genotype of one 'parent'. Repeat this to find the genotype of the other 'parent'. Now work out the possible genotypes and phenotypes of the F1 'offspring'. Note the results.

Repeat this procedure to obtain the F2.

Do your results show 'Mendelian inheritance'?

You can extend this exercise by altering the ratio of beads available or even using co-dominance.

3 ▷ VARIATION

Devise and perform suitable experiments to study variation amongst a group of human subjects of a similar age:

DISCONTINUOUS VARIATION

Conduct a survey of tongue-rolling ability, or the presence/absence of ear lobes. Draw a suitable graph of the results (see Appendix 2).

CONTINUOUS VARIATION

Conduct a survey of middle finger length (mm), from knuckle to finger-tip (right hand). Draw a suitable graph of the results (see Apendix 2).

4 ▷ SOURCES OF INFORMATION

Introduction to Genetics, D. G. Mackean (John Murray). This book is divided into the following three sections:

1. Chromosomes and heredity
2. Heredity and genetics
3. Evolution, and the theory of natural selection

Each section is clearly explained by text, diagrams and photographs.

STUDENT'S ANSWER - EXAMINER'S COMMENTS

When the mechanism of inheritance of flower colour in garden peas was investigated, red-flowered plants were crossed with white-flowered plants. The first generation of plants all had red flowers. However, when these red-flowered plants were allowed to self-fertilise, about 25% of the offspring had white flowers, the remainder having red flowers.

In a similar investigation with snapdragon plants, when red-flowered plants were crossed with white-flowered plants, the resulting first generation all had pink flowers. When these pink-flowered plants were self-fertilised, 25% of the offspring had white flowers, 25% had red flowers and 50% had pink flowers.

A good start to the answer; it is in fact co-dominance.

(a) Suggest why the results obtained with the garden pea are different from those obtained with the snapdragon plants.

there is incomplete dominance or co-dominance going on.

(1 mark)

(b) By means of a diagram, show how the results for the snapdragon can be explained genetically.

It *is* important to give a 'key' to the symbols being used.

The symbol *'R^w'* could be used instead.

This is a clear, well-organised genetics diagram.

Symbols :
R = red allele,
W = white allele

Parents   RR × WW
            red   white

gametes   (R) (R)   (W) (W)

first generation   RW RW RW RW
                    all pink

The *phenotypes* of this generation should be written in as well.

These are really the same phenotype; it would be less confusing if the genotype was written as *'RW'* in each case.

Parent (self-fertilised)   RW × RW
                           pink   pink

gametes   (R) (W)   (R) (W)

second generation   RR RW WR WW

(4 marks)

(c) Some barley plants are susceptible to attack by mildew (a fungus) whilst others are resistant to mildew attack. In an investigation by a plant breeder, it was found that susceptible plants produced only susceptible offspring when self-fertilised, but that a resistant plant produced a mixture of resistant and susceptible plants when self-fertilised.

(i) How would the plant breeder obtain a stock of barley plants which were all resistant to mildew?

This answer is far too vague; it should refer to the selection (by repeated 'crossings') of true-breeding (homozygous dominant) resistant plants.

find resistant plants which produce other resistant plants all the time.

(2 marks)

(ii) Assuming that resistance to mildew is controlled by a single gene, what must be the genotype of the resistant stock?

Correct answer, using the available facts.

heterozygote (Rr)

NEA

(1 marks)
(Total 8 marks)

EVOLUTION

GETTING STARTED

Evolution is the process by which living things gradually develop from earlier forms by progressive inheritable changes.

There are two important outcomes of evolution:

1 **Increase in complexity.** The change from one form to another usually involves the production of more complex organisms from simpler *ancestral* forms.

2 **Increase in diversity**. The formation of *new species* is a significant part of the process of evolution.

Theories of evolution have been proposed to explain the mechanism of the process in terms of the available evidence. The two main theories of evolution are:

1 Inheritance of acquired characteristics (Lamark, 1809)

2 Natural selection (Darwin and Wallace, 1858).

Most biologists now accept an updated **neo-Darwinian** theory of evolution, which incorporates more recent ideas on the inheritance of *genes* (Ch.8).

Evidence for evolution is available from various studies. These include **palaeontology** (the study of fossils), comparative **anatomy** (body structure), **biochemistry** (body chemistry), **classification** (Ch.5), **geographical distribution** and **artificial selection**.

Artificial selection is the application of the principles of natural selection by **selective breeding** of domestic plants and animals. This is important, for instance, in agriculture and the food industry.

THE HISTORY OF LIFE

EVOLUTION

EVIDENCE FOR EVOLUTION

NATURAL SELECTION

ARTIFICIAL SELECTION

ESSENTIAL PRINCIPLES

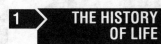

The way in which life began and has subsequently developed is clearly an important aspect of biology. There are several explanations for the origins of life, including:

    (i) **Special Creation.** Many people throughout the world believe that life was created at a particular time by God and that, once formed, species do not change.

    (ii) **Evolution**. Most biologists believe that life was created over a very long period of time by gradual changes, involving natural selection. New species are formed from pre-existing species as part of a continuing process. The origins of life through evolution involved the assembly of biologically important molecules during *chemical evolution*, followed by gradual development of increasingly complex organisms from simpler forms during **organic evolution**.

Evolution can explain both **similarities** and **differences** between organisms. Organisms are *similar* because they are descended from a common ancestor; each generation is related to previous ones by the **inheritance of genetic information** (Ch.8). Organisms are *different* because **variations** (Ch.8) occur between parents and offspring.

(a) NATURAL SELECTION

Natural selection is a process by which organisms which are better adapted to their environment tend to have an increased chance of survival; they therefore have a greater opportunity to reproduce and therefore pass on to their offspring those genetically determined characteristics which cause them to be better adapted.

    The theory of natural selection is based on the following related observations:

    1 **Reproductive Potential.** All organisms are capable of producing more than enough offspring to replace themselves. The potential for a very rapid increase in population was noted, amongst others, by **Thomas Malthus** in 1778. However, the number of surviving organisms in a population tends to remain, on average, *fairly constant*.

    2 **Competition.** Competition occurs when organisms require the same limited opportunities, such as access to food, oxygen, warmth and space and the avoidance of predators and disease. Competition is often more intense between members of the same species because their requirements tend to be similar. This leads to a 'struggle for existence'.

    3 **Variation**. Within any species there are variations caused by the *inheritance of different characteristics*. Variation occurs particularly in those organisms which reproduce sexually, because new genetic combinations are created. Whilst offspring are often different from their parents they also share many important similarities, too.

    4 **Adaptation.** Certain variations may allow particular individuals within a species to compete more effectively because they are better adapted. This increases their chances of survival in a given environment, and they are more likely to have the opportunity to reproduce. In this way, genetically determined characteristics may be 'selected' because they provide an advantage in comparison with other variations. This has been called 'survival of the fittest' i.e. survival of those best fitted to their environment.

How natural selection works

Natural selection occurs as the result of an *interaction of organisms with their environment*. Organisms are not always fully adapted to their surroundings, for example because their environment is *changing* or because they have *colonised* a new environment. In such circumstances any organism that becomes better

> some students find natural selection very difficult to understand and, therefore, to explain. If necessary spend some time on this topic until you feel really confident with it

adapted through a change in its inherited characteristics has a **selective advant-age**.

    Genetically-determined ('heritable') variation is an essential pre-requi-site for natural selection. This is because any variation which makes members of a species better adapted than others to survive can be passed on to subsequent generations. In other words, if the variation gives organisms a selective advantage it will tend to spread through the population.

    This idea can be demonstrated by a relatively simple example:

    The disease-causing bacterium *Neisseria gonorrhoeae* became resistant to the *antibiotic* (Ch.17) penicillin because of a new heritable variation. This variation was caused by a **mutation** (Ch.8); a change in the chromosome of one bacterium. The resistant cell was better-adapted because it had an **allele** (Ch.8) which could prevent the cell from being killed by penicillin. The offspring of the mutant bacte-rium inherited the resistance (Fig. 9.1) by natural selection; the allele providing re-sistance gave a selective advantage to the bacteria carrying it and so spread quick-ly through the population.

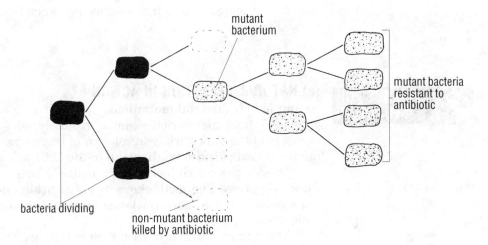

Fig.9.1 Resistance to antibiotics

(b) FORMATION OF SPECIES

Speciation is the formation of a new species and involves natural selection. In a population which can freely interbreed similar genetic information is, in a sense, shared by all individuals.

    The flow of **genes** (Ch.8) within the population is prevented if members of the species are not free to interbreed, for instance if they are separated by a physical barrier such a mass of land or water. If separation occurs for a sufficient period of time, separated groups of organisms will gradually become genetically different. This is because natural selection will be acting independently on each group. The cumulative differences may eventually be so great that the groups will not success-fully interbreed even if they become free to do so (Fig.9.2).

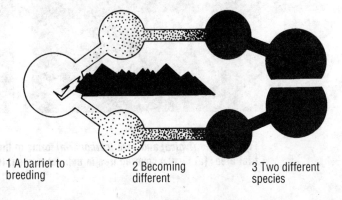

1 A barrier to breeding   2 Becoming different   3 Two different species

Fig.9.2 Mechanism of speciation (From Origin of Species pub. British Museum (Natural History))

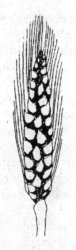

Fig.9.3 Wheat (Triticum aestivum): a hybrid from wild grasses.

the mule (Ch.5). However some hybrids, particularly in plants, may be fertile and may be considered to be a new species; for example, bread wheat (*Triticum aesitivum*) (Fig.9.3).

Barriers which prevent interbreeding and which therefore promote speciation include:

(i) **Geographical isolation**

Populations divided by the formation of oceans, rivers, mountains.

Example: different species of fruitfly (*Drosophila*) on the islands of Hawaii.

(ii) **Behavioural isolation**

Populations adopt different breeding cycles or courtship patterns.

Example: different species of grasshopper (*Chorthippus*) having different mating calls.

Even if interbreeding does occur, genetic differences may be such that the **hybrid** is infertile; for example in

3   EVIDENCE FOR EVOLUTION

(a) NATURAL SELECTION IN ACTION

Example 1: Industrial melanism

Dark (melanic) varieties occur in nearly 80 species of moth; the relative numbers of the dark variety in relation to the 'normal' paler forms increased during the period of **industrialisation** in the UK from about 1850 to 1950.

One species which has been particularly well studied is the peppered moth, *Biston betularia*. The moth shows two genetically- determined colour variations; the *dominant* (Ch.8) dark (melanic) form and the *recessive* (Ch.8) pale (non-melanic) form.

The relative number of each type of the (nocturnal) peppered moth eaten by birds may depend on how well camouflaged they are whilst resting on surfaces such as tree trunks during daytime. (Fig.9.4)

(a)   (b)

Fig.9.4 Pale *(typica)* and dark *(carbonaria)* forms of the peppered moth *(Biston betularia)* in an industrial area. (a) Lichen covered tree in unpoluted area; (b) blackened tree in polluted area.

Photos: J.S. Haywood

	PERCENTAGE OF EACH FORM	
YEAR	DARK	PALE
1848	1	99
1894	99	1

Fig.9.5 Increase in relative numbers of the dark form of the peppered moth *(Biston betularia)* in an industrial area.

The increase in numbers of the dark form in the Manchester, UK, area during nearly 50 years of industrialisation occurred very quickly as is shown in Fig.9.5. This increase corresponded with the blackening of tree trunks by smoke. At the same time, the growth of lichen, which is sensitive to **atmospheric pollution** (Ch.17) was seriously reduced. The relative distribution of dark and pale forms in 1958 (Fig.9.6) shows that the number of pale forms remained relatively high in the non-industrialised areas of Britain.

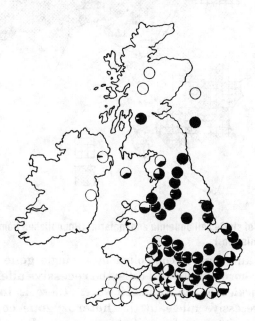

Fig.9.6 Distribution of pale and dark forms of the peppered moth *(Biston betularia)* in Britain in 1958. (Republished from the journal *Heredity*, with permission)

In this example, natural selection of the dark form may have occurred during a period of increasing pollution because they were better camouflaged on blackened tree trunks than the pale form. Being dark gave moths a selective advantage in industrial areas because they were better adapted to their environment. Since the Clean Air Act of 1959 air pollution has declined and so also have the numbers of the dark form of the peppered moth.

These observations have been confirmed by capturing and marking moths, releasing them and then recapturing them. This allows estimates to be made of the relative numbers of each type of moth in a given area.

Example 2: Sickle cell anaemia

Red blood cells (Ch.12) normally have what is known as a 'biconcave' shape and they carry oxygen around the body. **Sickle cell anaemia** is a genetically-determined disease in humans which affects the sequence of amino acids (Ch.4) in the **haemoglobin** molecule (Ch.12). The allele (Ch.8) which causes the disease is formed by a recurrent **mutation** (Ch.8). The result is that, in low oxygen concentrations, red blood cells 'collapse' and become distorted into a sickle shape (Fig.9.7).

Sickle cells are destroyed by the **spleen** (Ch.12) and so the oxygen-car-

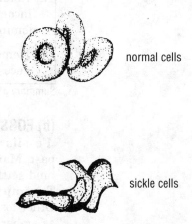

normal cells

sickle cells

Fig.9.7 Sickle cells compared with normal red blood cells

this is known as **anaemia**. Also, the shape and inflexibility of sockle cells prevents blood from flowing easily through narrow blood vessels. The sickle cell condition is obviously serious and can be fatal, yet it persists in some areas of the world. This is because in its milder forms the disease gives **resistance to malaria** (Ch.17), a disease caused by an organism *(Plasmodium falciparum)* which invades normal red blood cells. The distribution of sickle cell anaemia corresponds very closely to that of malaria. (Fig.9.8).

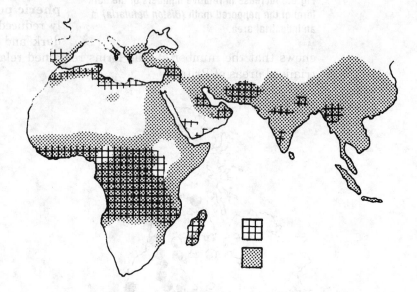

Fig.9.8 Distribution of sickle cell anaemia and malaria. (Republished from the journal Scientific American, with permission.)

Sickle cell anaemia is controlled by a single **gene** (Ch.8). The **dominant allele** (N) is for normal red blood cells; the **recessive allele** (n) may cause the development of sickle cell anaemia. However, there is **incomplete dominance** (Ch.8) of the recessive allele in the **heterozygous condition** (Fig.9.9). This results in an intermediate form of the disease, called **sickle cell trait**, which provides resistance to malaria. The sickle cell trait therefore gives a **selective advantage** and so the recessive gene remains in the population.

GENOTYPE	PHENOTYPE	ANAEMIA	MALARIAL RESISTANCE	OCCURENCE IN POPULATIONS IN MALARIAL REGIONS
NN Homozygous dominant	Normal	Not anaemic	Not resistant	25% surviving
Nn Heterozygous (incomplete dominance)	Sickle cell trait	Not anaemic	Resistant	50% surviving
nn Homozygous recessive	Sickle cell anaemia	Anaemic	Resistant	25% dying

Summary of the gentics of sickle cell anaemia (refer to Ch.8 for an explanation of the words used)

(b) FOSSIL EVIDENCE

Fossils are the preserved remains or traces of organisms which were living in the past. Many fossils were formed in **sedimentary rock** as particles of sand, silt or mud settled around dead organisms and then became compressed into solid rock. The **impression** embedded in the rock reveals the shape of the original organism. Other fossils have been formed by organisms being **preserved** in substances such as amber or peat.

The age of fossils can be estimated from the position where they are found; older fossils normally occupy a deeper position in a rock formation. Fossils provide a record of change of one form of organism into another; for example in the evolution of the modern horse (*Equus*) from its ancestral forms.

Fossils provide a record of those organisms that have become extinct; they probably failed to adapt to a changing environment. However, the fossil record is not continuous or complete. This may be because soft-bodied organisms do not readily form fossils and because other conditions may have been unsuitable.

(c) ANATOMICAL EVIDENCE

Organisms which are thought to have evolved in a similar way often have comparable structures within their body. **Homologous structures** are thought to have been derived from a **common ancestor** but do not necessarily perform the same function. Although they are thought to share common origins, homologous structures may have become adapted to different functions; this is known as **divergent** or **adaptive radiation** in evolution.

A good example of such homologous structures is the **pentadactyl limb** (Ch.14) in vertebrates (Ch.5) (Fig.9.10). This may perform different functions in locomotion (Ch.14) so is adapted in different ways. However, similarities in bone structure indicate that the pentadactyl limb may have been derived from a common ancestor.

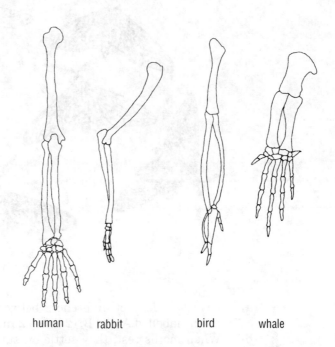

human　　rabbit　　　　bird　　　whale

Fig.9.10 the pendactyl limb of a homologous structure

Analogous structures are similar in function but do *not* indicate close evolutionary relationships between certain organisms. For example, the wings of the bat (*Plecotus*), bee (*Apis*) and a sycamore fruit (*Acer*) perform a similar function but have been derived very differently.

(d) ARTIFICIAL SELECTION

Artificial selection is the development of 'improved' types of **domesticated** organisms useful to humans by **selective breeding**. The main purpose of artificial selection is to provide useful varieties, but the process also shows how natural selection could operate. In the case of artificial selection, the selection of adaptations is by humans rather than by purely 'natural' means.

For example, farm animals and plant crops are selectively bred for increased yield and resistance to disease. Variation (Ch.8) naturally occurs, for instance because of mutations (Ch.8); organisms showing variations which are desirable are selectively bred with each other.

All domesticated plants and animals are closely related to living or recently extinct 'wild' types. The process of artificial selection results in new 'varieties' within a particular species but is not normally a means of forming a new species (Ch.9).

EXAMINATION QUESTIONS

QUESTION 1

A moth trap was set up on a roof in the middle of a large industrial town. In an experiment using this moth trap, a group of pupils collected several peppered moths. Most of the moths were similar to the ones labelled A but a few resembled moth B.

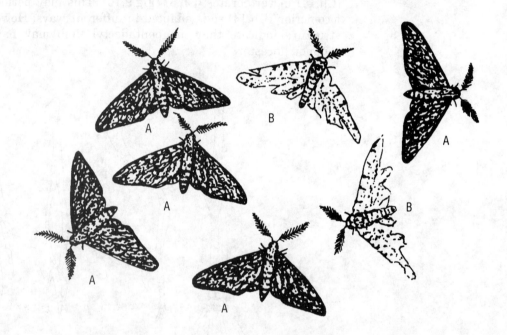

(a)   Give two distinct differences between the appearance of the wings of the moths labelled A and B. (2 lines) **2 marks**

(b)   When moths rest, they settle on surfaces such as trees or walls with their wings outstretched. The students decided to see whether or not most moths like A survived better than moths looking like B. Small marks were made on the undersides of the trapped moths' wings then the moths were released. A few days later the moth trap was set up again and the catch was examined to see how many marked moths were recaptured. The results are shown in Fig.9.12.

	Number of moths marked and released	Number of marked moths which were recaptured
Type A	416	119
Type B	168	22

Fig.9.12

(i) Why were the moths marked on the underside of their wings?

(1 line) **1 mark**

(ii) Which type of moth survived better in the industrial town?

(1 line) **1 mark**

(iii) Explain why this type of moth survived better.

(3 lines) **2 marks**
Total 6 marks (LEAG)

QUESTION 2

The kiwifruit originally grew wild in China. In the 1960s a New Zealand farmer planted a number of seeds intending to select plants with the best features.

(a)   What name is given to this form of selection?

(1 line) **1 mark**

(b)   Why was it important for the farmer to use seeds from a large number of different plants?

(2 lines) **1 mark**

(c)   The best variety is called Hayward after the farmer who discovered it. Most of the world's kiwifruit is now the Hayward variety.

(i) How must Hayward plants be reproduced to keep the variety the same?

(1 line) **1 mark**

(ii) What could research workers do if they want to improve on the Hayward variety?

(3 lines) **2 marks**
Total 5 marks (LEAG)

QUESTION 3

(a) What is meant by the term variation? **2 marks**

(b) Describe the effects of variation on the process of evolution. **10 marks**

(c) Discuss the causes of sickle cell anaemia and its effect in areas where malaria is common. **8 marks**

Total 20 marks (IGCSE)

A further practice question on the topics discussed in this chapter is provided in Chapter 18 (Question 6).

OUTLINE ANSWERS

ANSWER 1

(a)   (i) Colour: dark (A) or pale (B)

(ii) Wing margin: smooth/intact (A) or serrated/damaged (B)

(b)   (i) Marks allow identification but they are not visible when moth is resting.

(ii) Type A; dark

(iii) Better camouflaged against blackened surface, so not easily seen by predators.

ANSWER 2

(a)   Artificial selection

(b)   Increase the chances of variation in different genes/alleles.

(c)   (i) Asexually, by vegetative reproduction

(ii) Promote sexual reproduction, involving cross pollination, between many plants (alternative methods include genetic engineering and also inducing mutations, e.g. by radiation).

COURSEWORK – A STEP FURTHER

1 > NATURAL SELECTION

SURVIVAL
Visit a zoological or botanical garden or a natural history museum. Find examples of adaptations which provide organisms with a selective advantage and which increase the chances of survival.

EXTINCTION
Extinction is sometimes said to be the result of 'over-adaptation'. Using reference books and other sources, find an example of an organism that has become extinct. In what ways was it 'over-adapted'?

2 > ARTIFICIAL SELECTION

Choose a suitable domesticated plant or animal. Using reference material, prepare a brief description of its wild (ancestral) form. Compare the selected features in the plant or animal that you have chosen with the original features. Present your findings in the form of a table.

3 > FURTHER READING

There are numerous excellent books on evolution. Since there is much public interest in the subject, many of the books are written in a style which is fairly easy to understand. Here are some examples:
1 *Origin of Species*, (British Museum (Natural History), 1981)
2 *Evolution in Modern Biology*, K. J. R. Edwards (Institute of Biology/Arnold, 1977)
3 *Evolution*, Colin Patterson (British Museum (Natural History), 1978)
4 *Life on Earth*, David Attenborough (Collins/BBC, 1979)
5 *The Theory of Evolution*, John Maynard Smith (Penguin, 1975)
6 *The Selfish Gene*, Richard Dawkins (Granada, 1983)

STUDENT'S ANSWER – EXAMINER'S COMMENTS

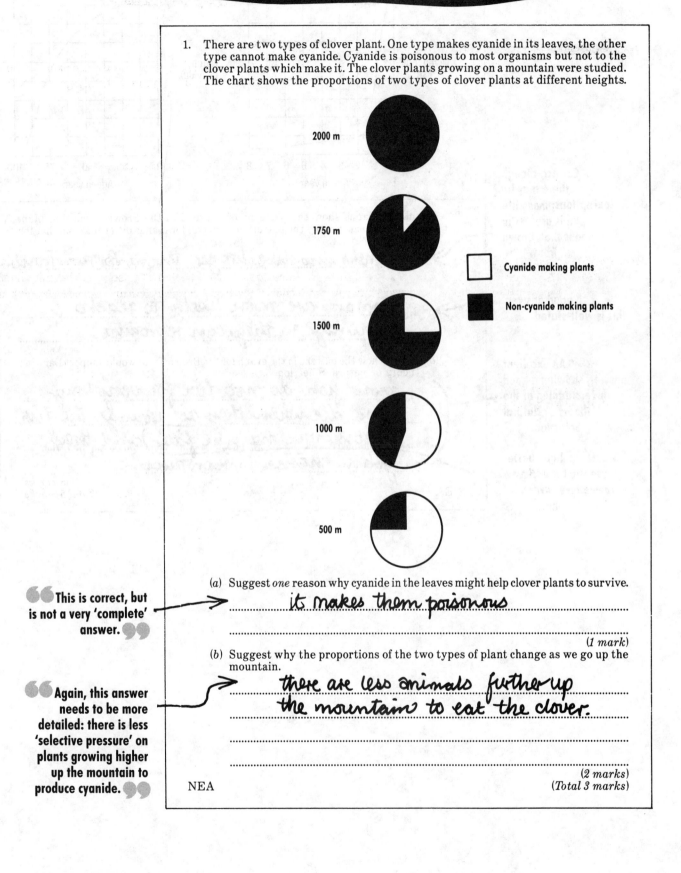

1. There are two types of clover plant. One type makes cyanide in its leaves, the other type cannot make cyanide. Cyanide is poisonous to most organisms but not to the clover plants which make it. The clover plants growing on a mountain were studied. The chart shows the proportions of two types of clover plants at different heights.

2000 m

1750 m

☐ Cyanide making plants

■ Non-cyanide making plants

1500 m

1000 m

500 m

(a) Suggest *one* reason why cyanide in the leaves might help clover plants to survive.

it makes them poisonous

66 This is correct, but is not a very 'complete' answer. **99**

(1 mark)

(b) Suggest why the proportions of the two types of plant change as we go up the mountain.

there are less animals further up the mountain to eat the clover.

66 Again, this answer needs to be more detailed: there is less 'selective pressure' on plants growing higher up the mountain to produce cyanide. **99**

NEA

(2 marks)
(Total 3 marks)

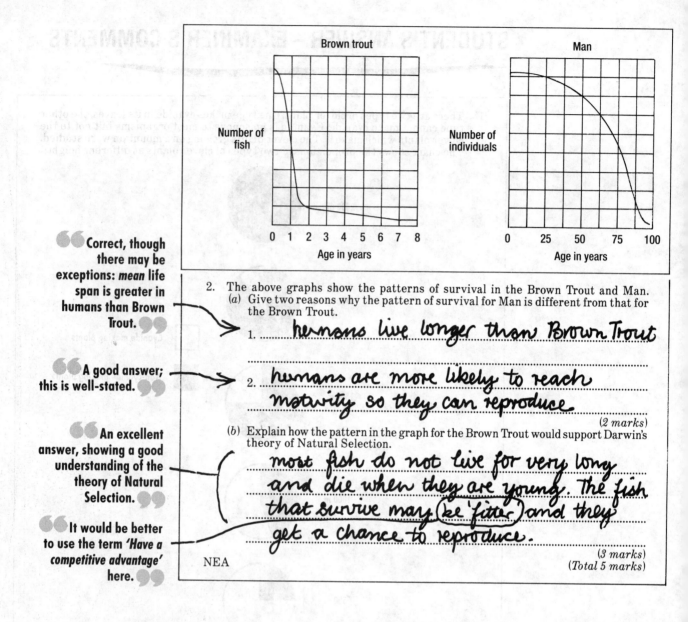

Brown trout

Number of fish

Age in years

0 1 2 3 4 5 6 7 8

Man

Number of individuals

Age in years

0 25 50 75 100

> **Correct, though there may be exceptions:** *mean* **life span is greater in humans than Brown Trout.**

> **A good answer; this is well-stated.**

> **An excellent answer, showing a good understanding of the theory of Natural Selection.**

> **It would be better to use the term** *'Have a competitive advantage'* **here.**

2. The above graphs show the patterns of survival in the Brown Trout and Man.
   (a) Give two reasons why the pattern of survival for Man is different from that for the Brown Trout.

   1.   humans live longer than Brown Trout

   2.   humans are more likely to reach maturity so they can reproduce

   (2 marks)

   (b) Explain how the pattern in the graph for the Brown Trout would support Darwin's theory of Natural Selection.

   most fish do not live for very long and die when they are young. The fish that survive may (be 'fitter') and they get a chance to reproduce.

   (3 marks)
   (Total 5 marks)

   NEA

GETTING STARTED

Respiration is the release of energy from the breakdown of food molecules within living cells. Respiration is a **characteristic** of life **since all living things require energy for essential activities.**

Respiration consists of a series of *chemical* and *physical* processes:

1 **Internal respiration** (also called *cellular* and *'tissue'* respiration) consists of *chemical* processes which release energy, mainly from glucose. These processes can be aerobic (with oxygen) or anaerobic (without oxygen). The word formulae are:

Aerobic: glucose + oxygen → water + carbon dioxide + energy
Anaerobic: glucose → ethanol + carbon dioxide + energy
(in *plants* and *fungi*)
Anaerobic: glucose → lactic acid + energy (in *animals*)

2 **External respiration** (also called **gaseous exchange**) consists of mainly *physical* processes involving the exchange of gases between the organism and its environment. The exchange occurs across a **respiratory surface**. This exchange may be made more efficient by **breathing** or **ventilation** movements.

**INTERNAL
   RESPIRATION
EXTERNAL
   RESPIRATION**

ESSENTIAL PRINCIPLES

Respiration is an essential series of processes resulting in the release of energy within all living cells of all organisms. The release of energy occurs as the outcome of a sequence of chemical reactions often involving gases which are exchanged between the organism and its environment.

For convenience, the overall process of respiration can, as we have seen, be divided into two distinct components:

1 **Internal respiration**, also known as cellular or 'tissue' respiration. Internal respiration is a *chemical* process involving the breakdown of organic molecules and the liberation of energy.

2 **External respiration**, also known as gaseous exchange. External respiration, is a *physical* process involving an exchange of gases between the organism and its external environment. In larger, more complex and more active organisms there may be a specialised **respiratory surface** across which the exchange can take place. **Breathing** known also as **ventilation** or **respiratory movements** may promote gaseous exchange in certain organisms.

Breathing is therefore *part* of respiration and should not be regarded as an alternative word for the same thing. Some organisms do not make any particular respiratory movements (for example, plants and very small animals). Also, the release of energy can occur without oxygen or carbon dioxide being involved (see 'Anaerobic respiration' below).

> 66 many exam candidates use the word 'breathing' to mean 'respiration'. It is worth noting that, far from releasing energy to the organism, breathing movements actually *consume* energy! 99

1 ▷ INTERNAL RESPIRATION

Internal respiration consists of the release of energy from the chemical breakdown of certain **organic molecules** (Ch.4), such as glucose. **Glucose** is in fact the main respiratory substrate in respiration; other organic foods can be converted into glucose for respiration. The amount of energy liberated during respiration depends on how completely the glucose molecules are broken down. This in turn is determined by the availability of **oxygen**. Consequently, there are two types of respiration: **aerobic** (*with* oxygen) and **anaerobic** (*without* oxygen).

(a) AEROBIC RESPIRATION

Aerobic respiration occurs in most living things, plant and animal. Aerobic respiration takes place in the *presence of oxygen* and results in the *complete breakdown of glucose* to water and carbon dioxide with the release of a relatively *large amount of energy*, enough to make 38 molecules of ATP (see below). This complete breakdown of glucose in the presence of oxygen is known as the **oxidation** of glucose. The process can be summarised as follows:

GLUCOSE + OXYGEN → WATER   +   CARBON DIOXIDE + ENERGY (2880 kJ/mol)
$C_6H_{12}O_6$ + 6 O_2 → 6 H_2O +   6 CO_2
(1 mole)

> 66 you should thoroughly learn this formula and those for anaerobic respiration 99

Note: the chemical formula which accompanies the word formula is not required by all examination boards.

The energy released from aerobic respiration is 2880 kJ/mol. 'kJ' means *kilojoule* and is a measurement of energy; '*mol*' means *mole* (see Appendix 1) which is a particular amount of a substance (for glucose, this is 180 g).

As a result of aerobic respiration, 38 molecules of ATP can be made. This 'chemical energy' can be used (see below) when the organism needs it.

The **experimental evidence** for respiration is based on the way in which substances are either used or produced during the processes of aerobic or anaerobic (see below) respiration. The uptake of oxygen and the production of energy (as heat) and carbon dioxide are relatively easy to observe. The use of glucose is difficult to demonstrate, however. The production of water from respiration (sometimes called '**metabolic water**') cannot be shown in a simple experiment, although this water is important for many organisms.

(b) ANAEROBIC RESPIRATION

remember that, by definition, oxygen is not involved in anaerobic respiration and in animals carbon dioxide is not involved either

Anaerobic respiration, or or '**fermentation**', occurs in plants and animals, although the chemical pathways involved are different. Anaerobic respiration takes place in the *absence of oxygen* and results in the *partial breakdown of glucose*, with the release of a relatively *small amount of energy*. The breakdown products of anaerobic respiration are different in plants and animals:

(i) Anaerobic respiration in plants (alcoholic fermentation)

Without oxygen glucose is broken down to **ethanol** (ethyl alcohol) and carbon dioxide in plants and in fungi (Ch.4) such as yeasts (*Saccharomyces*). Some energy is released, enough to make two ATP molecules:

GLUCOSE →   ETHANOL   + CARBON DIOXIDE + ENERGY (210 kJ/mol)

$C_6H_{12}O_6 \rightarrow$ $2\ C_2H_5OH + 2\ CO_2$

    (1 mole)

Experimental evidence for anaerobic respiration involves the production of carbon dioxide or heat energy (see below) from organisms respiring without oxygen. Ethanol can also be collected by **distillation**. Tests for ethanol include burning (distinctive blue flame) and smelling.

Experiment to demonstrate anaerobic respiration in yeast (*Saccharomyces cerevisiae*). Yeast is a **facultative anaerobe** (see below). The tube is set up (Fig.10.1) so that the yeast respires anaerobically; oxygen in the air is excluded by the layer of liquid paraffin, whilst boiling then cooling the water removes dissolved oxygen. Any anaerobic respiration which takes place results in the release of carbon dioxide; this produces a colour change in the **bicarbonate indicator**, from *red* to *yellow*. This colour change is explained in Ch.15. There will be an initial delay in this colour change after bubbles first appear at tube B. This is because the air in tube A above the liquid paraffin will contain small amounts of carbon dioxide.

In this experiment, the yeast in tube A may need to be **warmed gently**; respiration consists of **enzyme-controlled** (Ch.4) chemical reactions which are more rapid at higher temperatures, until an *optimum* temperature is reached. The rate of respiration can measured by the number of carbon dioxide bubbles appearing at tube B.

The release of carbon dioxide in tube B can be monitored using **limewater** instead of bicarbonate indicator. The limewater (calcium hydroxide) forms a **milky** appearance (calcium carbonate) in the presence of carbon dioxide.

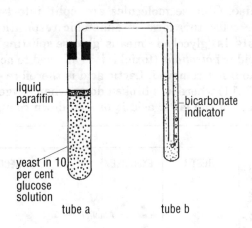

liquid paraffin

bicarbonate indicator

yeast in 10 per cent glucose solution

tube a   tube b

Fig.10.1 Anaerobic respiration in yeast

Experiment to demonstrate anaerobic respiration in germinating seeds. In natural conditions, most seeds begin their germination underground (Ch.7) where there is likely to be insufficient amounts of oxygen. For this reason, seeds often release energy for growth by anaerobic respiration.

Seeds such as those of pea (*Pisum sativum*) which have just begun to germinate are suitable. Their outer testa (seed coat) is removed to avoid the introduction of trapped air. The seeds are briefly dipped in mild antiseptic to kill any microbes which might interfere with the experiment. The experiment is set up as shown in Fig.10.2. A control (see Appendix 3) is set up using boiled (killed) seeds for comparison.

The gas that gathers in the tube after a few days can be shown to be carbon dioxide by introducing bicarbonate indicator, using a syringe and flexible tube. A change in the colour of the indicator to a characteristic yellow confirms the presence of carbon dioxide.

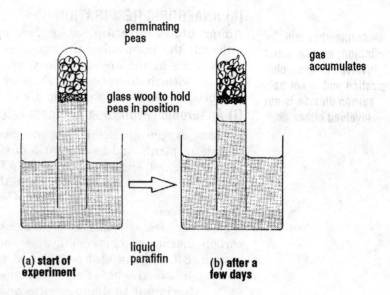

Fig.10.2 Anaerobic respiration in germinating seeds

(ii) Anaerobic respiration in animals (lactic acid fermentation)

When insufficient oxygen is available to meet the animal's energy requirements glucose is broken down to lactic acid. Some energy is released, enough to make two ATP molecules:

GLUCOSE $\rightarrow$ LACTIC ACID + ENERGY (150 kJ/mol)

$C_6 H_{12} O_6$ $\rightarrow$ $2 X_3 H_6 O_3$

    (1 mole)

This process occurs in the **muscles** (p..) of higher animals, including humans, during **exercise**. Glucose molecules are 'split' into two molecules of lactic acid within muscle cells; this form of anaerobic respiration is sometimes known as **muscle glycolysis** ('glycolysis' means 'glucose splitting').

Lactic acid is *poisonous* (toxic) if it is allowed to accumulate. It causes muscle ache or fatigue if not removed. Lactic acid is therefore carried in the blood system to the liver (Ch.11) where it is broken down when oxygen becomes available again. Twenty per cent of the lactic acid is broken down completely to water and carbon

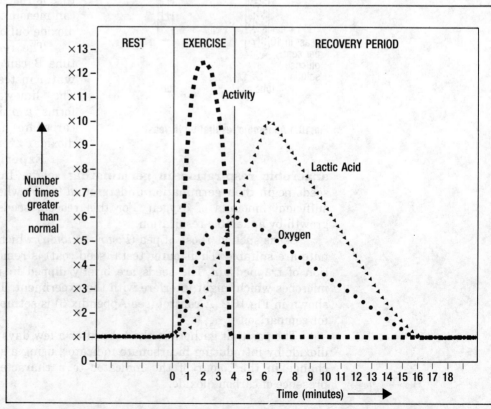

Fig.10.3 Lactic acid and the oxygen debt (After F.M. Sullivan, *Life Story*, Oliver & Boyd, 1986)

dioxide, during aerobic respiration. The energy yielded from this is used to reconvert the remaining (80 per cent) lactic acid to glucose, for future use in respiration.

The oxygen required to break down lactic acid is known as the **oxygen debt**, so called because the body has 'overdrawn' its energy resources during exercise. A human will continue panting after exercise to absorb the additional oxygen needed to 'pay off' the oxygen debt. The time taken to remove lactic acid from the body (Fig.10.3) is known as the **recovery period**. The length of the recovery period will depend on the amount of anaerobic activity and also the fitness of the individual concerned. Over short distances (e.g. 100 m sprints) athletes may not breathe at all during the actual race.

exam candidates often have difficulty with the idea of *oxygen debt*. Take care that you understand the principles involved

(c) COMPARISON OF AEROBIC AND ANAEROBIC RESPIRATION

Most organisms gain their energy from aerobic respiration. This is because relatively large amounts of energy are released during aerobic respiration (see Fig.10.5). However, many organisms are capable of anaerobic respiration, either *temporarily* or *permanently*, in the absence of oxygen:

Facultative anaerobes respire aerobically if oxygen is available, otherwise they respire anaerobically.

Example: yeast (*Saccharomyces*) and tapeworm (*Taenia*).

Obligate anaerobes respire anaerobically all the time; oxygen may even be toxic to them.

Examples: the soil-dwelling bacterium *Clostridium tetani*.

Aerobic and anaerobic respiration are *not* really alternatives, however. The breakdown of glucose begins anaerobically, in the **cytoplasm** (Ch.4) of the cell resulting in the formation of two molecules of a substance called **pyruvic acid**

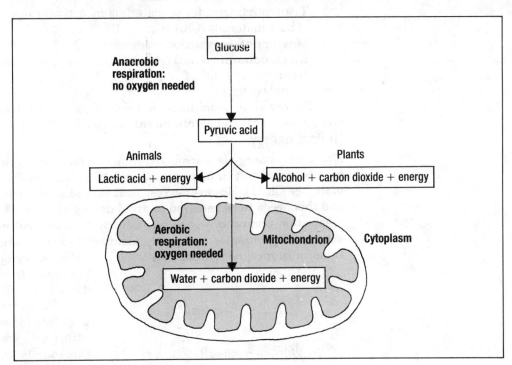

Fig.10.4 Chemical pathways in respiration

(Fig.10.4); this sequence is common to all cells. If enough oxygen (i.e. more than 2 per cent in air) is available and the cell is capable of aerobic respiration, the pyruvic acid enters a **mitochondrion** (Ch.4) within the cell.

Pyruvic acid is broken down to the *inorganic* molecules (Ch.4) water and carbon dioxide within mitochondria; it is here that most energy is released. For this reason, very active tissues tend to have proportionally more of these organelles (p..). It is worth noting that aerobic respiration yields about 20 times more energy than anaerobic respiration, so mitochondria clearly are very important to the cell. In the absence of oxygen, pyruvic acid is converted to *organic* molecules either lactic acid (animals), or alcohol and also carbon dioxide (plants).

Respiration	Respiratory substrate	Respiratory products	Energy yield (kJ/mol)	ATP yield	Location in cell
Aerobic	Glucose	Inorganic: water, carbon dioxide	2880	38	Cytoplasm and mitochondria
Anaerobic: plants	Glucose	Organic: ethanol, also carbon dioxide	210	2	Cytoplasm
Anaerobic: animals	Glucose	Organic: lactic acid	150	2	Cytoplasm

Fig.10.5 Comparison of aerobic and anaerobic respiration

(d) THE NEED FOR ENERGY

Energy is released from some **catabolic** ('breakdown') reactions and used for **anabolic** ('building up') reactions (see Appendix 1). Catabolic and anabolic reactions together comprise **metabolism**, i.e. all the chemical reactions in the body. Energy is constantly being exchanged between different metabolic reactions within living organisms.

Energy is needed, in a usable form, for many essential activities within organisms. Examples of energy-requiring activities include:

Synthesis: formation of new substances for growth, development and repair (Ch.7) and for general metabolism

Transport: transfer of materials by active transport (Ch.4) and movement of bulk materials (Ch.12)

Movement: contraction of muscles

Electrochemical activity: generation of a nerve impulse (Ch.13)

Heat: generation of a relatively high body temperature in endothermic animals (Ch.11)

Energy from respiration is released as *heat* (about 30–40 per cent of the energy liberated) and as '**chemical energy**' (60–70 per cent):

(i) Heat energy

Every time energy is transferred from one form to another, heat is released. This may be important in maintaining relatively high body temperature in some animals (see Ch.11). However excess heat may also be produced in very active tissues and this needs to be removed to avoid damaging cells. This is also one reason why respiration occurs in a succession of small stages. Although the overall effect of aerobic respiration is chemically identical to the **combustion** (**burning**) of the same substance, respiration is a much slower, controlled process. (The heat energy released from food combustion is described in Ch.15.)

Experiment to demonstrate that heat is released during respiration in germinating wheat (*Triticum*) seeds

The production of heat by living things is regarded as evidence of respiration. In this experiment, germinating seeds are **insulated** from temperature changes in the environment by being placed in a vacuum flask (Fig.10.6). A **control** (Appendix 3) consisting of boiled (killed) seeds is set up for comparison. In both cases, the seeds are soaked briefly in a weak antiseptic solution (e.g. TCP) to kill any surface micro-

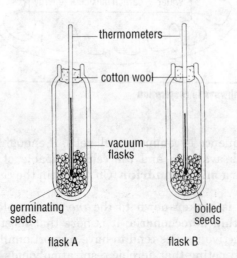

Fig.10.6 Production of heat during respiration

organisms which might interfere with respiration.

After a few days, the temperature in flask A is expected to be higher (by about 5–10°C) than that in flask B. This is because the seeds in flask A were living, and can respire. The temperature in each flask can be measured at regular intervals (e.g. 2 h), when convenient, over 48 hours; this allows estimates of the rate of respiration (see below) to be made.

(ii) Chemical energy

Organisms need other forms of energy besides heat energy. Also, energy is not always required at the time or the place where it is released during respiration. For these reasons, energy is temporarily 'stored', or transferred using special molecules. An example of an energy transfer molecule is **ATP** (**adenosine triphosphate**), which contains three ('tri-') phosphate groups. Energy is used to combine **ADP** (**adenosine diphosphate**) with another phosphate group to make ATP. The reaction is reversed when energy is needed again (Fig.10.7).

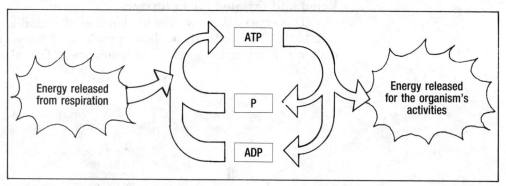

Fig.10.7 Energy transfer involving ATP

not all exam boards require a knowledge of ATP; check this by referring to your syllabus

2 ▷ EXTERNAL RESPIRATION

External respiration involves the exchange of certain gases between the organism and its external environment. The **respiratory gases** involved are oxygen and carbon dioxide. Oxygen is needed for **aerobic** respiration, a process which occurs in most organisms. Also, carbon dioxide is produced as a waste product which can be poisonous (toxic) if allowed to accumulate and which therefore has to be removed. The efficient exchange of gases during external respiration is an important part of the overall process of obtaining energy from aerobic respiration. Aerobic respiration yields about *20 times* more energy than anaerobic respiration (see Fig 10.5).

(a) THE RESPIRATORY SURFACE

The surface through which respiratory gases are exchanged between the organism's internal and external environment is called the **respiratory surface**. The actual design of of the surface depends on many factors, including habitat (aquatic or land) and size and activity of the organism. Examples of respiratory surface include **lungs** (mammals, birds, reptiles, amphibia), **gills** (fish, amphibia), **tracheoles** (arthropods), **body covering** (smaller animals) and **leaf cells** (plants).

(i) Characteristics of respiratory surfaces

All respiratory surfaces share certain *characteristics*, which in general promote the movement of gases by diffusion (Ch.4):

(a) **Permeability.** Respiratory surfaces need to be thin, because diffusion does not readily occur over distances of more than about 1 mm.

(b) **Moisture.** Respiratory gases need to be dissolved within the tissues of organisms; a moist respiratory surface is particularly important in land-dwelling (terrestrial) organisms (they secrete mucus to maintain the moisture).

(c) **Large surface area.** The surface area available for the exchange of gases must be large in comparison with the volume (or mass) of the organism. The outer surface of a large, active animal would not be sufficient in area for gaseous exchange, even if it was permeable and moist.   The reason for this is that large animals have a relatively small *surface area/volume ratio*; this is explained in Appendix 1.

(d) **Transport system.** The rate of diffusion of gases across the respiratory surface is increased if a steep *concentration gradient* (Ch.4) is maintained. For oxygen, this is achieved by carrying it away to the rest of the organism. In larger organisms, respiratory pigments such as haemoglobin (Ch.12) are important in carrying oxygen. There is a diffusion gradient for carbon dioxide, too, though this operates in the opposite direction.

(ii) Experimental evidence for gaseous exchange

There are several experiments which can be used to confirm that oxygen is used and that carbon dioxide is produced during respiration. The relative rate at which respiratory gases enter or leave an organism can be used to determine the **respiration rate**.

Experiment to demonstrate the relative amount of oxygen in inhaled and exhaled air in humans

This experiment involves the burning of a candle in inhaled and exhaled air (Fig.10.8). The **combustion time** in the two situations depends on the amount of oxygen present and is used as an indication of the relative amounts of oxygen in each case.

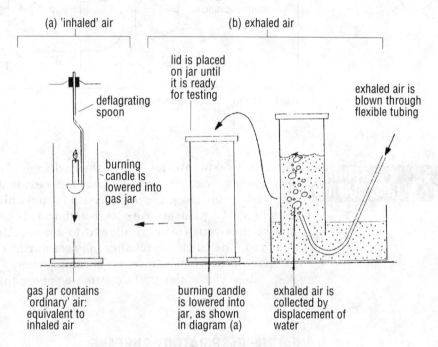

Fig.10.8 Experiment to compare oxygen in inhaled and exhaled air

It is normally found that a candle will burn for longer in 'inhaled' air than in exhaled air. Burning times of 'inhaled' air are typically 1–5 seconds, depending on the size of the jar; for exhaled air the times may be about 1–2 seconds. The results indicate that relatively more oxygen is contained in inhaled air than in exhaled air (the actual amounts are given in table 10.16)

Experiment to demonstrate the relative amount of carbon dioxide in inhaled and exhaled air in humans

The experiment is set up as shown in Fig.10.9. Each of the two test tubes contains a **carbon dioxide indicator** solution such as bicarbonate indicator (or limewater). The arrangement of delivery tubes causes inhaled air to bubble through tube A whilst exhaled air bubbles through tube B.

After a few seconds, tube B will show the presence of carbon dioxide; bicarbonate indicator will change colour from red to yellow (Ch.15); limewater will go 'milky'. Tube A will take much longer to give a positive result. This demonstrates that relatively more carbon dioxide is contained in exhaled air (the actual amounts are given in table 10.16).

note carefully the arrangement of tubes in Fig.109; this is important for the interpretation of the experiment

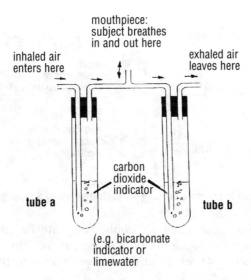

Fig.10.9 Experiment to compare carbon dioxide in inhaled and exhaled air

Experiment to demonstrate that carbon dioxide is given out by small organisms

Small organisms can be enclosed within the chamber into which carbon dioxide-free air is pumped (Fig.10.10). Air can be pumped into the system by an aquarium pump, or pumped out using a filter pump. Any carbon dioxide which emerges from the chamber can be tested with a carbon dioxide indicator such as bicarbonate indicator or limewater.

The indicator in **Tube 3** will show the presence of carbon dioxide, assumed to be from the organism, after several minutes. The apparatus can be modified to show that carbon dioxide is given off by a plant as a result of respiration. The chamber should be kept in darkness, for instance by being covered by black polythene, to prevent **photosynthesis** (Ch.15). The pot of a potted plant should be covered to prevent any carbon dioxide from soil organisms from interfering with the experiment. The respiration rate will be much slower in plants than in animals.

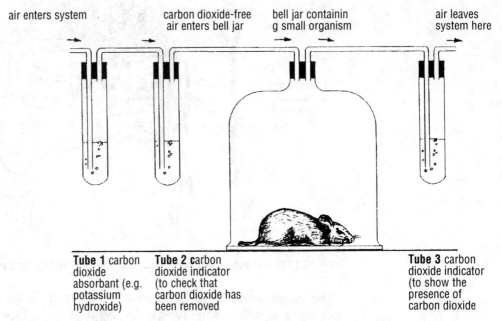

Fig.10.10 Experiment to show that carbon dioxide is given out by small organisms

Experiment to demonstrate rate of respiration using a respirometer

The **rate of respiration** can be determined by the rate of oxygen uptake by a living organism or tissue. The experiment is based on differences of **volume** (or, **pressure**) which result from oxygen being being removed from the air within the apparatus for aerobic respiration. The volume differences can be measured by a narrow graduated tube; a narrow tube is sensitive to small differences in volume due to respiration; the apparatus is known as a **respirometer** (Fig.10.11).

Since an equal volume of carbon dioxide is released, this needs to be absorbed by a **carbon dioxide absorbant**, such as soda lime, or sodium hydroxide. Volume differences can also result from a change in temperature, so a '**water bath**' of constant, known temperature is used.

Rate of respiration in this experiment can be estimated by measuring the distance moved along the scale by the dye 'marker' during a given time. The rate can be determined at different temperatures; **exothermic** (Ch.11) organisms will

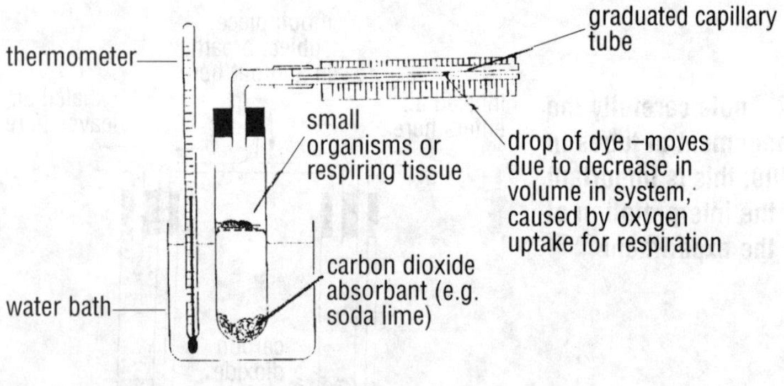

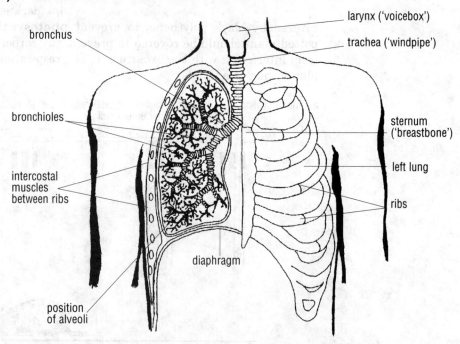

Fig.10.11 Experiment to measure the rate of respiration using a respirometer

tend to respire at approximately double the rate for each 10°C increase in temperature, within reasonable limits of temperature. This is because respiration involves **enzymes** (Ch.4), which are sensitive to temperature.

(b) THE HUMAN GAS EXCHANGE SYSTEM

Fig.10.12 Human respiratory system (vertical section of right lung; front view)

The **respiratory system** (shown in Fig.10.12) is located in the **thorax** (chest cavity) and includes the **lungs**. The respiratory surface in humans is the lining of the lungs. Lungs are used by all large, air-breathing animals, including those **mammals** (Ch.5) such as dolphins, seals and whales which live in water. The lungs have all the *characteristic features of respiratory surfaces*. They are **ventilated** by **breathing movements**. A brief description of the functioning of the main components of the respiratory system is given in Fig.10.13.

COMPONENT	DESCRIPTION
Lungs	Consist of *alveoli* and *bronchioles*. Each lung is covered by a double *pleural membrane*, enclosing *pleural fluid*; these membranes protect the lungs.
Alveoli	Alveoli are the sites of gaseous exchange. The total number of alveoli in the lungs is about 700 million, giving a combined surface area of 80 m^2.
Bronchioles	Bronchioles consist of a branching network of tubes, carrying air to and from the alveoli. The wider bronchioles are strengthened with *cartilage*.

Bronchi	Bronchi connect the bronchiole network with the trachea. Each ***bronchus*** is strengthened by ***cartilage***.
Trachea	The trachea (windpipe) connects the lungs to the mouth and nose cavities. ***Cilia*** (very fine hairs) cover the lining of the trachea; these beat rhythmically and move particles away from the lungs. ***Mucus*** secreted by the trachea, traps particles including microbes.
Ribs	The ribs protect the lungs (and heart) and are important in breathing movements. Ribs are fre to move at their points of attachment to the ***vertebral column*** (backbone) and to the ***sternum*** (breastbone).
Intercostal muscles	There are two sets of ***antagonistic*** (Ch.14) ***muscles*** between the ribs. ***External*** intercostal muscles are used for inhalation; ***internal*** intercostal muscles contract during exhalation. The muscles raise and lower the rib 'cage'.
Diaphragm	The diapragm consists of a muscle sheet which, when relaxed, become ***domed*** in shape (see Fig.10.15). Contraction of the diphragm muscles causes it to flatten, increasing the chest volume.
Nasal cavity	Air that is breathed through the nose is ***filtered*** by hairs, moistened by ***mucus*** and warmed by blood capillaries lining the nasal cavity. Breathing can contiue whilst ***chewing*** (Ch.15) occurs in the mouth cavity, but is temporarily interrupted by ***swallowing***. (Ch.15)
Epiglottis	The epiglottis is a muscular flap of tisue which automatically closes off the trachea during swallowing. This is an example of a ***reflex action***. (Ch.13).

Fig.10.13 Summary of the main components of the respiratory system.

The respiratory cycle

The **respiratory** (breathing) **cycle** is a rhythmic, alternating process involving inhalation (**inspiration**, 'breathing in') and exhalation (**expiration**, 'breathing out') (Fig.10.14). **Breathing rate** in a resting condition is about 16 cycles per minute. The **rate** and **depth** of breathing vary according to the individual's need for energy (see below). The cycle is mostly coordinated by **involuntary control** (Ch.13).

Air is moved into and out of the lungs by changes in the *volume* of the thorax; this results in corresponding changes in *pressure* within the thorax. Breathing movements involve the contraction and relaxation of muscles associated with the ribs and diaphragm (Fig.10.14). The *processes* of inhalation and exhalation are summarised in Fig.10.15.

Changes in **air** resulting from - inhalation and exhalation are summarised in Fig.10.16.

When the demands for energy change, there is often a corresponding change in breathing *depth* and *rate*:

(i) **Depth of breathing**. Although individual measurements vary widely the average **capacity** of human adult lungs is about 5 dm^3). During normal ('*quiet*') breathing, about 0.5 dm^3 of air (the tidal volume) is breathed in. This is increased to 4.5 dm^3 (the **vital**

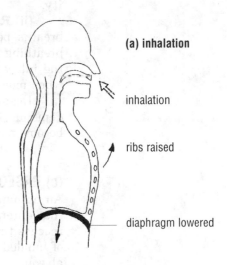

(a) inhalation

inhalation

ribs raised

diaphragm lowered

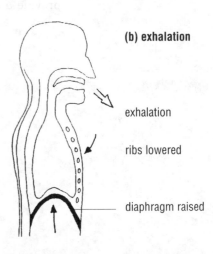

(b) exhalation

exhalation

ribs lowered

diaphragm raised

Fig.10.14 Breathing movements in humans (vertical section; side view)

CHANGE	INHALATION	EXHALATION
Intercostal muscles	***External*** muscles contract, causing the ribs to move upwards and outwards.	***Internal*** muscles contract, causing the ribs to move downwards and inwards; gravity may assist this
Diaphragm	Contracts and flattens, pushing down on the contents of the abdomen below.	Relaxes and becomes domed; displaced contents of abdomen push from below.
Lungs	Become inlflated against their elastic tendency.	Elasticity of lungs causes them to become deflated.
Volume of thorax	Increases	Decreases
Pressure in thorax	Decreases	Increases

Fig.10.15 Summary of inhalation and exhalation

COMPONENT	EXHALED	INHALED AIR
Oxygen	16%	21%
Carbon dioxide	4%	0.04%
Water vapour	Saturated = 6.2%	Variable, depends on humidity; average = 1.3%
Temperature	38°C	Ambient

Fig.10.16 Relative composition of inhaled and exhaled air

capacity) when more energy is needed. Some air (about 0.5 dm^3 during exercise) normally remains in the lungs at all times; this is known as the **residual capacity**.

(ii) **Rate of breathing**. The breathing rate is normally about about sixteen breaths per minute during 'quiet' breathing. Most (about 60 per cent) of the breathing movements in this situation are due to the diaphragm rather than to the intercostal muscles. The rate can increase to about 30 breaths per minute when more oxygen is needed.

Despite increases in the depth and rate of breathing during exercise, the demands for oxygen may not be fully met. In this situation, respiration may become partially **anaerobic** for a while and an **oxygen debt** is caused.

(c) GASEOUS EXCHANGE

An exchange of gases occurs at the **alveoli**; this results in a change in the air that enters the lungs (see Fig.10.16). Approximately 70 per cent of inhaled air reaches the alveoli and can take part in gaseous exchange; the other 30 per cent of inhaled air occupies the **dead space** of the impermeable tubes leading to the alveoli.

There are about 700 million alveoli in an average adult's two lungs; these provide a total surface area of about 80 m^2. This surface area is about forty-four

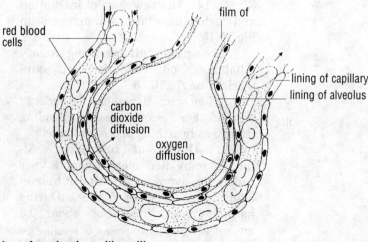

Fig.10.17 Structure of an alveolus, with capillary

The structure of a single alveolus is shown in Fig.10.17. Each alveolus has the characteristics of respiratory surfaces in general; they are permeable and thin (0.0001 mm), moist (with mucus), have a large surface area and are closely associated with a transport system. Steep concentration gradients of oxygen and carbon dioxide are maintained across the alveolus lining. The respiratory gases are carried to and from the lung by the blood (Ch.12) in slightly different ways:

(i) Oxygen

Oxygen is not very *soluble* (Appendix 1) in the liquid part of blood and is carried instead in **red blood cells**, where it becomes attached to **haemoglobin**. Haemoglobin is converted to the unstable molecule **oxyhaemoglobin** when it combines with oxygen. Haemoglobin is re-formed again when the blood reaches tissues in the body where the oxygen concentration is low:

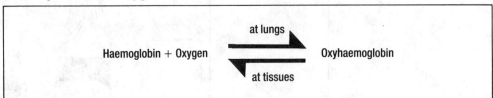

Red blood cells have a comparatively large surface area, allowing a more rapid uptake and loss of oxygen. The cell are pressed against the walls within the narrow capillaries; this increases the efficiency of oxygen uptake.

(ii) Carbon dioxide

About 90 per cent of the **carbon dioxide** is carried as **bicarbonate ions** (Appendix 1) which may combine with hydrogen ions to form **carbonic acid**. The remainder of the carbon dioxide is carried by haemoglobin molecules.

Refer again to the comparison of inhaled and exhaled air in Fig.10.16. The fact that a significant amount (16 per cent) of oxygen is exhaled is one reason why **expired air resuscitation** (E.A.R., the 'kiss of life') can be so effective in reviving an unconscious subject. **Nitrogen** is the most abundant gas (79 per cent) in air; it is not included in Fig.10.16 because it does not take part in chemical reactions (it is **inert**) within the body so it can be ignored for normal situations.

(d) ENVIRONMENTAL EFFECTS ON RESPIRATION

The quality of the air inhaled can have significant effects on an individual's health. Air that is inhaled through the nose is filtered, moistened and warmed before it reaches the delicate lung tissues. Air entering the body can cause damage, however, especially if it contains impurities. **Polluted air** (Ch.17) can cause disease and, directly or indirectly, even death. **Environmental pollution** includes the presence in the atmosphere of gases from industry and internal combustion engines.

Self-pollution by individuals who smoke is a major problem in many countries in the world. Smoking increases the risk of certain respiratory and circulatory (p..) diseases for smokers. Smoking also affects others who breathe smoke-laden air; this is known as '**passive smoking**'. Pregnant women who smoke may affect the growth of their unborn child because smoking reduces the oxygen available for the foetus. This is because *carbon monoxide* absorbed from the smoke displaces oxygen from haemoglobin molecules.

There are three main diseases, involving the respiratory system, which occur more frequently in smokers than non-smokers:

"questions on smoking and its effects on the respiratory system and on life expectancy are fairly common in GCSE Biology exams"

(i) Bronchitis

Inflammation (swelling up) of bronchi, caused by irritants and infectious microorganisms; this is accompanied by an accumulation of mucus. The narrowing of tubes causes difficulty in breathing. Cilia can be killed by substances in tobacco smoke, making the respiratory passages more vulnerable to disease.

(ii) Emphysema

Emphysema is a condition involving the breakdown of the alveoli. Irritants in tobacco smoke induce coughing, which damages already weakened lung tissue.

(iii) Lung cancer

Lung cancer is much more frequent in smokers than non-smokers; about 90 per cent of all lung cancers occur amongst smokers.

There is much evidence to indicate a strong relationship between smoking and diseases; life expectancy is, on average, decreased by increased smoking (Fig.10.19), especially if smoking was started in earlier life. Smokers who give up increase their life expectancy, for instance by reducing the chances of contracting lung cancer (Fig.10.20).

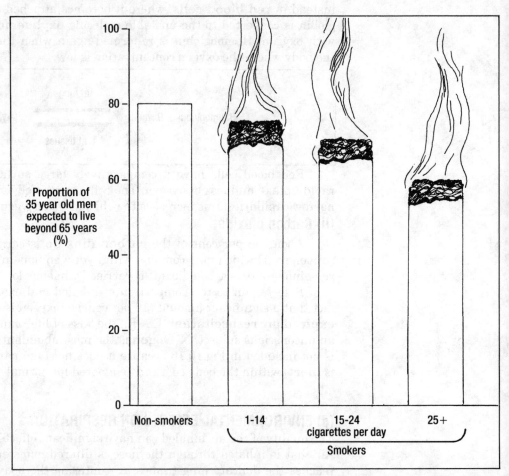

Fig.10.19 Proportion of men smokers and non-smokers (aged 35) who are expected to die or live beyond 65 years

(e) RESPIRATION IN PLANTS

Respiration is a constantly-occurring process in all living parts of plants. Respiration occurs at the same time as **photosynthesis** (Ch.15) in the light; they are *not* alternative processes. Plants do not really have specialised respiratory surfaces for the exchange of gases. The main reasons for this are:

(i) Plants are generally *less active* than animals; for instance, plants do not move about in their environment and do not maintain a relatively high internal temperature.

(ii) Plants have a *branching*, rather than compact form (Ch.7); the resulting high surface area allows an increased exchange of substances with the environment. The living tissues in a plant tend to be near the outer surface.

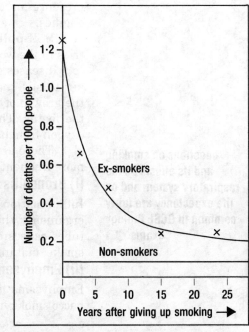

Fig.10.20 Death rates from lung cancer in ex-smokers and non smokers

(iii) Plants containing chlorophyll release oxygen when they are photosynthesising (this is explained in Ch.15).

Respiratory gases may be supplied or removed internally by photosynthesis, in the light. Oxygen and carbon dioxide may also be exchanged with the atmosphere in land plants through pores in the leaf called **stomata** (Ch.12). Gases may also enter woody stems and roots through pores called **lenticels**. Gases move by diffusion, along concentration gradients (Ch.4). Oxygen entering the air spaces becomes dissolved in the film of water surrounding the loosely packed cells mesophyll cells. Large air spaces and hollow stems (e.g. in marsh plants) allow gases to circulate within the plant.

EXAMINATION QUESTIONS

QUESTION 1

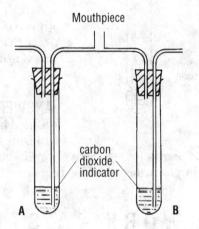

The diagram shows an apparatus which can be used to compare the carbon dioxide content of air breathed in and air breathed out. In using this apparatus a person breathes in and out through the mouthpiece.

(a) (i) Draw arrows on this diagram to show the direction which air would take in passing through the apparatus.

1 mark

(ii) Name a suitable carbon dioxide indicator which could be used in this apparatus.

(1 line) **1 mark**

(iii) Describe the appearance you would expect this indicator to have in each of test tubes A and B if a person breathed in and out through the mouthpiece several times.

(2 lines) **1 mark**

(b) (i) Name one chemical which is a common pollutant of the atmosphere.

1 mark

(ii) Briefly describe one effect which this substance can have on the body.

(2 lines) **1 mark**

Total 5 marks (SEB – Human)

QUESTION 2

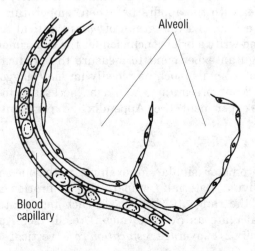

The diagram shows part of a blood capillary and alveoli in a lung.

(a) Name the blood cells shown in the capillary.

(1 line) **1 mark**

(b) Name the process by which oxygen moves from the alveoli into blood capillaries.

(1 line) **1 mark**

(c) Explain how the movement of oxygen into the blood is helped by:

(i) the thin walls of the alveoli and

(ii) the large number of alveoli in the lungs.

(5 lines) **2 marks**

Total 4 marks (LEAG)

A further practice question on the topics of this chapter is provided in Chapter 18 (Question 7).

OUTLINE ANSWERS

ANSWER 1

(a) (i)

Mouthpiece

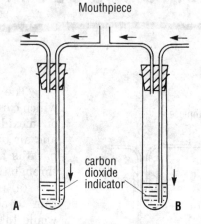

carbon
dioxide
indicator

A　　　　　　　　B

(ii) Bicarbonate indicator or limewater

(iii) Test tube A: bicarbonate indicator remains red, limewater remains clear; slight change may occur.

Test tube B: bicarbonate indicator goes yellow, limewater goes cloudy ('milky')

(b) (i) Carbon monoxide

(ii) Combines with haemoglobin, preventing oxygen from being carried.

ANSWER 2

(a) Red blood cells

(b) Diffusion

(c) (i) Diffusion occurs more effectively over short distances.

(ii) Provide a large surface area for diffusion.

COURSE WORK – A STEP FURTHER

An understanding of respiration can be developed by suitable experimental and survey work. Here are some suggestions:

1 ENERGY FROM RESPIRATION

(a) The heat energy from germinating seeds can be measured over a period of about 48 hours; measure temperature at convenient intervals, if possible every 2 hours. Present the results in the form of a line graph of *temperature* (vertical scale) against *time* (see Appendix 2). It is possible accurately to measure the mass of the seeds (together with the apparatus) when temperature readings are being taken. Present the results as a line graph of *mass* (vertical scale) against *time*. Explain each graph and write a brief conclusion for the experiment.

(b) Design an experiment to measure the production of heat energy from a small group of animals, such as blowfly larvae (maggots) (*Calliphora*) over a 48 hour period. What precautions would be necessary to ensure the accuracy and validity of the experiment? (See Appendix 3: Experimental Design).

2 RESPIRATION RATE

Set up a respirometer (similar, for example, to the one shown in Fig.10.11) containing suitable living material. Compare the respiration rate at four different temperatures, in the range 10°C–40°C. At each temperature, record the rate three times, and calculate an average (mean) result (see Appendix 1). Present a line graph (Appendix 2) of average *respiration rate* (vertical scale) against *temperature*.

3 > BREATHING RATE

Measure the breathing rate (number of breaths per minute) of resting individuals in a class/ year group. Calculate the average (mean) value (see Appendix 1). Present the results in the form of a bar graph. Repeat the experiment immediately after the individuals have undergone strenuous exercise for 2 min. Calculate the average (mean) rate, as before. Present the results in another bar graph. Summarise any differences between the two sets of results.

4 > THE EFFECTS OF SMOKING

Set up the apparatus shown in the diagram. This is designed to collect any tar contained in cigarette smoke. Smoke is drawn into the apparatus when a finger is placed over the tube at A.

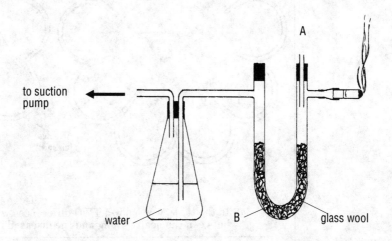

Carefully weigh the mass of the 'U'-tube B before and after the smoke from a cigarette has been sucked through. Repeat the experiment for different types of cigarette, containing low, medium and high tar. Compare also the relative amount of tar entering the 'U'-tube from filtered and unfiltered cigarettes.

Present the results in an appropriate way (Appendix 2) and write a brief conclusion for the experiment.

5 > FURTHER INFORMATION

The following address might be helpful with information on breathing:

Chest, Heart and Stroke Association
Tavistock House North
Tavistock Square
London WC1H 9JE
Tel. 01-387-3012
(Enclose 23cm x 15cm s.a.e.)

STUDENT'S ANSWER – EXAMINER'S COMMENTS

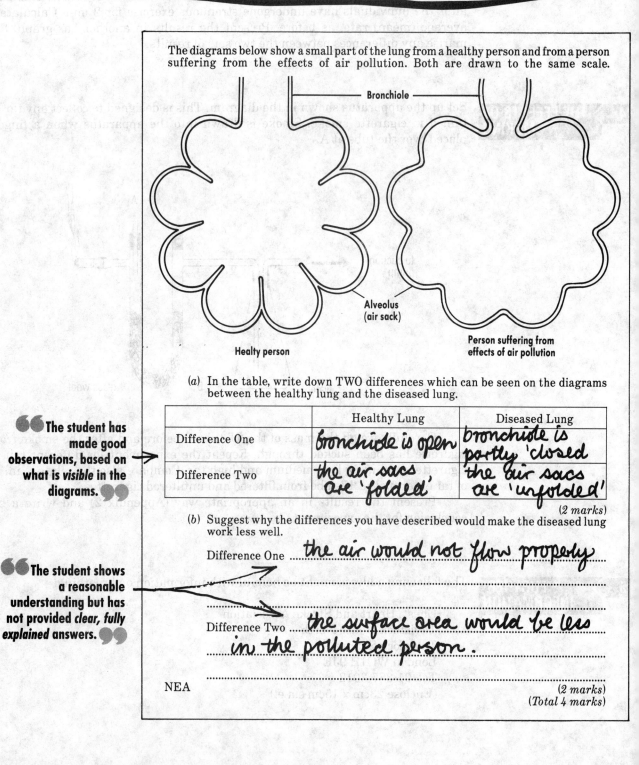

The diagrams below show a small part of the lung from a healthy person and from a person suffering from the effects of air pollution. Both are drawn to the same scale.

Bronchiole

Alveolus (air sack)

Healthy person

Person suffering from effects of air pollution

(a) In the table, write down TWO differences which can be seen on the diagrams between the healthy lung and the diseased lung.

	Healthy Lung	Diseased Lung
Difference One	bronchiole is open	bronchiole is partly 'closed'
Difference Two	the air sacs are 'folded'	the air sacs are 'unfolded'

(2 marks)

The student has made good observations, based on what is *visible* in the diagrams.

(b) Suggest why the differences you have described would make the diseased lung work less well.

Difference One ....the air would not flow propely....

The student shows a reasonable understanding but has not provided *clear, fully explained* answers.

Difference Two .... the surface area would be less in the polluted person.

NEA

(2 marks)
(Total 4 marks)

C H A P T E R

HOMEOSTASIS

GETTING STARTED

Homeostasis is the maintenance by organisms of a *constant internal environment* within a *changing external environment*. Homeostasis allows an organism to be relatively independent of its surroundings. The advantage of a controlled, fairly constant internal environment is that various essential processes can operate more efficiently at an **optimal level**.

Homeostasis is achieved by various *homeostatic control* systems. These keep internal *variables* such as temperature, pH and water content within acceptable limits. The optimal level for each of these variables is also called a **set point**, **norm** or **reference point**. The process of homeostasis requires a means of *detecting* and also *responding* to any changes in relation to the optimal level. This constantly occurring process involves **negative feedback**, which reduces the tendency for change away from the optimal level.

Homeostasis occurs to some extent in all organisms; more complex organisms show more elaborate patterns of control. This is because they perform a wider range of activities than simpler organisms. Examples of homeostasis which occur in mammals include **temperature regulation**, **excretion** and **blood sugar control**.

HOMEOSTATIC CONTROL
TEMPERATURE REGULATION
EXCRETION
GLUCOSE REGULATION

ESSENTIAL PRINCIPLES

1 > HOMEOSTATIC CONTROL

Homeostasis provides a relatively constant internal environment despite changes in an organism's external environment. Organisms live in an external environment whilst cells live in an internal environment. The internal environment contains fluids which surround cells and are contained within them. In many more complex animals the main fluid is blood (Ch.12), so homeostasis is primarily a means of keeping the composition and temperature of blood stable.

Homeostasis occurs to some extent in all living organisms and can be considered to be a **characteristic of life** (Ch.4). Homeostasis provides relatively stable conditions for chemical processes, or **metabolism**, to take place at an optimal level and therefore increases an organism's ability to survive. This stability is the result of continuous, energy consuming processes. Any variations from the optimal level are detected and responded to as part of the organism's **sensitivity** (Ch.15). Homeostasis reduces the effect of variations away from the optimal level; this is called **negative feedback**. Fig.11.1 shows how homeostatic control operates. The '**corrective mechanism**' shown in Fig.11.1 normally includes a receptor, control centre and a responding organ; this is more fully explained in Chapter 13.

> ❝the principle of negative feedback is important in understanding homeostasis, but it can be difficult to understand. Studying the following examples will help, however❞

```
            Change
         ┌──────────┐
         │          ▼
  ┌───────────┐  ┌───────────┐
  │  OPTIMAL  │  │ CORRECTIVE │
  │   LEVEL   │  │ MECHANISM  │
  └───────────┘  └───────────┘
         ▲          │
         └──────────┘
           Negative
           feedback
```

Fig.11.1 Homeostatic control

The more complex organisms tend to control their internal environment within a relatively narrow range; this allows them to be fairly independent of the external environment. Processes of homeostasis which occur for example in mammals include **temperature regulation**, **excretion** and **blood sugar control**.

2 > TEMPERATURE REGULATION

Temperature regulation, or **thermoregulation**, is a process by which an organism maintains a fairly constant internal temperature even if the external (*ambient*) temperature is changing. Ambient temperatures can vary considerably (see Ch.16), but most organisms can only function effectively within the **metabolic range** of about 0–45°C; living processes, especially those controlled by **enzymes** (Ch.4) operate efficiently at these temperatures. The *optimum* ('ideal') temperature for enzyme activity is about 40°C.

Temperature differences between the internal and external environment can cause a temperature exchange at the surface of the organism. The way in which this occurs is largely determined by the surface area of the organism; surface area depends on **size** and **shape** (Appendix 1: surface area to volume ratio).

TEMPERATURE REGULATION IN ANIMALS

There are two main types of temperature regulation in **animals**, *ectothermic* and *endothermic*, depending on how body heat is obtained:

(i) **Ectothermic (poikilothermic)**. Ectothermic (*or 'cold blooded'*) animals depend mostly on an *external* source of heat, mainly from the sun. They tend to have a **variable body temperature**. All animals other than birds and mammals are ectothermic. Such animals may control their body temperature but not usually within narrow limits; temperature regulation is mostly achieved by *behavioural* processes. For example, a lizard can regulate its body temperature to some extent by moving into or out of shade. However, the temperature of a lizard is likely to remain similar to that of the environment (see Fig.11.2). The body temperature of ectotherms may be relatively high, so the term 'cold-blooded' can

be misleading. At fairly low temperatures, ectothermic animals become inactive (*torpid*), so they live most successfully in warmer regions of the
world.

　(i) **Endothermic (homoiothermic)**. Endothermic (*or 'warm-blooded'*)
animals depend mostly on an *internal*
source of heat, mainly respiration
(Ch.10). They tend to have a **constant,
relatively high body temperature**.
Birds and mammals are endothermic.
Such animals control their body
temperature within narrow limits;
temperature regulation is mostly
achieved by *physiological* processes.

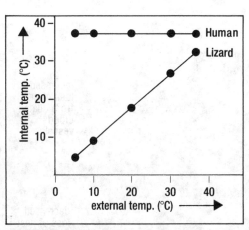

Fig.11.2 The relationship between internal and external temperature in ectothermic and endothermic animals

The body temperature of a bird or mammal is fairly independent of the surrounding temperature (Fig.11.2). Endothermic animals are regarded as being fairly advanced compared to ectotherms.

　Endothermic animals can operate effectively in fairly low temperatures and
this allows them to occupy colder as well as warmer regions of the world. Endothermic animals generally consume more food than ectothermic animals of a
similar mass: the food is used to release heat energy from respiration, for instance in the liver and the muscles.

TEMPERATURE REGULATION AT THE SKIN OF ANIMALS

The **skin** represents the boundary between an organism's internal and external
environments. Temperature exchanges between the organism and its surroundings occur at the skin, depending on the surface area of the skin.

(i) Surface area

　Surface area is a major factor in determining the rate at which heat is gained
or lost by the organism. In most parts of the world the external temperature is
less than the internal temperature of organisms. Smaller organisms have a relatively large surface area (they have a *large* **surface area/volume ratio**, see Appendix 1) so small animals tend to lose heat to their surroundings more readily
than large animals. For this reason endothermic animals, especially those living
in colder regions, are often fairly large. Young birds and mammals lose heat more
rapidly than adults. The **shape** of an animal will also affect the rate of heat loss;
flattened, extended surfaces such as ears and limbs provide a relatively large
area and are reduced in endothermic animals living in cold climates.

> ❝the surface area/volume ratio is one of the most difficult concepts in biology. Unfortunately it is also one of the most important! Study the text carefully and refer to Appendix 1 if necessary❞

　As well as surface area, there are three main factors which influence the
rate of heat loss at the skin; they are **evaporation**, **radiation** and **insulation**.
Each of these can be controlled, mostly by involuntary (Ch.13) responses; the surface of the skin can detect changes in temperature at the body surface. Also, the
temperature of blood flowing into the brain is monitored.

(ii) Evaporation

The evaporation of sweat has a cooling effect because heat energy (called the
'latent heat of vaporisation') from the organism is used in the process; this is the
energy needed to convert the liquid water in sweat into vapour. The rate of evaporation is affected by **humidity** and other factors in the environment; this is
similar to the situation in plants, during transpiration.

　The rate of sweating increases when the body temperature begins to rise, for
example as a result of exercise or because the surroundings are relatively warm.
An increase in the amount of sweat being produced (Fig.11.3) corresponds with
an increase in blood supply to the skin (see below). Sweating does not occur to
the same extent throughout the body, for instance because of an uneven distribution of sweat glands, or because some parts of the body are covered by hair or fur
(see below), and some animals lose water from their tongue; this is panting.
Sweating is also a form of **excretion** since sweat contains wastes including *urea*.

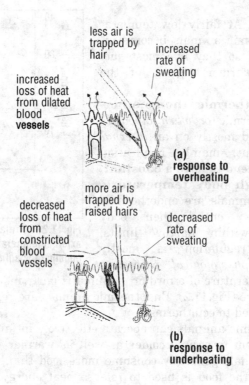

less air is
trapped by
hair

increased
rate of
sweating

increased
loss of heat
from dilated
blood
vessels

**(a)
response to
overheating**

more air is
trapped by
raised hairs

decreased
loss of heat
from
constricted
blood
vessels

decreased
rate of
sweating

**(b)
response to
underheating**

**Fig.11.3 Control of temperature at the skin
surface**

(iii) Radiation

Radiation involves the direct transfer of heat energy from the blood to the surroundings; this is affected by the amount of blood which reaches parts of the skin nearest to the surface:

Vasodilation increases the loss of heat by radiation. Vasodilation involves the widening of arterioles leading to the skin, allowing more blood through to the tissue just under the skin (Fig.11.3).

Vasoconstriction reduces the loss of heat by radiation. Vasoconstriction involves the narrowing of arterioles and the reduction of blood flow.

Variations in the amount of blood reaching the outer parts of the skin also affects the rate of sweat production (see above) since sweat is produced from blood.

(iv) Insulation

Insulation reduces the loss of heat at the skin surface; insulation is provided by **hair**, **fur** or **feathers** which trap a layer of air next to the skin. Air is a poor conductor of heat, so increasing the amount of air trapped reduces heat loss. This effect is achieved by the contraction of small **erector muscles**, shown in Fig.11.3. In humans, who have comparatively little hair, the result of these muscles contracting is visible as 'goose pimples'. Humans living in colder regions wear more clothing since the hair covering is insufficient insulation.

Insulation is provided more permanently by a layer of **subcutaneous fat** (adipose tissue), which is also a poor conductor of heat; this layer is likely to be quite thick in endothermic animals, including humans, living in cold regions. Fat is also a *stored food* which provides energy when the animal is unable to obtain sufficient food, for instance in cold conditions; fat has a high calorific value, yielding a lot of energy in respiration (Ch.10).

Structure	Function
Epidermis (cornified layer) (consists of dead cells)	**Protection** against physical damage, entry of microbes, excessive water loss. **Sensitivity** (Ch. 13); various different nerve endings which detect hot and cold temperature, touch, pressure and pain.
Dermis	**Nutrition** (Ch. 15): formation of vitamin D
Melanin	**Protection**, by 'blocking' excessive ultraviolet (u.v.) radiation. Skin is made darker permanently or temporarily in humans, depending on race. Darker skin radiates heat more rapidly than lighter skin.
Sweat glands and ducts	**Temperature regulation**: cooling effect of sweat. **Excretion** *and* **osmoregulation** (Ch. 11): sweat contains urea and excess water and salts.
Hair or feathers	**Temperature regulation**: trap a layer of air, for insulation. **Protection**: colour of fur or feathers provides camouflage, for prey and predators (Ch. 17). **Reproduction**: colour and position of feathers and fur may be important in courtship behaviour.

Fig.11.4 Summary of the functions of the skin

The skin is a large organ, having a wide range of functions, including that of temperature regulation. The functions of the skin are summarised in Fig 11.4.

Endothermic animals have various other ways of coping with cold conditions at certain times of the year. Birds may **migrate** to warmer regions, where food may also be more plentiful. Mammals are generally less able to move great distances. Small endothermic mammals may **hibernate**; this involves a period of inactivity, or **dormancy**.

Endothermic animals may fail to survive cold conditions, however. If the body temperature drops below the optimal level, **hypothermia** may result. In humans, hypothermia may occur in very cold conditions, when clothing is insufficient and when the individual is relatively inactive. In this sort of situation shivering may occur; this involves involuntary muscular action. Elderly people are particularly at risk because they may not be very active and because they may have difficulty in affording necessary clothing, food and fuel. Hypothermia is also a serious risk for people in cold water, because water rapidly conducts heat away from the body.

TEMPERATURE REGULATION IN PLANTS

Plants have very little direct control over their internal temperature which tends to be much more variable than that of animals. The metabolic level in plants is relatively low, and very little heat is generated internally. Plants have large surfaces for the absorption of light (Ch.15) and there is a possibility of overheating in hot conditions. Some cooling may occur by the evaporation of water from the leaves (Ch.12). Plants growing in hot regions are adapted in various ways, for instance to prevent too much water being lost from the leaves.

3 ⟩ EXCRETION

The removal of the waste products of metabolism is called **excretion**. The chemical processes of metabolism may lead to the formation of waste products, which are not required by the organism and which might be harmful. Some substances, such as alcohol, are *toxic* when they enter the body and they may be removed directly or after being made less harmful (e.g. in the liver). In practice, excretion in animals is also taken to include the removal of excess water and minerals absorbed from the diet (Ch.15). Excretion is necessary for two main reasons:

(i) to maintain the composition of an organism's fluids, including water content and pH.

(ii) to prevent the accumulation of poisonous (toxic) wastes which might otherwise interferes with metabolism.

❝candidates often confuse these three terms, each of which has a very differenct meaning❞

It is important to be able to distinguish **excretion** from **secretion**, which is the production of useful substances from cells. **Egestion** (Ch.15) is not really excretion because faeces contain undigested food which has not been absorbed or taken part in metabolism. Faeces do contain bile pigments (see Fig.11.8) which are the products of metabolism.

(a) EXCRETION IN ANIMALS

The main waste products of metabolism in animals are **carbon dioxide**, mineral salts and nitrogen-containing compounds such as **urea**. The main organs of excretion are the **skin, liver, lungs and the** kidneys **(Fig.11.5). The kidneys are also involved in the regulation of water content in the organism** (*osmoregulation*).

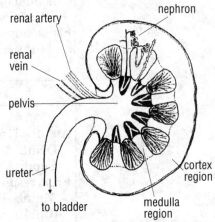

Fig.11.5 Vertical section through a mammalian kidney

THE KIDNEY

The **kidney** has two main functions; excretion of waste products and osmoregulation (the regulation of the water content of body fluid). Waste products leave the body in solution with water. Excretion therefore provides an opportunity for the concentration of body fluids to be adjusted.

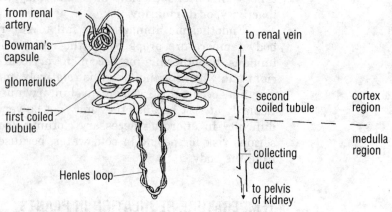

from renal artery

Bowman's capsule

glomerulus

first coiled bubule

Henles loop

to renal vein

second coiled tubule

collecting duct

to pelvis of kidney

cortex region

medulla region

Fig.11.6 Structure of a nephron

    The structural and functional unit of the kidney is the **nephron** (Fig.11.6), or **kidney tubule**. Each of the two kidneys in humans contains about one million nephrons. The nephron is a narrow tubule about 3 cm long; the combined length of the nephrons within each kidney totals about 30 km. This provides a very large surface area. There are also about 160 km of blood vessels in each kidney. The main function of the kidney is to filter blood. This is achieved during two processes:

(i) Filtration

Blood from a narrow branch of the renal artery enters‚the **glomerulus**; smaller molecules in the blood are forced under pressure into the surrounding **Bowman's capsule**. This process of filtration involves such molecules as water, urea, glucose, amino acids and also minerals.

(ii) Reabsorption

About 99 per cent of the filtered fluid (filtrate) in the nephron is reabsorbed. The useful components re-enter the blood by **active transport**, **diffusion**, and **osmosis** (Ch.4). The active transport uses energy released by respiration. Oxygen is therefore used by the kidney; carbon dioxide is produced.

    Substances which are normally totally reabsorbed are glucose and amino acids. This occurs mostly in the first coiled tubule. Water is reabsorbed throughout the nephron; minerals are reabsorbed in the two coiled tubules. The relative amounts of water and minerals which are returned to the blood can be varied and the process is controlled by hormones, including **ADH** (antidiuretic hormone, or *vasopressin*). This control allows the body to adjust the concentration of its fluid (osmoregulation).

    Urea is not reabsorbed. Instead, it forms a solution in water called **urine**; this is only about 1 per cent of the solution originally entering the nephron during filtration. This empties from nephrons into collecting ducts; it accumulates in

Gain (cm³)		Loss (cm³)	
		From kidney:	
Absorbed in gut:		**Urine**	1500
Drink	1500	From skin:	
Food	700	**Sweating**	500
From respiration:		From lungs:	
Metabolic water		**Exhalation** (Ch. 10)	400
(Ch. 10)	300	From egestion:	
		Faeces	100
Totals	2500		2500

Fig.11.7 Relative daily gain and loss in a human (an average adult male, resting, in moderate

the pelvis of the kidney, then the urine drains down the **ureter** to the **bladder** where it is temporarily stored (about 400 cm^3) before being released at intervals through the **urethra**; the release of urine is called **micturition**.

The exact composition of urine depends to a large extent on how much water has been gained or lost by the body (Fig.11.7). This, in turn, is affected by such factors as external temperature; in hot weather less urine is formed because more water is lost by sweating, but the urine is more concentrated.

(iii) Diabetes

Diabetes (*diabetes mellitus*) is a condition caused by a lack of sufficient **insulin** (Ch.13); this results in an increase in glucose concentration in the blood. Excess glucose filtered out of the blood is not necessarily all reabsorbed in the kidney; the presence of glucose in the urine is an indication of diabetes. The disorder can be treated by low-sugar diets and also by regular injections of insulin.

(iv) Kidney failure

Kidneys may fail because of disease or because blood pressure drops too low to maintain filtration. There are two main ways in which the failure of kidneys can be treated:

(a) **Artificial kidney**. The **artificial kidney** or **dialysis machine** performs some of the functions of a normal kidney. Blood from the patient is temporarily diverted from an artery in the arm through the machine and is then returned to a vein in the arm. Blood in the machine is passed over a **dialysis membrane**, which functions as a synthetic living membrane, which is **selectively permeable** (Ch.4). This membrane is surrounded by a solution containing the 'ideal' concentrations of substances. Certain small molecules such as urea and salts pass from the blood through the dialysis membrane by diffusion because they are above a certain concentration. Useful substances such as glucose, amino acids and some salts and water are retained in the blood. A patient requiring dialysis treatment needs to undergo this process every 2–3 days. Artificial kidneys are relatively expensive and not necessarily available to all patients with kidney failure.

(b) **Kidney transplantation**. A kidney from a suitable **donor** can be **transplanted** into the patient, normally in the lower abdomen. The tissues of the donor kidney must be similar to the patient's own tissues, otherwise an **immune reaction** (Ch.12) may result and the transplanted kidney will be rejected. Kidneys may be donated by someone closely related to the patient; the donor can live healthily with just one kidney. Kidneys may also be obtained, for instance, from the victims of road accidents. Kidney transplants allow patients to conduct a relatively independent life; however, there may not be enough suitable donor kidneys available to meet the need for them.

> ❝this topic is an example of a technological application in biology; questions on such topics are relatively common in GCSE Biology❞

(b) EXCRETION IN PLANTS

Plants produce relatively small amounts of waste substances because they only form organic molecules which they actually need; animals, however, may absorb molecules in their diet which are not necessarily required. Plants are generally less active than animals so accumulate wastes more slowly. The main excretory products from plants are **oxygen** and **carbon dioxide**. Oxygen is a waste product of **photosynthesis** (Ch.15) and is released in comparatively bright light. Carbon dioxide, produced from respiration, is released in darkness and in dim light (this is explained in Ch.15). Waste gases are mostly lost from the leaves; they are given off through the large surface area of the mesophyll cells then diffuse out of the leaves through the stomata (Ch.12). More complex wastes may be transported to metabolically inactive parts of the plant such as non-living xylem tissue or the vacuoles of living cells. Some wastes are converted into an insoluble form, for example as crystals. Wastes may also be transported into structures such as leaves, petals and fruits which are later lost from the plant.

4 ▶ GLUCOSE REGULATION

Glucose is a very important molecule because it can be used in **respiration** to release energy. However, if too much glucose is allowed to accumulate in the body fluids, excessive water may be lost from tissues by osmosis. In vertebrate animals the concentration of glucose in blood is controlled within quite narrow limits by the activities of various organs, including the **pancreas** and **liver**.

In humans, the average concentration of glucose in the blood is about 90 mg/100 cm^3. The concentration of glucose in the blood is regulated by the conversion of glucose to and from glycogen. Glycogen is a stored form of glucose which is insoluble and which is therefore not osmotically active (p..). The interconversion of glucose and glycogen is controlled by the hormones (p..) **insulin** and **glycogon**. Both hormones are produced by the **pancreas**, from tissue called **islets of Langerhans**.

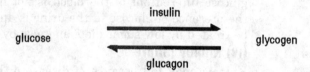

Insulin is released when the concentration of glucose in the blood is increased, for instance after a meal containing carbohydrate; the absorption of glucose from the gut (Ch.15) may raise the blood glucose concentration to about 140 mg/100 cm^3. Insulin decreases glucose concentrations by converting it to glycogen.

Function	Description
Glucose regulation	Storage of glucose as glycogen.
Protein breakdown	Breakdown (**deamination**) of excess amino acids and proteins forming carbohydrates, and also **urea**, which is carried to the kidneys for excretion (Ch. 11).
Fat metabolism	Conversion of fats into different forms, for metabolism.
Formation of bile	Formation of **bile**, which is temporarily stored in the **gall bladder** before being passed down the **bile duct** to the **duodenum** (Ch. 15). Bile contains sodium **bicarbonate**, which neutralises the acidic contents of the gut. Bile also contains **bile salts**, which are used in fat digestion, and **bile pigments**, which are from the breakdown of haemoglobin (Ch. 12) and which are excreted in faeces.
Iron storage	Iron from the breakdown of **haemoglobin** (Ch. 12) is stored in the liver until it is needed to make new haemoglobin molecules.
Vitamin storage	Storage of some fat-soluble vitamins (Ch. 15), including *A* and *D*.
Detoxification	Detoxification of poisons (toxins) involves converting them to less harmful forms. Poisons include those which are produced by **pathogens** (Ch. 17) and also those taken as **drugs**, e.g. alcohol.
Deactivation	Deactivation of certain **hormones** (Ch. 13) is important after they have performed their function.
Heat production	Heat energy may be released from some of the chemical reactions within the liver; this helps to maintain body temperature (Ch. 11).

Fig.11.8 Summary of the main functions of the liver

❝the hormone *glucogon* has the same effect as adrenalin on glycogen conversion in the liver❞

Diabetic individuals are unable to produce sufficient insulin and need to reduce the glucose content of their diet to avoid excess glucose in the blood. At concentrations above 160 mg/100 cm^3, glucose cannot all be reabsorbed in the kidney and some will appear in urine. Diabetics may also need to inject insulin so that sufficient glucose can be stored as glycogen.

Glucagon is released when the level of blood glucose is decreased, for instance during exercise. Glucagon increases glucose concentrations by converting it from glycogen. Diabetics may not have sufficient glucose or glycogen available to meets the body's needs. This condition, known as **hypoglycaemia**, can lead to a coma (unconsciousness) if glucose is not obtained in the diet.

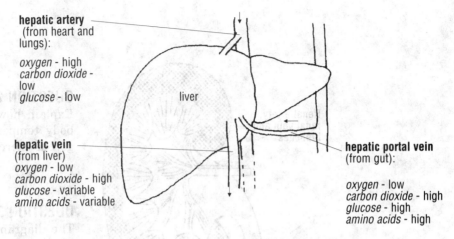

hepatic artery
(from heart and lungs):

oxygen - high
carbon dioxide - low
glucose - low

liver

hepatic vein
(from liver)
oxygen - low
carbon dioxide - high
glucose - variable
amino acids - variable

hepatic portal vein
(from gut):

oxygen - low
carbon dioxide - high
glucose - high
amino acids - high

Fig.11.9 Relative concentration of some blood components entering and leaving the liver

Muscles store most (about 60 per cent) of the body's glycogen; the rest is stored in the **liver**. This is one of many functions of the liver, the largest organ in the body. Some of these functions are summarised in Fig.11.8 and many are involved directly or indirectly in homeostasis. The liver occupies a dominant position in the circulatory system (Ch.12,Fig.12.8), receiving a supply of blood from the gut, through the hepatic portal vein as well as directly from the aorta, through the hepatic artery. The composition of blood is adjusted in various ways (see Fig.11.8) before leaving through the hepatic vein. The relative concentrations for certain substances are shown in Fig.11.9.

EXAMINATION QUESTIONS

QUESTION 1

Fig.11.10 shows a vertical section of human skin.

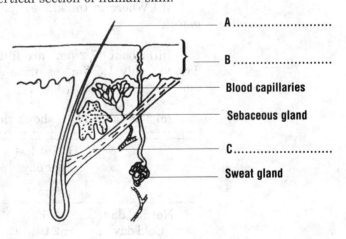

A ....

B ....

Blood capillaries

Sebaceous gland

C ....

Sweat gland

Fig.11.10

(a)   Name the parts A, B and C on the lines provided.

             3 marks

(b)   After running a race, your skin is wet and you face is hot.
      (i) Why is your skin wet and how does this help to cool your body?

             (7 lines) **4 marks**

      (ii) Why is your face hot and how does this help to cool your body?

             (7 lines) **4 marks**

(c)   How do you think the sebaceous glands help to keep hair and skin healthy?

(4 lines) **4 marks**
Total 14 marks (LEAG)

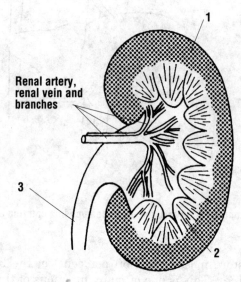

Renal artery, renal vein and branches

QUESTION 2
Explain how the skin helps to return body temperature to normal after vigorous exercise.
      Total 14 marks (LEAG)

QUESTION 3
The diagram shows a section through a mammal's kidney.
    (a) Name the parts 1, 2 and 3.
      3 marks

Rate of blood flow in kidneys	Rate of filtration into kidney tubules (nephrons)	Rate of urine passing out of kidneys
1.2 dm³ per minute	0.12 dm³ per minute	1.5 dm³ per day

Fig.11.12

(b) The table 11.12 gives information about the human kidney.

(i) What percentage of blood passing into the kidney is filtered into the kidney tubules?

      1 mark

(ii) Where in the kidney (part 1, 2 or 3 in the diagram) does filtration take place?

      1 mark

(iii) About 17.2 dm³ are filtered from the blood into the kidney tubules per day, yet only 1.5 dm³ of urine are excreted. What happens to the other 17.05 dm³?

      2 marks

(c) The table 11.13 shows the average amounts of urine, sweat and salt (so-

	Urine lost per day	Sweat lost per day	Salt (sodium chloride) lost per day	
	(dm³)	(dm³)	In urine (g)	In sweat (g)
Normal day	1.5	0.5	18.0	1.5
Cold day	2.0	0.0	19.5	0.0
Hot day	0.375	2.0	13.5	6.0

Fig.11.13

dium chloride) lost on a normal day, a cold day and a hot day. (Assume that food and drink are the same on all days.)

(i) Why is more urine lost on a cold day than a normal day?

      2 mark

(ii) Why do you think the total amount of salt lost on each of the three days is the same?

2 marks

(iii) The minimum amount of urine excreted in a day is 0.375 dm^3. Why do you think the kidneys always produce some urine?

2 marks

(iv) What *must* someone losing more than 7 dm^3. of sweat in a day do in order to remain healthy?

2 marks
Total 15 marks (SEG)

QUESTION 4

(a)   Explain the terms *homeostasis* and *negative feedback* in relation to body temperature of a mammal. (A detailed account of temperature regulation is **not** required.)

7 marks

(b)   (i) Describe the homeostatic control of the water content of the body.

7marks

(ii) Describe the influence of the liver, pancreas and adrenal glands on the sugar content of the blood.

6 marks
Total 20 marks (IGCSE)

OUTLINE ANSWERS

ANSWER 1

(a)   A = hair; B = epidermis; C = erector muscle (erector pili muscle)

(b)   (i) Sweat is produced, from sweat glands and ducts in the skin. The sweat uses heat energy from the body to evaporate, and this has a cooling effect on the body, including the blood. Blood which has been cooled then circulates around the body.

(ii) Arterioles in the epidermis dilate (vasodilation), allowing more blood near the surface of the skin. This blood loses heat to the external environment by radiation. The cooler blood then circulates around the body.

(c)   The sebaceous glands produce oil/grease which keeps the epidermis and hair fairly supple and waterproof. The grease contains substances which inhibit the growth of bacteria.

ANSWER 2

Excess body heat is generated in muscles after vigorous exercise. The tendency for body temperature to increase is offset by heat losses at the skin. This is achieved in three ways:

(i)   More sweat is produced by the sweat glands. The sweat passes through the sweat ducts and emerges at the sweat pores. Water in the sweat then evaporates, causing cooling. The heat energy required to convert the water in sweat into a vapour (i.e. the latent heat of vaporisation) is taken from the blood.

(ii)   More blood flows into the small blood vessels near the surface of the skin. This increased flow of blood is caused by vasodilation (widening) of vessels closer to the epidermis, for instance by the relaxation of muscles in the walls of certain arteries and arterioles. Heat is lost from the blood at the surface by radiation, convection and, if the skin is in contact with another surface, conduction. The increased flow of blood also causes more sweat to be formed.

(iii) Less air is trapped by hairs, which lay flat against the skin. This results from the relaxation of erector muscles and reduces the insulation at the surface of the skin. Blood which is cooled at the skin is then carried by the circulation to the rest of the body which is then cooled.

ANSWER 3

(a)   1 = cortex; 2 = medulla; 3 = ureter

(b)   (i) 10 per cent

       (ii) 1

       (iii) It is reabsorbed from the nephron into the blood.

(c)   (i) Less water is lost through sweating on a cold day; the water is lost instead in urine.

       (ii) The salt content of the body is maintained at a constant level to avoid problems of osmosis; if a constant amount of salt is present in the diet, a constant total amount will be lost.

       (iii) Urine is a solution of the waste urea and other toxins, which must be removed at intervals from the body.

       (iv) Consume enough water and salts to maintain minimum amounts in the body.

COURSE WORK – A STEP FURTHER

Below are four fairly simple investigations of temperature control and excretion.

1 > EXPERIMENT 1

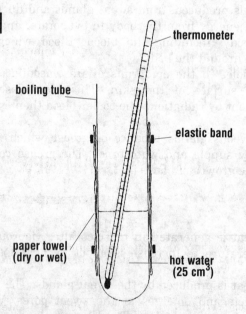

Set up two boiling tubes, each wrapped with a paper towel, secured by elastic bands (Fig.11.14). Soak the paper towel of one tube with cold tap water; this is the 'wet' tube. Do not soak the towel of the other, 'dry', tube.

Carefully pour 25 cm^3 of boiling water, for instance from a kettle, into each tube and immediately note the temperature of each tube. Begin timing. Note the temperatures in each case at regular intervals, for instance every minute, for about 8 minutes. Plot the cooling curves for the wet and dry tube as line graphs (Appendix 2) on the same axes; *temperature* (vertical scale) should be plotted against *time*.

Comment on the results; note that most of the cooling in each tube occurs in the first 1–2 minutes. Suggest possible improvements to the experimental technique. If this is a 'model' of a sweating person, say what each of the following components represent: boiling water, boiling tube, and wet paper towel.

Fig.11.14 Experiment to show the cooling effect of evaporation

EXPERIMENT 2

Set up two different-sized flasks, for instance by clamping a 100 cm^3 and 250 cm^3 round-bottomed flask in a retort stand.

Half-fill each flask with boiling water, then immediately begin timing and note the temperature of each flask. Record the temperatures at regular intervals, for instance every minute, for about 8 minutes. Plot the cooling curves for the small and large flasks as line graphs (Appendix 2) on the same axes; *temperature* (vertical scale) should be plotted against *time*.

Comment on the results and also on the accuracy of the experiment. If the flasks represent endothermic (homoiothermic, 'warm-blooded') animals, which one, large or small, would have the most difficulty in staying warm. Explain your answer.

EXPERIMENT 3

Design a suitable experiment, using simple equipment, to show the effect of insulation on heat loss. Use experiments 1 and 2 above for guidance, and refer if necessary to Appendix 3 ('Experimental Design'). Present your results in an appropriate way (Appendix 2) and comment on your findings.

EXPERIMENT 4

Put a small quantity of each of the following separately into three labelled test tubes:

Tube A = urine
Tube B = plasma (from centrifuged blood)
Tube C = distilled water

Test the contents of each of the tubes in the follow ways:

Test 1 = litmus (test for pH)
Test 2 = 'Clinistix' (test for glucose)
Test 3 = 'Albustix' (test for protein)

Write an account of your experiment, including a summary of results and comments.

SOURCES OF INFORMATION

The following address may be useful for further information on diabetes:

British Diabetic Association
10 Queen Ann Street
London W1M 0BD
Tel. 01-373-1531

STUDENT'S ANSWER – EXAMINER'S COMMENTS

(a)   The table shows the approximate composition and volume of the fluid entering the kidneys by the renal arteries, passing into the nephrons and then leaving the kidney as urine.

percentage composition	entering kidneys	entering nephrons	leaving as urine
proteins	8.0	0	0
salt	0.7	0.7	1.2
urea	0.03	0.03	2.0
sugar	0.1	0.1	0
Fluid volume in cm per minute	750	125	1

(i) From the table,

   (a) Which substances are unable to pass through the membrane of the Bowman's capsule?

proteins

(1 mark)

   (b) which substances are completely reabsorbed by the tubule?

sugar

(1 mark)

(ii) Why must urea be expelled in the urine?

because it will poison the body if it builds up.

(1 mark)

(iii) What differences in composition of urine would you expect in

   (a) a starving refugee living on starch and water,

it would contain less urea

(1 mark)

   (b) a weight lifter eating lots of steak,

more protein would enter the kidney

(1 mark)

   (c) a jockey trying to keep his mass down by rationing his fluid intake?

a more concentrated urine, less urine is produced.

(1 mark)

(c) Some young children pass through a developmental stage in which they sometimes urinate whilst asleep rather than awaking before this happens (they wet the bed), possible treatments involve

   (i) not having an evening drink,

   (ii) using a special pad in the bed which, as soon as it is dampened by the first urine, rings a bell to wake the child,

   (iii) giving a medicine in the evening to reduce the blood supply to the kidney during the night.

In each of the three treatments, give a brief explanation of the body mechanism which is being altered to prevent bed-wetting.

(i) *less water is filtered by the kidney so there is less water in the urine and less urine.*

(2 marks)

(ii) *The bell tells the child to wake up*

(2 marks)

(iii) *less water reaches the kidney, so less urine is produced.*

(2 marks)

WJEC

(2 marks)
(Total 12 marks)

Correct answers.

This is correct; the water content (and the volume) of the urine would *increase*.

Protein does not enter the urine so this answer is not relevant. There *would* be an increase in urea concentration in urine, from the breakdown of excess protein in the liver.

Correct.

This is correct; it is worth using the word 'volume' in relation to amount.

For two marks another point needs to be made, eg that this produces a conditioned reflex.

This is correct, though some explanation is needed; a reduction in the volume of blood reaching the kidney decreases the volume of urine produced.

TRANSPORT SYSTEMS

G E T T I N G   S T A R T E D

Transport systems are used to move important substances within the organism. These substances may enter through **exchange surfaces or may be formed in cells within the organism. Various transport systems then move them to regions where they are used in** metabolism, **any waste molecules being subsequently transported to exchange surfaces for removal.**

Transport systems include processes such as **active transport, diffusion** and **osmosis** which move substances over relatively *short* distances, such as within and between cells. The movement of materials over relatively *large* distances within the organism is called **mass flow** (**bulk flow**). Mass flow in both animals and plants involves the use of specialised tubes which form a **vascular system.** The movement of substances within vascular systems tends to be an active process in animals, for instance involving a pump such as the heart. In plants, substances are moved by mainly passive processes.

ESSENTIAL PRINCIPLES

Transport systems are used for **distribution** within organisms; to move substances from where they are made available to where they are needed. In larger, more complex organisms, different tissues and organs are specialised for different functions. Substances which are made or absorbed in one region of the organism may be required in another region. In large organisms specialised cells may need to supply or obtain substances to or from other tissues, including exchange surfaces. Specialised transport systems allow the movement of materials to occur more efficiently.

Transport occurs over both short and long distances:

(i) **short distance transport** within and between cells, by **active transport**, **osmosis** and **diffusion**; diffusion is a relatively slow, passive process.

(ii) **long distance transport** between tissues and organs of relatively large organisms, by **mass flow** through specialised tubes which form a vascular system. Mass flow transport systems occur in both animals and plants.

Animals which are *very small* (less than about 1 mm across) or which are thin have a *relatively large surface area to volume ratio* (Appendix 1); substances can be exchanged directly between cells within the organism and the environment surrounding the organism. Individual cells can obtain or remove substances over short distances by active transport and diffusion.

Larger animals have a *relatively small surface area to volume ratio*. Larger animals tend to be fairly complex and active, performing a wide range of activities. Such animals have many cells which do not have immediate access to the other parts of the body which supply or receive materials. Specialised tissues are used to allow mass flow of substances over large distances. The specialised system consists of three main components:

(i) **transport fluid**, e.g. blood, lymph

(ii) **vascular system**, e.g. blood or lymph vessels

(iii) **pumping mechanism**, e.g. the heart.

The **vascular system** can be 'open' or 'closed'. In an *open* vascular system, the transport fluid drains into body spaces before re-entering vessels; this form of circulation occurs in arthropod animals for example the insects. In a *closed* vascular system, the transport fluid remains within vessels during much of the circulation. Certain vessels are permeable, and substances enter or leave the circulation through the walls of the vessels. The closed system occurs in many animals including vertebrates. The advantage of closed circulatory systems is that they allow a much higher pressure to develop in the transport fluid, such as blood; this additional pressure is used to circulate the fluid more efficiently. A closed system also allows the distribution of the fluid within the animal to be controlled more easily.

2 ⟩ BLOOD SYSTEM

The three main components of the blood system are **blood**, **blood vessels** and the **heart**. Each of these is described below for a mammal such as the human.

(a) BLOOD

Blood is a transport fluid which also has an important function in protecting the body against infection. Blood consists of two main components; these can be separated when blood is spun in a centrifuge:

plasma (55 per cent of the blood volume)

cells and cell fragments (45 per cent of the blood volume)

The total volume of blood in an average adult human is about 5.5 dm^3; this represents about 10 per cent of the body mass. The exact composition of the blood varies throughout the body as substances are added or removed in different regions.

(i) Plasma

Plasma is the liquid part of blood; it consists of water (91 per cent) which contains dissolved and suspended particles:

(a) **water**. Water is a solvent; it also carries heat around the body. The amount of water in the blood is important in determining blood pressure (see below) and in osmoregulation, and is controlled by various processes including the activities of the kidney.

(b) **blood proteins**. Blood proteins are made in the liver. They are important in various processes and include:

fibrinogen and prothrombin; important in blood clotting; plasma with these proteins removed is known as serum

globulin; some globulins function as antibodies, others are used to carry hormones and vitamins in the blood-albumen; used in osmoregulation

(c) **control proteins**. Hormones ('chemical messengers') and enzymes are important in regulating various metabolic processes.

(d) **dissolved food and wastes**. Food includes glucose, amino acids, fatty acids, glycerol, vitamins and minerals; wastes include urea and carbon dioxide.

(e) **dissolved gases**. As well as waste carbon dioxide, plasma contains small amounts of nitrogen and oxygen; most of the oxygen is not very soluble and most is carried within red blood cells (see below).

(ii) Cells

There are two main types of **cells** contained in blood. Blood also contains **cell fragments**, called **thrombocytes**. Each type of cell is quite different in structure and function:

(a) **Red cells**. Red cells, (or **erythrocytes**, red blood corpuscles) are formed (at the rate of about 1 million per second) in the bone marrow of the ribs, sternum and vertebrae (Ch.14). The outer membrane of the red cells may include certain proteins which determine the individual's blood group. In the foetus, red cells are mostly made in the liver and spleen. Mammalian red blood cells have a relatively short life time (about three months) because they lack a nucleus; the cells are broken down in the spleen and liver, and the iron and some of the protein is re-cycled. The nucleus is lost from each cell during its formation, creating a depression in the central part of the cell; this produces the characteristic **biconcave disc shape** of red blood cells (Fig.12.1). The shape provides a large sur-

Cell type	Site of manufacture	Function	Relative no./mm^3 of blood*	Structure
Red cell	Bone marrow	Carry oxygen and some carbon dioxide	5 000 000	
White cells:			7 000	
Phagocyte	Bone marrow	Engulf bacteria	4 900	
Lymphocyte	Lymphatic system	Antibody production	1 680	
Thrombocyte	Bone marrow	Part of blood clotting mechanism	250 000	

*1 mm^3 of blood is about one small drop.

Fig.12.1 Comparison of different types of blood cells

face area for the exchange of gases. The total surface area of all red blood cells in the human body is estimated to be about $3500m^2$! Exchange is further promoted by the fact that red cells need to squeeze through *capillaries* (Ch.12) one after the other; the relatively slow movement and the close contact between the cells and the vessel wall allows diffusion (Ch.4) to occur more readily.

Each red cell contains about 300 million **haemoglobin molecules**, which combine with oxygen in a reversible way to form **oxyhaemoglobin molecules** Haemoglobin increases (by about ten times) the capacity of the blood to carry oxygen. Red cells also carry carbon dioxide as **bicarbonate ions** p... The uptake or loss of oxygen or carbon dioxide is determined by the relative concentration in side and outside the red cell; this is explained in Ch.4.

The rate of production of red cells can be increased during growth, when new tissues require the supply of oxygen or the removal of carbon dioxide. Additional red cells will be needed as a result of blood loss. Individuals living at altitude also make extra red cells, because the amount of oxygen available is relatively low. In any situation in which insufficient iron is available in the diet fewer red cells than normal will be made. This condition is called **anaemia** and occurs because iron is needed in the manufacture of haemoglobin.

(b) **White cells (leucocytes)**. White cells are generally less numerous (by about 700 times) and also larger (by about twice) than red cells. White cells are however, very thin and can, unlike red cells, enter or leave the circulation through small gaps in capillaries (see below). Each white cell has a nucleus. In general, white cells form part of the body's internal defences against disease, or immunity. There are several types of white cell, but two types occur in relatively large numbers; these represent about 94 per cent of all white cells:

(i) **Phagocytes** (70 per cent). Phagocytes (or **polymorphs, granulocytes** have a lobed nucleus (see Fig.12.1) and the cell shape is variable. Phagocytes surround, engulf and destroy bacteria; they are not effective against viruses. The engulfing process of phagocytes is very similar to that in *Amoeba* (Ch.4). The bacteria may have previously been clumped together by the action of lymphocytes.

(ii) **Lymphocytes** (24 per cent) Lymphocytes have a large, rounded nucleus and a fairly regular cell shape (Fig.12.1). Lymphocytes produce **antibodies** (or **antitoxins**) in the presence of 'foreign' or '*non-self*' proteins (or **antigens**) in the blood, such as **pathogens** (disease-causing microbes) Antibodies are effective against many viruses, as well as bacteria. Antibodies have different effects, for example they may clump pathogens together (**agglutination**) or split pathogens open Antibody production is a complex process (Fig.12.2) involving the recognition of an antigen and the synthesis of an appropriate antibody by lymphocytes This is called the **immune response** and may involve chemical 'memory'

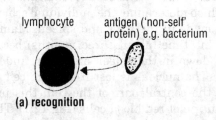
(a) recognition
lymphocyte   antigen ('non-self' protein) e.g. bacterium

(b) synthesis and release of antibody
Fig.12.2 The immune response system

the lymphocytes 'remember' which antibodies have proved effective against which antigens. The 'memory' is genetic and can be inherited by other lymphocytes This is one of several types of immunity, some of which are summarised in Fig.12.3.

Most trypes of specific immunity only provide protection against a particular type of disease. Immunity may not be effective for the remaining lifetime of an individual, especially in the case of passive immunity or active induced immunity. Lymphocytes may lose the 'memory' of how to make certain antibodies Another problem is when the immune system itself gets attacked and is prevented from producing a range of antibodies. This has occurred in the case of AIDS (Acquired Immune Deficiency Syndrome). AIDS is caused by a virus which invades certain lymphocyte cells which are then unable to produce antibodies for what would otherwise be relatively mild infections.

The immune system unfortunately operates against transplanted tissue including blood and various organs from a donor organism (the kidney is one example, see Ch.11. Tissue rejection is avoided by the use of **immuno-suppressant** drugs, though the patient is then susceptible to infections.

Type of immunity	Description and examples
Non-specific immunity	Involves mechanisms which respond generally to non-self proteins. Examples: the action of phagocytes (Ch. 12), also the action of chemicals such as **interferon** and **lysozyme** produced by the body.
Specific immunity	Involves mechanisms which respond specifically to non-self proteins.
Active immunity	Is based on antibody production and action within one organism; the **immune response** (see Fig. 12.2).
Active natural immunity	Involves the immune response resulting from a naturally occurring **infection** by a pathogen (disease-causing) organism. Examples: immunity to German measles (rubella), whooping cough.
Active induced (acquired) immunity	Involves the immune response resulting from an artificial introduction, e.g. by **vaccination (inoculation)**, of a modified type of antigen. Examplex: cowpox, polio vaccine; much 'weaker' than the actual pathogen.
Passive immunity	Is based on antibodies produced by *another* organism which then have their action within a particular individual. This provides immunity for a fairly limited period.
Passive natural immunity	Involves the transfer of antibodies from a mother to a foetus across the **placenta** (Ch. 6). Examples: measles and polio.
Passive induced (acquired) immunity	Involves the transfer of antibodies by **injection**, e.g. of **serum** (Ch. 12). Example: diptheria.

Fig.12.3. Summary of immunity

(c) **Thrombocytes** Thrombocytes (**platelets**) are cell fragments rather than complete cells; however they may contain nuclei, (see Fig.12.1 above). The function of thrombocytes is to restrict blood loss at wounds by taking part in the blood clotting (**coagulation**) mechanism, by producing substances which cause blood vessels to constrict and by releasing **thromboplastin** (**thrombokinase**).The release of thromboplastin sets in motion a complex series of reactions which results in the conversion of **fibrinogen** to **fibrin** at the site of the wound (Fig. 12.4). Fibrin binds together the edges of the wound and causes the formation of a clot which prevents further blood loss and pathogen entry.

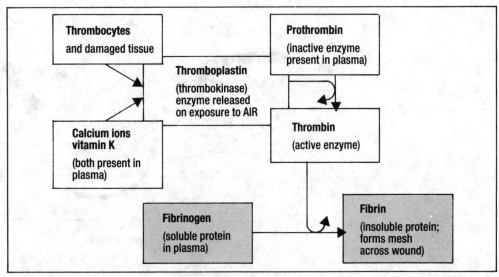

Fig.12.4 Summary of the blood clotting mechanism

Comparison	Artery	Vein	Capillary
Cross-section	Muscle / Fibrous coat / Lumen		Single cell
Internal (lumen) diameter	Fairly narrow; can expand (= pulse)	Fairly wide.	Very narrow; red blood cells squeeze through.
Wall structure	The wall is relatively thick and also elastic, to withstand pressure.	The wall is relatively thin; there are **valves** to keep blood moving in one direction (see Ch.12).	Wall is composed of a single cell layer; gaps between cells allow exchange of materials with surrounding tissues.
Blood direction	Blood flows away from the heart.	Blood flows towards the heart.	Blood flows from arteries to veins.
Blood pressure	High.	Low.	Very low.
Blood flow rate	Rapid, irregular.	Slow, regular.	Very slow.

Fig.12.5 Comparison of the main types of blood vessel

(b) BLOOD VESSELS

Blood vessels are tubes which form the circulatory system and which direct blood around the body in a particular direction. There are three main types of blood vessel; the **artery**, **capillary** and **vein**. These are compared in Fig.12.5.

The structure of each of type of blood vessel is an adaptation to its function. The function of **arteries** and **veins** is to carry blood to or from the capillaries respectively. The function of the **capillaries** is to allow materials in the blood to be exchanged with surrounding tissues; no living cell is more than about 0.5 mm from the nearest capillary. The relatively high pressure of blood in capillaries forces some of the plasma through the permeable capillary walls (Fig.12.6), which sometimes have special pores. The plasma which has leaked out is known as

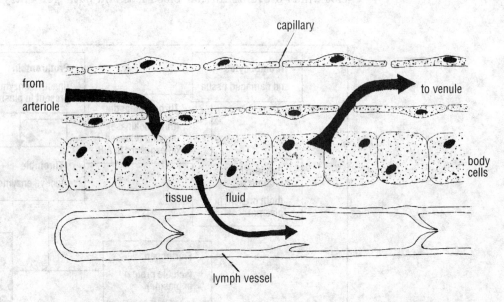

Fig12.6 Tissue fluid formation

tissue fluid; this contains nutrients and oxygen, as well as antibodies and hormones. White cells may also move from the capillary. Larger protein molecules and red blood cells remain within the capillary. Tissue fluid allows an exchange of substances between the blood and surrounding tissues; wastes are carried from tissues back into the circulation. Most of the tissue fluid re-enters the capillary (by osmosis, Ch.4); excess tissue fluid drains into the lymphatic system where it becomes known as **lymph**. Blood pressure drops in the capillaries during tissue fluid formation. The drop in pressure also occurs because the total space inside a group of capillaries is much greater than the space of the artery that supplies them.

 Arteries divide repeatedly into smaller **arterioles** which eventually lead to the capillaries. These re-join to form **venules** and then **veins**. This sequence is

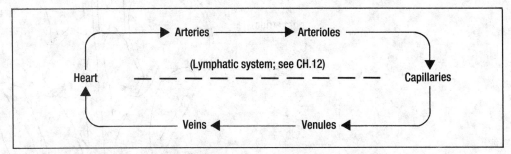

Fig12.7 Summary of the sequence of blood vesels in the circulation

shown in Fig.12.7.

 The double (**dual**) circulation, typical of mammals, is shown in a simplified form in Fig.12.8., and is composed of the **pulmonary circulation** serving the lungs and the **systemic circulation** serving the rest of the body. Most **arteries**, except pulmonary arteries, contain **oxygenated blood** and most veins, except pulmonary veins, contain deoxygenated blood. The fundamental distinction between arteries and veins is that arteries carry blood *away from the heart*, and veins carry blood *towards the heart*.

> **exam candidates are not always clear about the difference in function of arteries and veins**

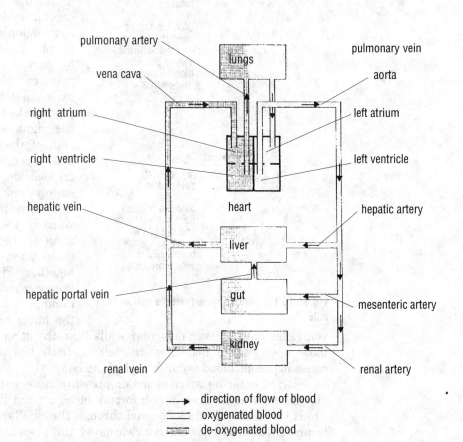

Fig.12.8 Simplified diagram of the double circulation in mammals

(c) THE HEART

The **heart** is a muscular pump which keeps blood moving through the circulatory system. The heart in mammals such as humans consists of two fused pumps, which pump either **oxygenated blood** (*left side*) or **deoxygenated blood** (*right side*). Each side of the heart is further divided into two compartments (Fig.12.9) the **atrium** (**auricles**) and **ventricles**, which allows blood to be pumped in two stages.

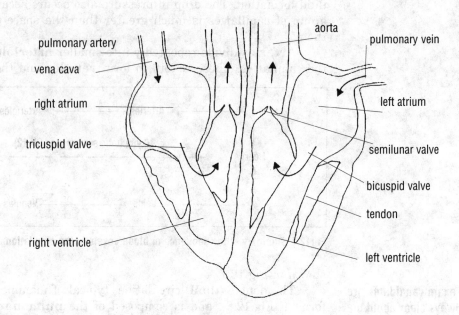

Fig.12.9 Vertical section through a mammalian heart

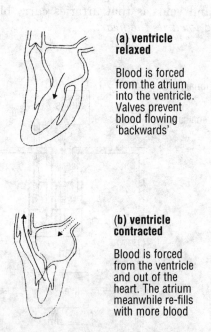

(a) ventricle relaxed

Blood is forced from the atrium into the ventricle. Valves prevent blood flowing 'backwards'

(b) ventricle contracted

Blood is forced from the ventricle and out of the heart. The atrium meanwhile re-fills with more blood

Fig.12.10 The cardiac cycle (verticle section; left side

The heart beats in a continuous series of rhythmic muscular contractions; each repeating sequence is called a *cardiac cycle*. The frequency of cardiac cycles and the power of each contraction depends on the body's need for blood and is regulated by the brain, by nerves and hormones (Ch.13). The heart can also regulate its own activity by a small patch of tissue, called the **pacemaker**, embedded in the wall of the right atrium. The average adult rate of the cardiac cycle is about 72 beats per minute. This can be increased dramatically, for instance to supply and remove more materials to exercising muscle. Blood from all the veins in the body drains into the two atria of the heart at the beginning of each heart beat. Both atria contract together (Fig.12.10), forcing blood into the ventricles. These then contract, pumping blood into arteries leading to the lungs or the rest of the body. The ventricles have thicker muscular walls than the atria because they need to push blood over greater distances; the left ventricle has particularly thick walls because it pumps blood around most of the body.

Blood entering arteries under pressure causes them to expand against the elastic walls which then recoil, forcing blood around the circulation. Blood pressure is lost when blood has passed through the capillaries. The low-pressure blood is prevented from flowing backwards by the presence of valves in the walls of veins. This is very similar to the arrangement in the **lymph vessels** (see below). The movement of blood towards the heart is assisted by pressure from surrounding **skeletal muscle** when it contracts; this may be particularly important when gravity is acting on the blood returning to the heart.

The heart muscle itself requires a constant supply of blood. This is provided by the **coronary artery**. If the flow of blood through the coronary artery is reduced the heart muscle cannot function properly; this may result in a coronary thrombosis (heart attack), caused by a blood clot which blocks the flow of blood to the heart muscle. The problem begins with artherosclerosis, the build up of fatty deposits on the lining of the arteries. The chances of heart disease can be significantly reduced by avoiding too much fat (especially animal fat) in the diet. Other possible causes of heart disease include obesity (Ch.15), smoking, excess alcohol, severe stress and insufficient exercise.

(d) LYMPHATIC SYSTEM

The **lymphatic system** consists of a network of fine tubes called **lymph vessels**. The lymphatic system has two quite distinct functions; transport of lymph and defence against pathogens:

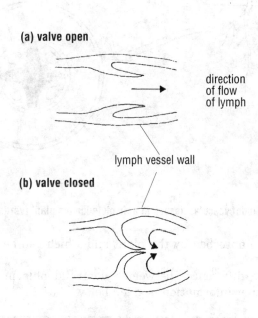

(a) valve open

direction of flow of lymph

lymph vessel wall

(b) valve closed

Fig.12.11 The action of valves in a lymph vessel

(i) Transport of lymph

Lymph fluid is formed from tissue fluid (see Fig.12.6). The lymph is a fairly clear liquid, similar in composition to plasma; however, the lymph from the lacteals, within the villi of the small intestine (Ch.15), is 'milky' because it contains many small lipid droplets. Lymph vessels from throughout the body eventually join together into two large **lymphatic ducts**. These drain the lymph back into the blood system near the **vena cava** (see Fig.12.8). The lymphatic system does not have its own pump; instead, it relies on the pressure of surrounding skeletal muscles. Valves in the lymph vessel walls, functioning like those in veins, keeps lymph moving towards the heart (Fig.12.11)

(ii) Defence against pathogens

At intervals along the lymph vessels are swellings called **lymph nodes**. These are regions where stationary **phagocytes** (see Fig.12.1) extract and engulf any bacteria from the lymph

flowing past them. **Lymphocytes**, which produce antibodies against pathogens, are formed in the lymph nodes and then enter the blood circulation.

PLANT TRANSPORT SYSTEMS

Specialised transport tissues occur in the larger, more advanced **plants**. Many of these plants belong to the **Spermatophyte** group and they live on land; these include 'flowering plants' (**Angiosperms**, Ch.5). Transport tissues are particularly important for large plants living on land because tissues in any region of the plant are unlikely to have access to all the materials that they need from the environment. Also, large, land-living plants may need the additional support (Ch.14) which transport tissue provides. Mass flow of substances occurs over relatively large distances through specialised vascular tissue (conducting tissue).There are two main types of vascular tissue; **xylem** and **phloem**. In young, herbaceous (non-woody) plants these are situated together in **vascular bundles**, or veins. Vascular bundles are often arranged in a characteristic pattern; this is more regular (Fig.12.12) in dicotyledonous plants than in with monocotyledonous plants. The distribution of vascular tissues can be studied by using

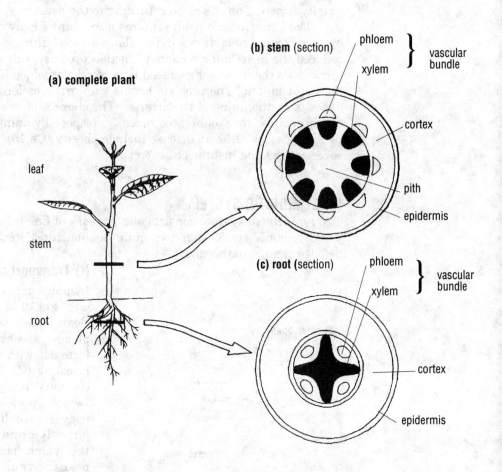

Fig12.12 Distributionof vascular tissues in a dicotyledonous plant (vertical and transverse sections)

dyes which are absorbed by the plant and which can be revealed in a transvers (cross) section.

The main differences between xylem and phloem are summarised in Fig 12.13 and further information is given below.

Comparison	Xylem	Phloem
Description	Consists of non-living woody *(lignified)* cells (**elements**) joined together to form continuous tubes (**vessels**).	Consists of living cells (**seive elements**).
Substances carried	**Sap:** water and mineral salts.	Solution of organic molecules (Ch. 4) made by the plant, including hormones (Ch. 13) and the products of photosynthesis (Ch. 15).
Direction of transport	*Unidirectional*; mostly upward, from root to stem and leaves.	*Bidirectional*; movement of substances occurs downward and upward.
Mechanisms of transport	Mostly passive processes including osmosis, capillary action and evaporation.	Mostly active processes, involving the use of energy; the mechanisms are not fully understood.

Fig.12.13 Comparison between xylem and phloem

Plants absorb substances from the environment through exchange surfaces these are typically *branching* and provide a large surface for materials to enter o leave the plant tissues. The movement of water and dissolved minerals throug **xylem tissue** results to a large extent from **evaporation**, or **transpiration**, o water from the aerial parts of the plant, especially the leaves. The movement c organic molecules through the **phloem** is a more active process and can b referred to as **translocation**, although this word is sometimes used to describe all mass flow transport of substances within the plant.

(a) MOVEMENT OF WATER THROUGH A FLOWERING PLANT

Transpiration is the process by which water is evaporated from the leaves and replaced by water drawn from the roots, where it enters the plant, this upward flow of water is called the transpiration stream. Transpiration is important because it causes the upward flow of water and mineral salts which are needed for metabolism. Water is also needed to provide **turgor** for support in non-rigid tissues (Ch.14). However, it should be noted that only a small proportion (less than 1 per cent) of water absorbed by the plant is retained. The complete process of transpiration occurs in three distinct phases:

   (a) absorption by roots
   (b) movement up the plant
   (c) transpiration from the leaves

(i) Absorption by roots

Roots are important for anchoring the plant in the soil as well as for absorbing substances from the soil. In land-living plants, water is mostly absorbed through the younger, more permeable parts of the root. The surface area for absorption is considerably increased (by about ten times) by **root hairs** (Fig. 12.14). These extensions of epidermis cells occur about 4–10 mm behind the root tip and make close contact with the water films on the surface of surrounding soil particles.

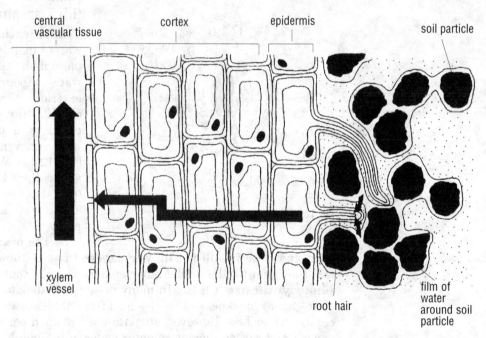

Fig.12.14 Absorption of water and minerals in the root (arrows show direction of water movement)

Minerals are also needed for the plant to make many organic molecules, using the carbohydrates formed by **photosynthesis** (Ch.15). The type and relative amount of minerals present depends on various factors (Ch.16). The way in which water and mineral ions enter the plant can be considered separately:

(a) The absorption of water is by **osmosis**, which is a *passive* process. The cells of the root contain relatively concentrated solutions compared with water in the soil. Water therefore enters the outer cells, including the root hairs. The solution inside these cells then becomes more dilute than that of cells situated nearer the central part of the root. The result is a **concentration gradient** across the root, causing water to be drawn towards the central vascular bundle. Those cells nearest the centre are constantly losing water to the vascular tissue (see below) and this also maintains the concentration gradient. It is worth noting that, whilst the absorption of water is a passive process, it relies on living cells and the accumulation of solutes (Appendix 1) by active processes.

(b) The absorption of mineral salts can occur by **diffusion** if the mineral involved is present in relatively small amounts within the plant. **Active transport** allows the plant to accumulate particular minerals above the concentration found in the surrounding soil; this requires energy derived from **respiration**. The relatively high concentration of minerals within the root tissues results in root pressure, which probably helps push water up the plant.

(ii) Movement up the plant

Water enters the open-ended **xylem vessels** in the central part of the root. Xylem tissue forms an almost continuous system of thin woody (lignified) tubes connecting the roots with the stem and leaves. The mechanisms for water movement must be sufficient to overcome gravity, for example in raising water over 30m in tall trees. There are three possible ways in which water is made to move up the plant:

(a) **root pressure**, which arises from active transport of minerals into the root cells (see above). This probably accounts for less than 5 per cent of the force necessary to move water through the plant.

(b) **capillary action**, which results from water molecules 'climbing' the narrow xylem vessels; *adhesion* occurs between the water and the lining of the xylem tubes. This 'pulls' water up the plant, although only for fairly short distances.

(c) **transpiration pull**, which is caused by the evaporation of water from the leaves; *cohesion* occurs between water molecules, which may form a continuous column throughout the plant. Transpiration is likely to account for most of the water movement up the plant.

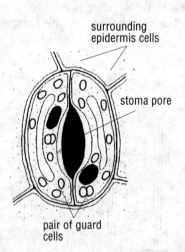

surrounding
epidermis cells

stoma pore

pair of guard
cells

Fig.12.15 A stoma

(iii) Transpiration from the leaves

Transpiration is the evaporation of water mainly from the surfaces of mesophyll cells in the leaves. The water vapour produced escapes to the exterior through specialised pores called **stomata**. Each stoma is bordered by a pair of guard cells which have unevenly thickened cell walls (Fig.12.15) When these cells take in water they become firmer, or **turgid** (p..); this results in a distortion of their shape and an opening of the stoma pore.

The mechanism by which stomata open and close is still not fully understood but is known to be based on the the fact that guard cells, unlike other epidermis cells, contain **chloroplasts** and can **photosynthesise** (Ch.15). In many plants the stomata open during daylight and close during darkness. The closure of stomata allows the plant to prevent excessive water loss. However, stomata need to open periodically to allow the gases oxygen and carbon dioxide to enter or leave the plant as part of the processes of respiration and photosynthesis.

Water evaporates mainly from the surfaces of the loosely packed **mesophyll cells** (see Ch.15) and then is lost mainly through the stomata. Most leaves have a **waxy cuticle** which limits water loss directly from the epidermis. Water is replaced by a constant supply from the vascular bundles within the leaves; these are continuous with the vascular system and, ultimately, the soil. If the rate of transpiration exceeds the rate of uptake of water in a herbaceous (non-woody) plant, cells may lose their **turgor**. This results in wilting and **loss of support** (Ch.14); the plant may not recover from damage caused to the tissues by wilting. Some plants live in areas of the world where water is not readily available or where the rate of transpiration can be very rapid. Such plants may be adapted, for instance to retain water or reduce transpiration.

The **rate of transpiration** depends on internal and external factors:

(a) **Internal factors** affecting the rate of transpiration include leaf area, thickness of the cuticle layer, the number and distribution of the stomata.

(b) **External (environmental) factors** affecting the rate of transpiration include temperature, humidity, wind and the availability of water from the soil (see Ch.16). An increased transpiration rate would occur at relatively high temperatures, low humidity and in fairly windy conditions.

(b) EXPERIMENT TO INVESTIGATE THE RATE OF TRANSPIRATION

The **rate of transpiration** is measured in terms of the water lost in a period of time by an intact plant or by a shoot (stem and leaves), or just leaves. This can be determined by two main methods:

(i) loss in mass (mass potometer)

The mass of the plant tissue is measured periodically, for instance on a top pan balance. Any loss in mass is assumed to be mainly due to loss of water by transpiration. Any container which supplies water to a shoot or whole plant should be covered to prevent direct evaporation, which would cause a loss in mass. Water in a container can be covered by oil; a pot of soil can be enclosed in a plastic bag.

(ii) rate of water uptake (volume potometer)

The potometer (Fig.12.16) is really designed for measuring water uptake rather than transpiration. However, since most (over 99 per cent) of water absorbed by the plant is lost by transpiration, the volume potometer is often used to measure transpiration rate. For convenience, a shoot is used; the roots of the plant are removed under water to prevent air bubbles entering the vascular tissue and causing a blockage. The potometer incorporates a fine capillary tube which measures water uptake; a small bubble or the water–air boundary moves

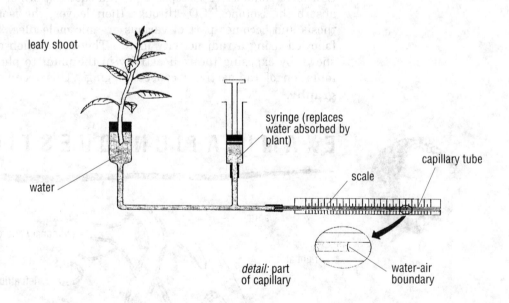

Fig.12.16 The potometer

towards the plant. The rate of (transpiration) uptake can be measured under different external conditions. Care must be taken to avoid leaks and air bubbles in the system and also variations in conditions not actually being tested.

(c) MOVEMENT OF ORGANIC SUBSTANCES THROUGH A FLOWERING PLANT

Organic substances are all derived from the products of **photosynthesis**. For instance, plants combine the carbohydrates made during photosynthesis with nitrates absorbed from the soil (Ch.16) to form **amino acids** . **Carbohydrates**, - especially **sucrose** and **amino acids** are transported in the plant by **phloem tissue**. These organic materials are carried, often from the leaves, to regions in the plant where they are needed; for instance, to the root and shoot tips, for **growth** (Ch.7). Organic molecules may be accumulated in food stores including **perennating organs**. Sugars may be important in the production of nectar in flowers. Various foods may be needed in seed and fruit formation.

The **rate** and **direction** of substances in the **phloem** can be measured in various ways, including ringing experiments and radioactive isotopes:

(i) Ringing experiments

Phloem is situated in the outer part of stems, just underneath the epidermis or bark. If a ring of epidermis and

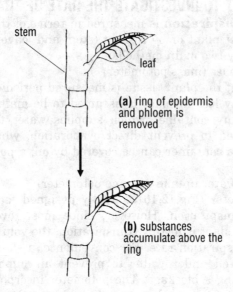

stem

leaf

(a) ring of epidermis and phloem is removed

(b) substances accumulate above the ring

Fig.12.17 Ringing experiment

phloem is stripped away, substances which would normally be moving down the stem accumulate (Fig.12.17). Water movement in the xylem is not directly affected by ringing.

(ii) Radioactive isotopes

Low-level radioactive isotopes emit radioactivity which can be measured. Plants absorb the isotope $^{14}CO_2$ through their leaves; the isotope is used in photosynthesis and becomes part of various organic molecules. The route of these can be followed using a radioactivity meter. The distribution of these molecules can be shown by exposing the radioactivity in the plant to photographic film; any accumulation of radioactivity causes 'fogging'. This technique is called **autoradiography**.

EXAMINATION QUESTIONS

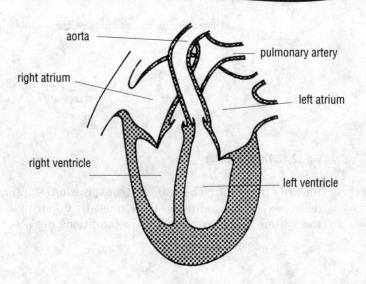

aorta

pulmonary artery

right atrium

left atrium

right ventricle

left ventricle

Fig.12.18

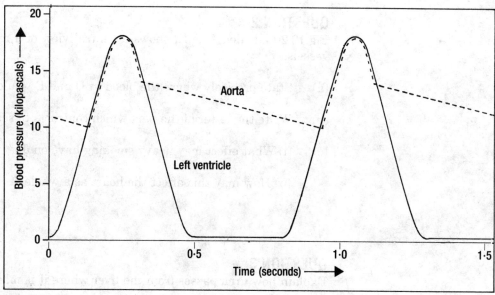

Fig.12.19

QUESTION 1

(a) Fig.12.18 shows a section through a mammal's heart and some of its major blood vessels.
(i) What route does blood take from the lungs to the aorta?

3 marks

(ii) Explain how the valve between the left ventricle and the aorta works.

4 marks

(b) Fig.12.19 shows blood pressure in the left ventricle and the aorta throughout two cycles of the heart. Using the graph:
(i) How long is a heart cycle (the time interval between the start of one heartbeat and the start of the next)?

1 mark

(ii) For how long during each heart cycle is the valve between the aorta and the left ventricle closed? How did you work out your answer?

2 marks

(iii) What is the difference between the maximum and minimum pressure in the aorta?

2 marks

(c) Explain how blood pressure is increased in the left ventricle.

3 marks
Total 15 marks (SEB)

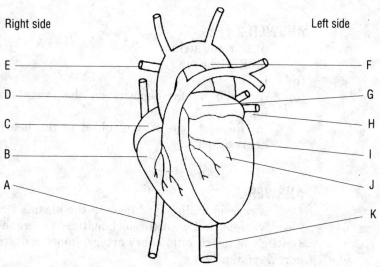

Fig.12.20

QUESTION 2

Fig.12.20 labelled A to K, shows a ventral view of a mammalian heart and blood vessels.

(a) State precisely where the blood in D and E would go to next. (2 lines)

2 marks

(b) Write the letter of the part which contracts to send blood to the brain.

(1 line) **1 mark**

(c) (i) What effect may heavy smoking have on J?

(1 line) **1 mark**

(ii) How may this affect the heart as a whole?

(1 line) **1 mark**
Total 5 marks (LEAG)

QUESTION 3

Explain how urea passes from the liver where it is made to the bladder.

Total 14 marks (LEAG)

Further practice questions on the topics discussed in this chapter are provided in Chapter 18 (questions 8 and 9).

OUTLINE ANSWERS

ANSWER 1

(a) (i) Pulmonary vein, left atrium, left ventricle, aorta

(ii) The valve is opened by the flow of blood when the left ventricle contracts; the blood pressure in the aorta causes blood to start returning to the heart when the left ventricle relaxes; returning blood fills the valve flaps and closes the valve, so preventing back flow.

(b) (i) 0.8 seconds

(ii) 0.6 seconds; this is the time during each cycle when the pressure in the aorta is greater than that in the left ventricle. This pressure difference is maintained by the closed valve.

(iii) 7.77 kilopascals

(c) Contraction of the muscles in the wall reduces the internal volume of the left ventricle; closure of the bicuspid valve prevents blood returning to the left atrium.

ANSWER 2

(a) (i) D: right atrium

(ii) E: right lung

(b) I

(c) (i) Build up fat deposits on the inner surface, causing a more narrow lumen.

(ii) Restricts the flow of blood to the heart muscle; this may result in a heart attack.

ANSWER 3

Urea is carried in dissolved form in the plasma through the following sequence of blood vessels and structures: hepatic vein, vena cava, right atrium and right ventricle of heart, pulmonary artery, lungs, left atrium and left ventricle of heart, aorta, renal artery.

In the kidney, urea, which is a relatively small molecule, is filtered from the glomerulus into the Bowman's capsule. Urea passes down the nephron (kidney

tubule), through the first coiled tubule, loop of Henle, second coiled tubule, and collecting duct; urea is not reabsorbed because it is a waste product. Urea by now forms a solution called urine. Urine is passed, by peristalsis, from the kidney down the ureter to the bladder.

COURSE WORK – A STEP FURTHER

1 ▷ EXPERIMENT TO INVESTIGATE VARIATIONS IN PULSE RATE

Some experimental work is suggested below:

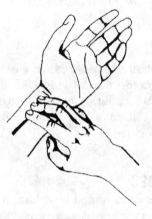

Fig.12.21 Taking a pulse

The pulse is caused by waves of high pressure blood which results in arteries rhythmically swelling. Each pulse corresponds to a heart beat so measuring the pulse rate is a means of determining heart rate. Pulse can be measured at any point on the body where an artery is situated close to the skin surface, for instance at the wrist. The pulse (of the radial artery) can be found on the wrist below the joint of the thumb. If three fingers are held next to each other along the position of the artery the pulse can normally be found (Fig.12.21).

Measure the pulse for one minute with the subject resting. The subject should then undergo strenuous exercise, for instance by running on the spot, for two minutes. The pulse rate should then be determined again, immediately after the period of exercise, and for every minute until the pulse rate returns to its resting value. The pulse rate should be noted each time.

The variations in pulse rate can be shown as a line graph (Appendix 2), with pulse rate (vertical axis) plotted against time. The recovery time is the period taken to reach the resting pulse rate after exercise. The recovery time can be determined for different periods of exercise, or with different individuals.

2 ▷ EXPERIMENT TO INVESTIGATE THE DISTRIBUTION OF VASCULAR TISSUE IN PLANTS

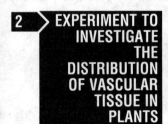

Complete plants or shoots can be made to draw up coloured dyes, for instance eosin dye. Suitable plant material includes Busy Lizzie (*Impatiens*) or celery (*Apium*). The plant is allowed to draw up the dye for about 30 minutes. Different parts of the plant can be sectioned using a sharp knife or razor; the distribution of the xylem vascular tissue is shown by the dye on the exposed surfaces. A hand lens may be needed to see enough detail. A comparison can be made of stem, root and leaf tissue. In each case, the distribution of tissue can be shown on a large, labelled diagram.

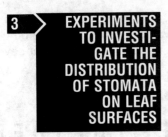

3   **EXPERIMENTS TO INVESTI-GATE THE DISTRIBUTION OF STOMATA ON LEAF SURFACES**

There are various ways of showing, directly or indirectly, the relative number of stomata on leaf surfaces:

(a) EPIDERMAL PEELING

The epidermis peels away from underlying tissues quite readily in some leaves, for instance those of tulip (*Tulipa*). If a small nick is made in a leaf, the epidermis can be carefully peeled away, using fine forceps. The epidermal peel can then be mounted on a microscope slide and examined. The characteristic green colour in guard cells should be clearly visible.

(b) LEAF IMPRINT

A clear nail varnish can be coated on the lower leaf surface of a suitable plant, e.g. privet (*Ligustrum ovalifolium*). The varnish will dry in a few minutes; it can then be carefully peeled off and examined under a microscope. An impression of the epidermis cells, including the guard cells, should be clearly seen.

(c) COBALT CHLORIDE

In the presence of water, cobalt chloride paper will change colour from blue to pink. The paper can be mounted onto a living leaf and held in position by clear adhesive tape, to prevent atmospheric water affecting the experiment. If held tightly against the leaf, the position of the stomata will be revealed by small pink areas on the paper after a short time.

(d) PREVENTING WATER LOSS

Water loss from plants can be determined by a loss in mass. If one surface (upper or lower) of a detached leaf is covered by a thin layer of Vaseline, water cannot be lost from that surface. If the petiole (leaf stalk) is also coated with Vaseline, it is assumed that any loss in mass over a period of time represents water loss from the exposed leaf surface. The experiment can be repeated by coating the other leaf surface of a similar-sized leaf and conducting the experiment over the same period of time. The relative water loss from each surface indicates the density of stomata on each side of the leaf.

This experiment can involve weighing the leaf at regular intervals in each case. Line graphs (Appendix 2) should be drawn using the same axes to allow an easier comparison; *mass* (vertical axis) is plotted against *time*. The distribution of stomata in different species, for example, broad and narrow leaved can be compared using this method. Design and, if possible, conduct a series of simple but effective experiments to investigate the effects of different conditions on the rate of transpiration of a potted plant. Care should be taken to keep all factors constant except the one actually being investigated. The investigation should include controls (Appendix 3) and any results should be suitably presented (Appendix 2). A concise account of the investigation, including conclusions and comments, should be given.

STUDENT'S ANSWER – EXAMINER'S COMMENTS

This potometer can be used to demonstrate the rate of water movement through a leafy shoot.

- leafy shoot
- Syringe
- Shoot inserted through a hole in the plunger
- Water
- Rubber tube
- Capillary tube

RULER (mm)

The following results were obtained by measuring under different conditions, the time taken for the water in the capillary tube to move through a distance of 100 mm.

Conditions	Time taken for the water to move 100 mm (minutes)
Cool, moving air, in daylight	2
Cool, still air, in daylight	6
Warm, moving air, in daylight	1
Warm, still air, in daylight	3
Warm, still air, at night	60

(a) Name the process by which the plant loses the water through its leaves.

transpiration

(1 mark)

(b) From the table, state *three* conditions which affect the rate of movement of water through the plant.

(i) *air movement* (ii) *air temperature* (iii) *light*

(3 marks)

(c) In cool, moving air, in daylight, state the rate of water movement in mm per minute.

2 mm per minute

(1 mark)

(d) If the leafy shoot was covered by a transparent polythene bag, in the light, state *two* ways in which the air in the bag would be affected.

(i) *it would stop moving*

(ii) *carbon dioxide would increase*

(2 marks)

(e) Suggest what would happen to the rate of water movement if the lower surface of the leaves were smeared with grease.

it would decrease because the stomata get covered.

WJEC

(1 mark)
(Total 8 marks)

Examiner's comments (margin):

"Good; correct answers."

"Incorrect; this is the *time* taken for water to move 100mm. Correct answer is $\frac{100}{2}$ = 50 mm per min."

"Correct; also, the oxygen and water content would increase."

"Incorrect; carbon dioxide would *decrease* in the light."

"Correct, although a *reason* is not asked for."

SENSITIVITY

GETTING STARTED

Sensitivity (**irritability**) in organisms means detecting and responding appropriately to changes in the internal and external environment. The response of an organism is *adaptive* because the organism becomes adapted to a new situation in such a way as to improve its chances of survival.

A change in an organism's internal or external environment which may result in a response is called a **stimulus**. A stimulus is detected by a **receptor** which relays the information to a coordinator. An appropriate impulse may then be sent to an **effector** which then produces a response. This arrangement (shown in Fig.13.1) occurs, in various forms, in all organisms.

Sensitivity is a **characteristic of life** and occurs in all organisms. Sensitivity in more advanced plants tends to involve growth responses under the control of hormones. Animals generally have a more complex arrangement for achieving sensitivity. Many animals are coordinated by a nervous system as well as by hormones.

ANIMAL SENSITIVITY
THE NERVOUS SYSTEM
THE ENDOCRINE SYSTEM
PLANT SENSITIVITY
PHOTOTROPISM
GEOTROPISM

ESSENTIAL PRINCIPLES

Sensitivity or **irritability** allows an organism to detect and respond appropriately to stimuli, that is, to any changes in its internal or external environment. Sensitivity is a characteristic of life and all organisms are capable of some awareness of those changes in their environment which may affect their chances of survival. Larger, more complex organisms perform a relatively wide range of activities and require more elaborate mechanisms for sensitivity. The basic mechanism of sensitivity is shown in Fig.13.1.

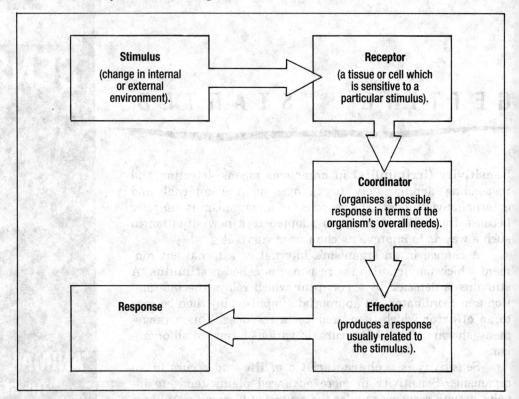

Fig.13.1 The mechanism of sensitivity

A **stimulus** represents information which the receptor converts into a form that that can be relayed within the organism, for instance by the release of a chemical message that is a hormone, or an electrochemical message, a nerve impulse. Coordination is especially important in *multicellular* (Ch.4), complex organisms, within which different tissues can communicate with each other.

Simpler animals respond to relatively few stimuli and the range of possible responses is fairly limited. **More complex animals** tend to have specialised tissues for sensitivity, for instance including sense organs and a relatively developed coordinating system, for example involving a brain.

The two main systems which have a direct role in sensitivity in higher animals are the **nervous system** and the **endocrine (hormone) system**. These operate together but perform their overall function of sensitivity in different ways. The nervous and endocrine systems are compared in Fig.13.2.

(a) THE NERVOUS SYSTEM
The **nervous system** in higher animals consists of two main parts: the **central nervous system** (CNS), which is composed of the brain and spinal cord, and the **peripheral nervous system** (PNS), which includes all other nerves.

Comparison	Nervous system	Endocrine system
Message	Nerve impulse	Hormones
Route	Nervous system	Blood system
Transmission rate	Rapid	Slow, depends on circulation
Origin of 'message'	Receptor	Endocrine gland
Destination of 'message'	Effector	Target organ or organs
Speed and duration of effect	Immediate, brief	Delayed, prolonged

Fig.13.2 Comparison of nervous and endocrine systems

The structural unit of the nervous system is the nerve cell, or **neurone (neuron)** (see Fig.13.3). Neurones are adapted for the transmission of nerve impulses, for instance by being elongated. Groups of neurones are arranged together in bundles, known as nerves.

There are three main types of neurones:

(i) **Sensory** (*afferent*) **neurones** carry a nerve impulse from a receptor (sensory cells) to the spinal cord and/or brain.

(ii) **Intermediate** (*relay, associate*) **neurones** connect sensory and motor neurones within the central nervous system.

(iii) **Motor** (*efferent*)) **neurones** (Fig.13.4) carry a nerve impulse from the brain and/or spinal cord to an effector, which may be a muscle or a gland, which produces a response.

Adjacent neurones are not connected directly to each other but are separated by very small gaps called **synapses**. Nerve impulses arriving at one side of the synapse cause the secretion of a *chemical transmitter* substance which diffuses across the gap. Synapses ensure that nerve impulses travel in one direction only.

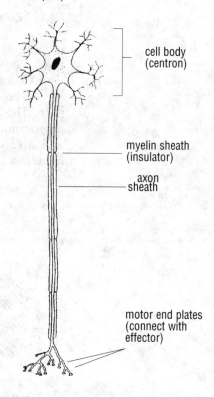

dendrites (connect with receptor)

cell body (centron)

myelin sheath (insulator)

axon sheath

motor end plates (connect with effector)

Fig.13.3 Structure of a motor neurone

Nerve pathways

A functional unit of the nervous system is the **reflex arc** (Fig.13.4). The reflex arc is the direct pathway from a **receptor** (sensory cells) to an **effector**, via the central nervous system. Connections between sensory and motor neurones may occur directly or, more usually, through an intermediate neurone. These connections occur in the grey matter of the inner part of the spinal cord and the outer part of the brain. White matter in the central nervous system carries nerve impulses to and from the grey matter. White matter is situated in the outer regions of the spinal cord and in the inner regions of the brain. There are two main types of reflex pathway; the simple reflex and the conditioned reflex.

Simple reflex

A **simple reflex** involves a pathway consisting of the reflex arc only. The pathway may involve the brain (cranial reflex) or the spinal cord (spinal reflex). A simple reflex results in a very rapid, involuntary (automatic) response to a stimulus. Simple reflexes are instinctive and often have a survival value, for instance in allowing the animal to escape danger. Examples of reflexes include eye blink-

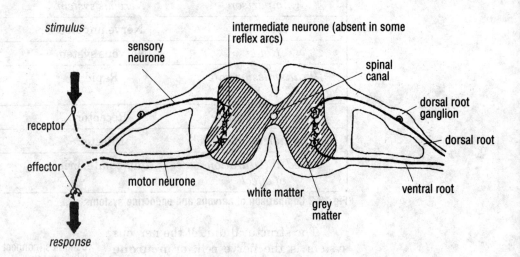

Fig.13.4 Reflex arc

ing and eye focusing (see below), withdrawing a limb from a source of pain, and the knee-jerk reflex (Fig.13.5).

Conditioned reflex

A **conditioned reflex** is a simple reflex which has been adapted by experience. The original (primary) stimulus is gradually replaced by another (secondary) stimulus which produces the same effect. This process is called **learning** and involves the brain which can store experience as **memory**. Intermediate neurones in the brain and spinal cord are important because they allow connec-

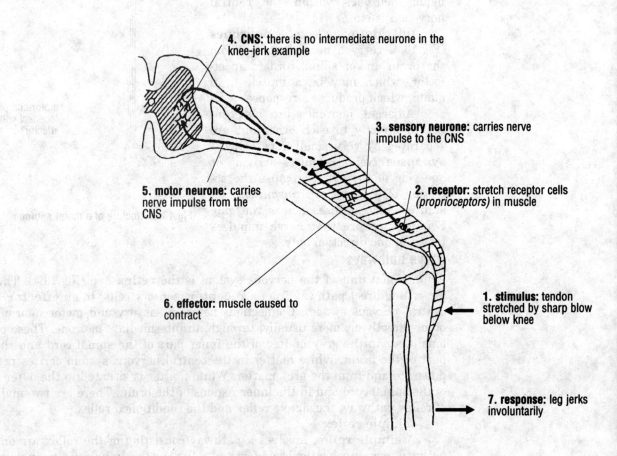

Fig.13.5 Simple reflex: the knee jerk

tions to be made with many other neurones; this increases the range of activities that an animal can perform.

(b) THE BRAIN

The **brain** is a much enlarged part of the central nervous system in vertebrates which coordinates many of the activities of the body. In particular, the brain organises information from the sense organs (see below), many of which may be closely situated in the head region. Some of the main regions of the brain are shown in Fig.13.6.

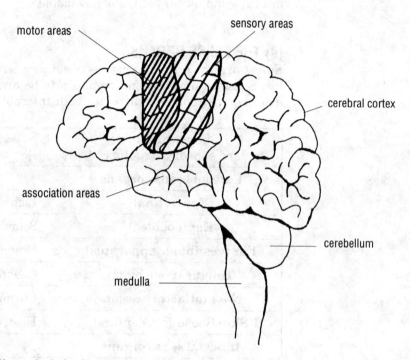

Fig.13.6 Human brain (surface view)

The cerebral cortex, cerebellum and medulla have quite distinct functions:

(i) The cerebral cortex

The **cerebral cortex** coordinates many complex, voluntary processes; this region is particularly well developed in higher vertebrates, especially humans. The cerebral cortex is the folded outer 3 mm of the cerebral hemispheres (cerebrum) and consists of grey matter within which many connections are made between adjacent neurones. The cerebral cortex contains three main regions: sensory areas, which receive input from the sense organs (see below); motor areas, which send out instructions to effectors such as muscles and glands; association areas, which interpret and analyse information. The association areas contain brain tissue which determines memory and learning.

(ii) The cerebellum

The **cerebellum** coordinates learned processes which become may become involuntary, such as speech, balance and movement. The cerebellum is important in organising the activity of voluntary (skeletal) muscle, for instance in limb movements such as walking.

(iii) The medulla

The **medulla** coordinates involuntary, automatic processes such as breathing, heart rate and swallowing.

(c) DRUGS AND THE NERVOUS SYSTEM

A **drug** is a chemical which is introduced into the body and which affects the activity of the body. The three main groups of drugs which affect the nervous system are sedatives, analgesics (painkillers or pain relievers) and stimulants.

(i) **Sedatives** (**depressants**) induce a state of relaxation and diminished anxiety. Examples include barbiturates and alcohol.

(ii) **Analgesics** (**pain-killers**) affects the part of the nervous system which produce a sense of pain. Examples include aspirin and paracetamol.

(iii) **Stimulants** reduce feelings of fatigue and induce a sense of alertness. Examples are caffeine and amphetamines.

Many drugs are used in medicine and some, such as alcohol, are socially acceptable to many people for recreational purposes. Other such drugs are illegal in many societies. Drugs which affect the nervous system may result in increased tolerance, so that the drug needs to be taken in greater quantities to produce a certain effect. Such drugs can be habit-forming, or addictive, and may cause withdrawal symptoms if not readily available.

(d) THE SENSE ORGANS

Sense organs consist of groups of sensory cells which detect a particular stimulus. Sense organs allow an organism to be aware of changes in the internal and external environment; there are both internal and external sense organs. Many

Sense organ and sensory structure	Stimulus
External sense organs	
Eye (retina)	Light
Ear (cochlea)	Sound vibration
Ear (vestibular apparatus)	Gravity and changes in body position
Tongue (taste buds)	Chemicals, taste
Nose (olfactory tissue)	Chemicals, smell
Skin (various receptors)	Heat, cold, touch pressure, pain
Internal sense organs	
Muscle stretch receptors	Muscle movement
Hypothalamus (part of brain)	Blood glucose levels, blood concentration

Fig.13.7 Summary of the main sense organs

sense organs are arranged on the outer surface of the body, particularly in the head region. Sense organs may be complex structures which have other, non--

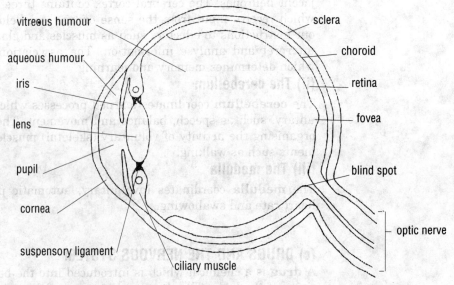

Fig.13.8 Human eye (vertical section)

sensory, cells associated with them. Examples of sense organs and the stimuli to which they respond are given in Fig.13.7.

The **eye** and the **skin** are two good examples of sense organs in humans.

Structure	Function
Eyelid	protects eye by *blinking* (a **reflex action**, Ch. 13). Blinking washes eye surface with **tears** (they contain a mild antiseptic), prevents the contact of harmful substances with the eye surface, and protects the retina against bright light.
Conjunctiva	Protects part of the cornea.
Cornea	*Refracts* (bends) light entering the eye.
Aqueous humour	Supplies nutrients to the lens and cornea.
Iris	Controls the amount of light entering the eye by adjusting the size of the **pupil**.
Pupil	Aperture which allows light into the eye.
Lens	Allows fine focusing by changing *shape*.
Suspensory ligament	Attaches lens to **ciliary muscle**.
Ciliary muscle	Changes the shape of the lens by altering the tension on the **suspensory ligaments**.
Vitreous humour	Maintains the shape of the eye.
Retina	Contains light-sensitive **rod** and **cone cells** which convert light energy into a nerve impulse.
Fovea	Very sensitive region where most light is focused.
Optic nerve	Carries nerve impulses to the brain, where they are interpreted.
Choroid	Supplies retina with nutrients; also, contains pigments which reflect the light (about 80%) not absorbed by the retina.
Sclera (sclerotic coat)	Protect and maintain the shape of the eye.

Fig.13.9 Summary of functions of main eye components

> **❝questions on the structure and functioning of the eye are fairly common – make sure you understand this section❞**

(i) The eye

Each **eye** is a spherical structure composed of layers and open on one side to admit light. The structure of the eye is shown in Fig.13.8. The function of various components of the eye are summarised in Fig.13.9.

The eye can respond to variations in light conditions, for instance in the distance, direction and brightness of an object. The eye is able respond to different light conditions by the activities of muscles inside and outside the eye. The contraction and relaxation of these muscles also provides information which the brain can use to estimate the distance of an object. This is important in animals, for instance in allowing them to judge distances from prey or predators. The overlapping fields of vision from the two eyes is called **binocular vision** and also allows distances to be estimated. Predator animals, for example the owl (*Strix*) and fox (*Vulpes*), have good binocular vision for hunting. Prey animals, for example the rabbit (*Oryctolagus*) and wood mouse (*Apodemus*), have good **monocular vision** (side vision) to increase awareness of possible predators.

Focusing (accommodation)

Most (about 70 per cent) of the bending (**refraction**) of light occurs as light passes through the cornea. The angle at which light enters the lens is different for distant and near objects. However, the eye can allow for this by movements of the lens; this is called focusing or accommodation and is a reflex action.

The lens is important in focusing and this is achieved by changes in its shape. This is brought about by a ring of ciliary muscles. The lens is pulled into a relatively thin shape (made *less convex*) by a tension of the suspensory ligaments; this tension is caused by the outward pressure of the vitreous humour and also by the contraction of radial ciliary muscles. The lens thickens (is made *more convex*) if this tension is reduced by a contraction of the circular ciliary muscles.

Focusing depends on the flexibility of the lens and ciliary muscle and this flexibility may be lost to some extent in humans as they become older. The shape of the eye is very important in focusing because it determines the distance be-

Eye defect	Cause	Correction
Long sight (hypermetropia)	Short eyeball: near objects cannot be focused	Converging lens
Short sight (myopia)	Long eyeball: distant objects cannot be focused	Diverging lens

Fig.13.10 Human eye defects

tween the lens and the retina, where the image is formed. The eye may become slightly distorted in shape as it grows. There are two main eye defects which involve difficulties in focusing; they are long sight *(hypermetropia)* and short sight *(myopia)*, shown in Fig.13.10.

Adjustments to changing light intensity

The amount of light entering the eye can be controlled by changes in the size of the pupil aperture, for instance a narrowing of the pupil in bright light; this protects the retina, which might otherwise be temporarily 'bleached'. Open-

(a) In bright light

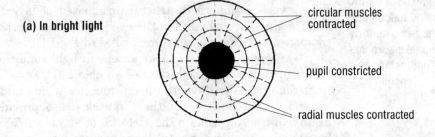

circular muscles contracted

pupil constricted

radial muscles contracted

(b) In dim light

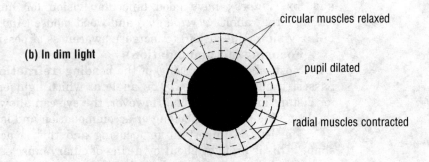

circular muscles relaxed

pupil dilated

radial muscles contracted

Fig.13.11 Variations in pupil size

ing and closure of the pupil is a reflex action and is achieved by contractions of muscles within the iris. There are two types of **antagonistic muscles** (Ch.14) in the iris (Fig.13.11); they are the **radial muscles**, which widen the pupil, and the **circular muscles**, which narrow the pupil.

The retina

The retina is the part of the eye which is sensitive to light. An inverted image is formed on the retina because of the bending (**refraction**) of light by the front part of the eye. The function of the retina is to convert the information carried by light into nerve impulses, which are transmitted to the brain. The sensation of sight is formed in the brain, which interprets visual information in terms of experience. The retina consists of two main types of light-sensitive (**photo-sensitive**) cells; the **rods** and the **cones** (Fig.13.12). These contain pigments which

Comparison	Rods	Cones
Structure		
Distribution	120 million cells spread throughout retina; much less in fovea.	Six million cells concentrated in the fovea.
Sensitivity: light intensity	Sensitive to **low** light intensities.	Sensitive to **bright** light intensities only.
Sensitivity: colour	Not sensitive to different colours (sensitive to **monochromatic** light only); used mainly in dim light.	Sensitive to colour. Different types of cones respond to the **primary colours red, green and blue**; the relative amounts of each type of colour allows humans to detect about 200 different colours.
Nerve connections	Rods share **common nerve connections**. This increases sensitivity to dim light, and decreases **acuity** ('visual accuracy').	Cones have **individual nerve connections**. This decreases sensitivity to dim light and increases acuity.

Fig.13.12 Comparison of rods and cones

are 'bleached' in light, generating a nerve impulse. The pigment in rod cells is derived from vitamin A (Ch.15) and is important for vision in dim light.

(ii) The skin

The **skin** is the outer covering of vertebrates and is therefore important in detecting stimuli in the external environment. The skin is sensitive to a range of stimuli and can be considered as a sense organ, although it has many other functions. The skin is the largest organ of the body and consists of an outer **epidermis** layer and an inner **dermis** layer. The outer part of the epidermis in many animals including humans is largely composed of dead cells which have an important function in protection. The **dermis** is a living layer, containing various types of cells, including sensory cells (Fig.13.13).

Sensory cells occupy different relative positions in the skin, some being nearer the outer surface than others. The density of certain sensory cells varies throughout the body surface; for instance, touch receptors in humans are particularly numerous in the finger tips, where the ability to discriminate closely placed

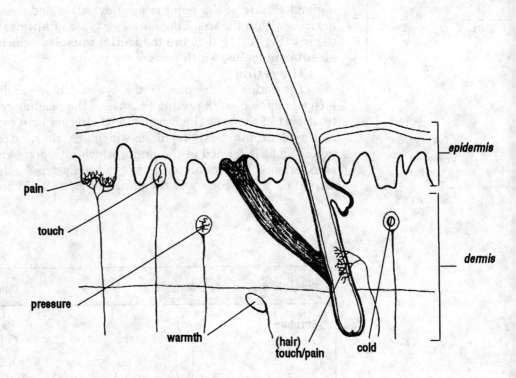

pain

touch

pressure

warmth

(hair)
touch/pain

cold

epidermis

dermis

Fig.13.13 Receptors in the human skin (vertical section)

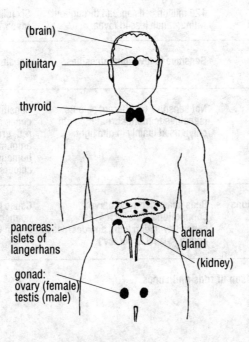

(brain)

pituitary

thyroid

pancreas:
islets of
langerhans

adrenal
gland

(kidney)

gonad:
ovary (female)
testis (male)

Fig.13.14 Position of the main endocrine glands in humans (the relative position of some other organs is also shown)

stimuli may be important. Different types of sensory cell in the skin may be stimulated together, increasing the capacity of the body to interpret the environment.

(e) THE ENDOCRINE SYSTEM

The **endocrine system** coordinates the activities of the animal by 'chemical messengers', or **hormones**. Hormones are proteins and are secreted by **endocrine glands** (sometimes called 'ductless glands'). These glands produce and store particular hormones, which are released directly into the bloodstream when required. The *activities of endocrine glands* are controlled by other hormones, called **trophic hormones**, by the **nervous system** and by **negative feedback** (see below). The overall function of the endocrine system, like that of the nervous system, is to coordinate the body's activities; a comparison of the two systems is given in Fig.13.2.

The position of the main endocrine glands is shown in Fig.13.14; some of these glands have other functions which may not necessarily be related to that of the endocrine system. Some of the functions of the main endocrine glands are summarised in Fig.13.15. Hormones have their effects on target tissues which are particularly sensitive to the hormone. Whilst hormones may have a long term effect, such as in growth and development, they do not permanently remain in the blood; they are broken down in the liver. The presence of a hormone in the body may cause the endocrine gland which produced it to slow down the rate of secretion; this is an example of negative feedback.

Gland	Hormone	Effects
Pituitary	Trophic hormones	Cause other endocrine glands, e.g. thyroid, adrenal and gonads, to release their hormones.
	ADH vasopressin	Increases water reabsorption in **nephrons of the kidney** (Ch. 11).
	Oxytocin	Causes contraction of the **uterus** during birth (Ch. 6).
	Prolactin	Stimulates milk production from **breasts** (Ch. 6).
Thyroid	Thyroxine	Increases the general rate of **metabolism** (chemical reactions in the body) and stimulates **growth**.
Adrenal gland	Adrenalin	Sometimes called the **fight, flight or fright hormones**; prepares the body for potentially difficult or dangerous situations, for instance by increasing **heart rate** (Ch. 12), efficiency of **muscles** (Ch. 14) and **breathing rate** (Ch. 10). Adrenalin also raises the *blood glucose* level (see below).
Pancreas (islets of Langerhans)	Insulin	Causes the conversion of glucose to glycogen (Ch. 11).
	Glucagon	Causes the conversion of glycogen to glucose (Ch. 11).
Gonads: ovary	Oestrogen	Promotes the development of female secondary sexual characteristics (Ch. 6).
	Progesterone	Maintains the uterus during pregnancy (Ch. 6).
Testis	Testosterone	Promotes the development of male secondary sexual characteristics (Ch. 6).

Fig.13.15 Summary of some of the main hormones in humans

(f) BEHAVIOUR

The observable outcome of all the coordinating processes of an organism is called **behaviour**. The range of behaviour that is expressed by an organism depends on the range of stimuli that it can respond to. The type of behaviour may depend on the direction of the stimulus, and the response may be by part of or by the whole organism. The outcome of all behaviour is often to increase an organism's chances of survival. Patterns of behaviour are characteristic of different species but also vary between individuals within a species. Plants show much less obvious behaviour than animals; plant behaviour consists of tropic and nastic responses. Animals generally show relatively elaborate behaviour. Behaviour is especially complex in social animals, including insects such as ants and bees, and also in more advanced animals such as birds and mammals.

There are two main types of behaviour, **instinctive (innate)** and **learned (conditioned)**. Instinctive behaviour is genetically determined and therefore is inherited. This increases an organism's chances of survival without the need to learn behaviour during the early, critical period of development. Examples of instinctive behaviour include the **simple reflex** , **courtship**, **mating** and **territorial behaviour** and **tactic responses**. Tactic response (**taxes**) involve a movement of the whole organism in response to a directional stimulus. For example, woodlice (*Oniscus*) may move towards regions of high moisture or low light intensity within a choice chamber (Fig.13.16).

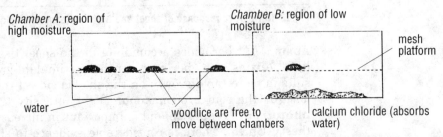

Fig.13.16 Taxic behaviour in a choice chamber

PLANT SENSITIVITY

❝biology students often struggle with the mechanism of tropic responses; you may need to re-read this section❞

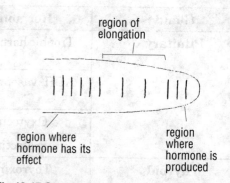

Fig.13.17 Growth at shoot or root tip

Plants adapt to changes in their immediate environment mainly by growth responses. These are coordinated within the plant by **hormones** (plant growth substances), for example the **auxins**, including IAA (*indol acetic acid*). Hormones either stimulate or inhibit various processes within the plant; their main function is to affect germination (p..) and growth.

Hormones produce **tropic responses**, or **tropisms**, which are related to the direction of the stimulus. If a shoot or root tip is exposed to a unidirectional stimulus, it will tend to grow away from or towards the stimulus. A **positive tropic response** involves growth *towards* a stimulus, whilst a **negative tropic response** involves growth *away from* the stimulus. Hormones are made in the shoot and root tips in the **meristem** area. Hormones are thought to move through tissues by **diffusion** and they may also be transported through **phloem**. Hormones have their actual effect in the region of **elongation**, behind the shoot and root tips, where cells expand and increase in length. In germinating seedlings, elongation occurs about 2–10 mm behind the plumule (young shoot) and radicle (young root). This can be shown by the separation of regularly spaced marks on the surface of a shoot or root tip of a germinating seedling (Fig.13.17).

The mechanism for the action of plant hormones such as auxin is not fully understood; it is thought that a unidirectional stimulus causes an unequal distribution of auxin. This causes uneven (*differential*) growth, resulting in a curvature. The sensitivity of shoot and root tissues to increasing concentrations of the hormone auxin is often quite different (Fig.13.18).

Tropic responses are classified according to the stimulus which causes them. The main tropisms are **phototropism** and **geotropism**, for which the stimuli are light and gravity respectively. These tropisms are compared in Fig.13.19.

(a) PHOTOTROPISM

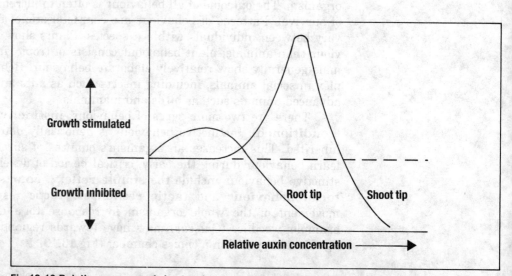

Fig.13.18 Relative response of shoot and root tips to increasing auxin concentration

Auxin (IAA) hormones accumulate in the shoot tissues away from unidirectional light. Auxins at higher concentrations stimulate growth in shoot tissue. This results in more rapid growth on the shaded side of the shoot. The shoot then grows *towards* the source of maximum light intensity (Fig.13.20). This is a **positive phototropic response** and is important in increasing the efficiency of photosynthesis (Ch.15). There is considerable evidence to show the action of auxin (IAA) hormones in phototropism. Some of the techniques used in experiments are brief-

Comparison	Phototropism	Geotropism
Stimulus	Light	Gravity
Response in shoot tip*	Positive	Negative
Response in root tip*	Negative in some species; neutral in others.	Positive
Importance of positive response	Shoot and leaves are held towards light, for photosynthesis (Ch. 15).	Roots grown down into soil for anchorage (Ch. 14) and the absorption of water and minerals (Ch. 12).

* positive = growth *toward* stimulus
negative = growth *away from* stimulus

Fig.13.19 Comparison of phototropism and geotropism

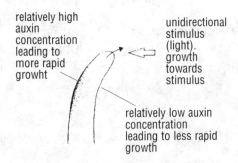

Fig.13.20 Positive phototropism in a shoot tip

ly summarised in Fig.13.21). Many of these experiments have been conducted with coleoptiles (a protective sheath around the shoot) of cereal plants such as oat (*Avena*).

(b) GEOTROPISM

Auxins accumulate in the root tissues towards the unidirectional stimulus of gravity. Auxins at higher concentrations inhibit growth in root tissue. This results in more rapid growth on the upper surface of the root. The root then grows downwards, towards the direction of the stimulus (Fig.13.22). This **positive geotropic response** causes roots to grow towards a source of water and minerals. Lateral (side) roots do not show a fully positive geotropism.

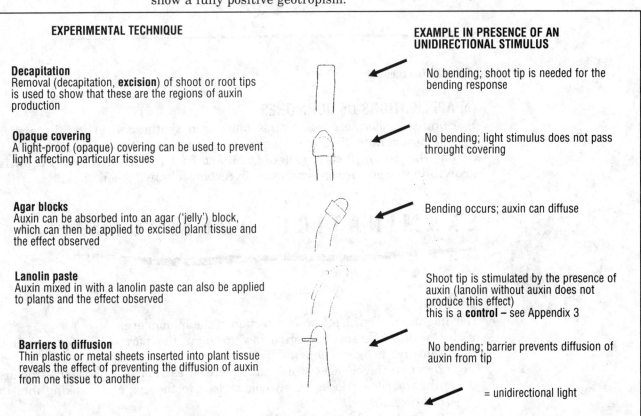

Fig.13.21 Techniques used in phototropism experiments

Shoots showing **negative geotropism** grow upwards, away from the direction of the stimulus (see Fig.13.19). This is because shoot tissue is stimulated by higher concentrations of auxin (see Fig.13.18). This response is important in plumules (young shoots) of germinating seedlings because they need to grow upwards, from below soil level, towards light, so that photosynthesis (Ch.15) can take place; positive phototropism (see above) cannot take place until a young shoot has emerged from the soil into light.

Experiments to show the mechanism of geotropism involve similar techniques to those described for phototropism (see Fig.13.21). The gravity stimulus cannot be removed unless the experiment is conducted in space; instead, gravity is 'cancelled out' by rotating seedlings on a clinostat (Fig.13.23); the speed is normally about 1 revolution per 15 mins.

relatively low auxin concentration leading to more rapid growth

relatively high auxin concentration leading to less rapid growth

unidirectional stimulus (gravity)

Fig.13.22 Positive geotropism in a root tip

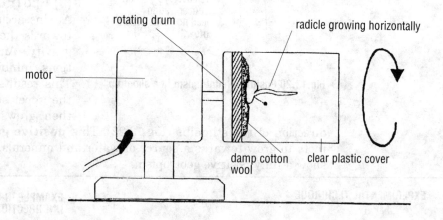

rotating drum

radicle growing horizontally

motor

damp cotton wool

clear plastic cover

Fig.13.23 The clinostat

(c) APPLICATIONS OF HORMONES

Hormones or hormone substitutes have been synthesised artificially and are used in horticulture. Two important applications are in **promoting growth**, including the rooting of cuttings (see Ch.6) and fruit formation, and in **inhibiting growth** in weeds; hormones are used in certain selective weedkillers.

EXAMINATION QUESTIONS

QUESTION 1

The diagram in Fig.13.24 shows a section of the human eye.
(a)   On the diagram, use an arrow to show the part of the eye which is sensitive to light. **1 mark**
(b)   Describe the changes which take place in each of the following structures when a person looks at an object close to the eye after looking into the distance.
      (i) The lens. (2 lines) **1 mark**
      (ii) The ligaments. (2 lines) **1 mark**

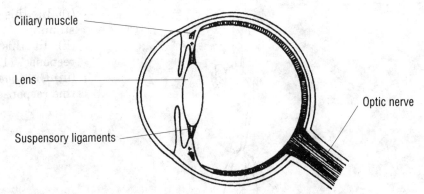

Fig.13.24

       (iii) The ciliary muscles. (2 lines) **1 mark**

(c)   Explain why damage to the optic nerves can cause blindness. (2 lines)

                                               1 mark

                                 Total 5 marks (LEAG)

QUESTION 2

In an experiment, three plant shoots were treated as shown in Fig.13.25.

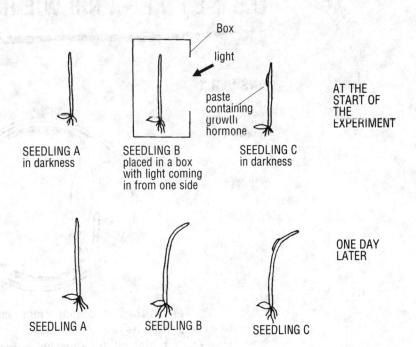

Fig.13.24

(a)   What name is given to the response made by seedling B? (1 line) **1 mark**

(b)   How does the hormone in the paste affect the growth of seedling C? (2 lines)

                                               1 mark

(c)   Which side of seedling B has the more hormone? (1 line) **1 mark**

                                 Total 3 marks (LEAG)

QUESTION 3

Fig.13.26 shows a young plant growing towards the light, which came from one side only.

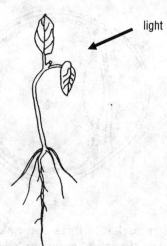

(i)) In this example what was the stimulus? (1 line) **1 mark**
(ii) In this example what was the response? (1 line) **1 mark**
(iii) Give *one* advantage to the plant of this response. (1 line) **1 mark**
         Total 3 marks (LEAG)

Fig.13.26

Further practice questions on the topics discussed in this chapter are provided in Chapter 18 (questions 10 and 11).

OUTLINE ANSWERS

ANSWER 1
(a)

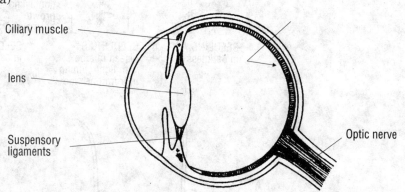

(b)   (i) The lens is thickened; made more convex.
       (ii) The ligaments become slack.
       (iii) The circular ciliary muscles are contracted. (radial ciliary muscles are relaxed.)
(c)   The optic nerve is necessary to carry impulses from the retina to the brain where it is interpreted as sight.

ANSWER 2
(a) Positive phototropism.
(b) The hormone stimulates more rapid growth on the side where it is applied.
(c) There is more hormone on the side away from the light.

ANSWER 3
(a)   (i) Light
       (ii) Growth curvature was caused, resulting from an uneven distribution of hormone.
(b)   The plant can absorb more light for photosynthesis.

COURSEWORK – A STEP FURTHER

Three investigations on animal and plant sensitivity are suggested. In each case a concise account should be written of method, and conclusion (see Appendix 3), and the results should be presented in a suitable way (Appendix 2). For each investigation, the method should be critically discussed and possible improvements suggested.

1 ▷ INVESTIGATION 1: REACTION TIME

A 1 metre ruler is held by the experimenter vertically above and in front of the subject, who should be ready to catch the ruler between finger and thumb when it is released by the experimenter. The experimenter releases the ruler without warning. The subject should detect a movement in the ruler either (i) by sight or (ii) by touch. The distance (in cm) the ruler falls before it is caught can be used as an indication of 'reaction time'. If the subject's hand was at 100 cm at the start of the experiment, a high distance value indicates a fast reaction time.

The experiment can be repeated to investigate any of the following conditions:
– the difference in reaction time for an individual subject when using sight and touch
– the difference in reaction time for an individual subjects over several attempts
– the difference in reaction time for different individuals using the same experimental conditions.

2 ▷ INVESTIGATION 2: SKIN SENSITIVITY

Two pins mounted 1 cm apart in a cork or bung are needed for this experiment. The sensitivity of the different parts of the skin can be tested by touching the skin with one and then two pins, keeping the eyes closed. The ability of the skin to discriminate two pins can be assessed. The experiment can be developed by varying (a) the distance between the pins from 0.5 cm to 2 cm and, (b) the pressure with which the pins are applied.

3 ▷ INVESTIGATION 3: PHOTOTROPISM IN PLANTS

Plan and, if possible, conduct an experiment to show phototropism in seedlings such as cress or oats (*Avena*). The experiment should involve simple materials such as black paper and kitchen foil.

STUDENT'S ANSWER – EXAMINER'S COMMENTS

The diagram represents a section through the human eye.

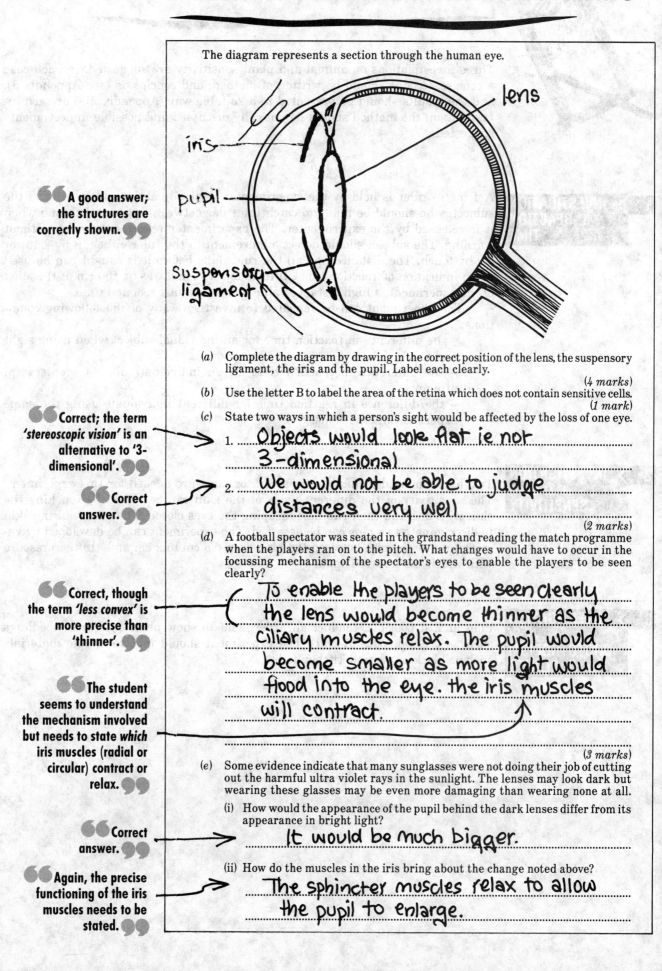

lens

iris

pupil

Suspensory ligament

66 A good answer; the structures are correctly shown. **99**

(a) Complete the diagram by drawing in the correct position of the lens, the suspensory ligament, the iris and the pupil. Label each clearly.

(4 marks)

(b) Use the letter B to label the area of the retina which does not contain sensitive cells.

(1 mark)

(c) State two ways in which a person's sight would be affected by the loss of one eye.

66 Correct; the term *'stereoscopic vision'* is an alternative to '3-dimensional'. **99**

1. Objects would look flat ie not 3-dimensional

66 Correct answer. **99**

2. We would not be able to judge distances very well

(2 marks)

(d) A football spectator was seated in the grandstand reading the match programme when the players ran on to the pitch. What changes would have to occur in the focussing mechanism of the spectator's eyes to enable the players to be seen clearly?

66 Correct, though the term *'less convex'* is more precise than 'thinner'. **99**

66 The student seems to understand the mechanism involved but needs to state *which* iris muscles (radial or circular) contract or relax. **99**

To enable the players to be seen clearly the lens would become thinner as the ciliary muscles relax. The pupil would become smaller as more light would flood into the eye. the iris muscles will contract.

(3 marks)

(e) Some evidence indicate that many sunglasses were not doing their job of cutting out the harmful ultra violet rays in the sunlight. The lenses may look dark but wearing these glasses may be even more damaging than wearing none at all.

(i) How would the appearance of the pupil behind the dark lenses differ from its appearance in bright light?

66 Correct answer. **99**

It would be much bigger.

(ii) How do the muscles in the iris bring about the change noted above?

66 Again, the precise functioning of the iris muscles needs to be stated. **99**

The sphincter muscles relax to allow the pupil to enlarge.

(iii) Why could wearing thes defective glasses be more damaging than not wearing any at all?

> By wearing the glasses the pupil would be letting in damaging rays that if the glasses were not worn would not be let in as the eye would be able to sense that the light was so intense.
>
> By not wearing them the eye senses the intensive light and so the pupil becomes smaller allowing less light to enter.

(2 marks)

NISEC

(Total 15 marks)

❝This is a good answer, but it needs to be more concise; the student should use the space and mark allocation as a guide for answer length.❞

CHAPTER 14

MOVEMENT AND SUPPORT

GETTING STARTED

Movement (**locomotion**) is a **characteristic of life**; most organisms can move all or part of themselves. Movement is important as a means of **dispersal** and **colonisation**. Movement allows organisms to move towards potentially beneficial stimuli, such as food and warmth, and away from harmful stimuli such as predators and cold. In this way movement allows individual organisms to seek *optimum* (ideal) conditions.

Support allows organisms to maintain their **shape**; this may be important for movement. The shape of organisms is also important in determining the exchange of substances with the environment, for instance heat or gases. Terrestrial (land) organisms require additional support because they are surrounded by low-density air; organisms are subjected to the force of gravity, and support systems allow them to resist this. Support systems are often also **protective**, whilst permitting essential movement.

LOCOMOTION
PLANT MOVEMENT
AND SUPPORT
ANIMAL MOVEMENT
AND SUPPORT

ESSENTIAL PRINCIPLES

Movement and support allow organisms to determine their position in the environment, and therefore exploit the resources available to them more effectively. **Locomotion** is the ability of the whole organism to move from one place to another. In many cases organisms move by specialised systems of locomotion and using their own energy. Organisms may also use 'external' forces for movement, such as air and water currents; some examples of this are given below. Though movement is a **characteristic of life**, plants generally are not capable of locomotion. The relative amount of movement shown by plants and animals is a major difference between them, and is mainly due to their very different modes of nutrition (Ch.15).

Small, relatively simple organisms in the Protista group are capable of movement in fluid towards or away from a **directional stimulus**; this is called **taxis** and the movement is brought about either by a flowing of the cell cytoplasm, as in *Amoeba*, or by the use of hair-like **cilia** and **flagella**, which create small water currents. Cilia in particular are also important within larger organisms, where they are used to move fluids along tubes. In humans. for instance, cilia line the **trachea** and **oviduct** (Ch.6). **Sperm** cells, including those of humans use flagella to achieve movement.

Movement in most large animals tends to involve **muscles** (see below). A significant proportion of an animal's body mass is muscle; about 45 per cent of a mammal's mass is muscle. This muscle is important not just in locomotion but also in various control processes, such as with **valves** and **sphincters** in the **gut** (Ch.15), **bladder** and **arterioles** . Muscle is also important in the functioning of internal **transport systems** (Ch.12) in higher animals; for instance in the **heart** and **arteries** .

(a) MOVEMENT

Most plants are **non-motile** and **sessile**; they remain located in a particular place. Plants can obtain all their nutrients from their immediate environment and are adapted for the absorption of substances by having a *branched* body (Ch.7). Plants can respond to stimuli by **growth responses**, or **tropisms** (Ch.13), at their shoot and root tips. Tropisms allow plants to obtain more resources such as light and water from the environment. Individual plants are likely in this way to exploit their immediate environment effectively. Each plant becomes established in its environment from a 'parent' plant by reproduction. This often involves the production of **spores** and **seeds** which become detached and **dispersed.** In sexual reproduction in higher plants, **pollen** is carried during **cross pollination** (Ch.6) from one plant to another, for instance by **wind** or **insects**.

(b) SUPPORT

Plants have a fairly rigid structure. This limits movement but allows plants to maintain a shape and position to exchange substances with the environment. Plants use mostly **carbohydrates** for support. Most plant cells have **cellulose walls** which give cells mechanical strength and also allows them to swell and become **turgid** (firm) (Ch.4). The turgid tissue exerts an outward force which is resisted by a tension from the **epidermis** layer. This turgidity is very important in small, 'non-woody' herbaceous plants; these plants tend to complete their life cycle within one year; they are **annuals**.

Additional support is provided by the distribution of **vascular bundles** (Ch.12) in the roots and shoots (Fig.14.1). The vascular bundle contains xylem tissue which, consisting of **lignified** cells, provides the plant with support, as well as being part of the transport system. Vascular tissue is arranged towards

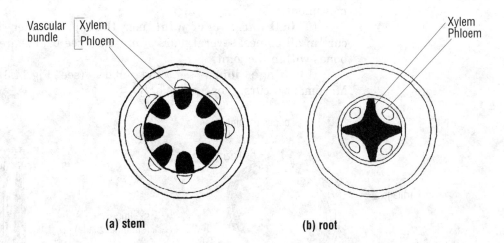

Fig.14.1 Distribution of vascular tissue in a typical dicotyledonous plant (transverse sections)

the outer part of the stem in the dicotyledenous ('broad-leaved') plants (Ch.5), and provides stability against *bending* forces. Plants need to be able to support their shoot system, so that, for instance, leaves may absorb light for **photosynthesis** (Ch.15), flowers take part in *pollination* and fruits and seeds be dispersed (Ch.6). *Vascular tissue is arranged centrally in roots; this resists the pulling* forces that roots are subjected to. Vascular tissue (veins) in leaves resists *tearing* forces and help maintain the flat shape of these organs; this is very important for photosynthesis.

Larger, 'woody' plants, mainly shrubs and trees, have a life cycle extending over more than one year; they are biennials and perennials. Such plants may reach a relatively large size and need to be supported by additional deposits of wood within their tissues; this is called **secondary thickening**, and results in a large proportion of the stem and root consisting of woody tissue. Some of this non-living tissue also conducts water and minerals through the plant.

(a) MOVEMENT

Animals are generally **motile**; they can move all or part of their body from one place to another. This **locomotion** is important as a means of *locating food* which may not be available from the animal's immediate environment. Some aquatic animals are **sessile**; they obtain their nutrients as suspended matter from the surrounding water. However, such animals show a relatively large amount of movement of their body parts. Many animals may need to move to **avoid predators** (Ch.17), or to seek other organisms for **reproduction**. hard **skeletons** (see below) incorporate various type of **joints** to allow movement. In vertebrates (Ch.5), joints occur where bones meet. There are three main types of joint:

(i) Immovable joints

where bones are **fused** or held together by a protein called collagen, for example the bones of the **cranium** (part of the skull).

(ii) Partially movable joints

where bones **slide** or **glide** over each other; the **articulating** ('rubbing') **surfaces** of the bones are covered with a layer of cartilage. Examples of partially movable joints include the vertebrae (see below) and the wrist and ankle.

(iii) Movable, or synovial joints

where some movement of bones can occur. Synovial joints are **lubricated** by **synovial fluid**, produced by a synovial membrane which surrounds the joint (Fig.14.2). Friction between bones is also reduced by flexible **cartilage** which covers the articulating surface of each bone within the joint. The cartilage acts as a **shock absorber**, for instance in land animals during running and jumping.

There are two main types of synovial joint, each allowing a different amount of movement:

(a) **ball and socket joint**, e.g., the hip, shoulder (Fig.14.2). Movement occurs in all planes; several pairs of muscles (see below) are attached to each of the bones within the joint.

(b) **hinge joint**, e.g. the elbow (see Fig.14.3), knee, finger joints. Movement occurs in one plane only.

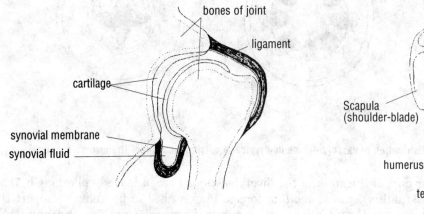

Fig.14.2 Typical synovial joint (shoulder)

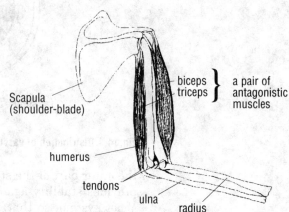

Fig.14.3 Typical arrangement of antagonistic muscles (elbow region)

Movement at a joint

Movement is caused by the contraction of muscles attached to bones (**skeletal, voluntary muscles**) which are coordinated by **nerves**. Muscles are therefore examples of **effectors** (Ch.13) because they produce an effect, normally as a direct consequence of a stimulus. Each skeletal muscle is usually attached to two bones, one being anchored to the muscle (at the **point of origin**), the other being free to move (at the **point of insertion**). Muscles are attached to bone by **tendons**; these are *inelastic* (non-stretching) and transmit the power of muscles directly to the bone. Bones are attached to other bones by **ligaments** (see Fig.14.2); these are *elastic* (stretching) and allow bones to move, whilst holding the joint together.

Muscles are only capable of *contracting* (pulling) or *relaxing*, but not pushing. For this reason most muscles operate in **antagonistic pairs**; the contraction of one antagonistic muscle often corresponds with the relaxation of the other. **Non-skeletal** (*smooth, involuntary*) **muscles** occur in antagonistic pairs, too; for instance, the *circular* and *longitudinal* (or *radial*) muscles of the gut (Ch.15) and iris. Skeletal muscles which straighten a limb are called **extensors**. Those which bend a limb are called **flexors**. A good example of an antagonistic pair of muscles is the **biceps** and **triceps** in the human arm (Fig.14.3). The biceps muscle is a flexor, whilst the triceps is an extensor.

(b) SUPPORT

Animals require a system of support to allow movement and, like plants, to maintain their body shape. Animals tend to use **protein** (Ch.4) for support. Most animals have some sort of skeleton for support. This is especially important in animals living on land because they need to be able to resist the force of gravity; air has a low density compared to that of water (about 800 times lower). There are three main types of skeleton:

(i) Hydrostatic skeleton

This occurs in smaller, soft-bodied animals, for example the earthworm (*Lumbricus*). The hydrostatic skeleton consists of a muscular body wall enclosing a fluid-filled **body cavity**, which the muscles contract against.

(ii) Exoskeleton

This occurs in the arthropod group of animals and is an outer hardened covering. This covering is composed of various substances; in insects, for instance, it is composed mainly of the protein **chitin**. The exoskeleton provides protection for the soft inner tissues. The exoskeleton is arranged as a system of jointed tubes, with muscles attached inwardly. The exoskeleton is **moulted** at intervals (Ch.7) to allow growth. Arthropods living in dry conditions on land secrete an additional layer of wax, preventing them from losing water; this has been a very important adaptation (Ch.9) of insects to their life on land. Exoskeletons would not provide adequate support for larger, heavier organisms on land, however.

(iii) Endoskeleton

This occurs in all vertebrate and in some invertebrate animals. The endoskeleton consists of living tissues such as cartilage and bone. These can increase in size throughout the animal's period of growth, without the need for moulting. In humans, bones represent only about 15 per cent of body mass; bone is about 25 per cent lighter than a solid structure of the same volume, yet has a very similar mechanical strength. Bone contains cavities which actually give added strength, as well as lightness; this is especially important in flying vertebrates such as birds. Skeletons composed mostly of bone have allowed animals to exploit land more effectively and to be larger and move faster than many other organisms. On land, limbs are used to lift animals away from the ground, and this increases the efficiency of their locomotion.

Bone tissue consists essentially of 'grit' (inorganic deposits of **calcium** and **phosphate**) and 'glue' (a **protein**). The tissue is supplied with new materials by a network of blood vessels; for example, calcium from the diet (Ch.15) can provide for growth or repair. Bone also functions as a **calcium store**, for example supplying calcium during pregnancy (Ch.6). Apart from support and movement, bone is important in **protecting organs** such as the brain (Ch.13) and organs in the thorax (chest capacity); the ribs are also involved in **breathing** (ventilation). Some bones are sites of red and white **blood cell production** (Ch12).

Cartilage is a much softer, more rubbery tissue than bone. In some aquatic animals (for example the sharks) the entire skeleton is composed of cartilage. In most adult vertebrates, cartilage is confined to certain regions of the body; in humans, cartilage **lubricates** and **cushions** joints (see above) and **supports** various structures, such as the trachea, nose and ear pinna.

The human skeleton

The human skeleton consists of many (204) bones, ranging in size from the tiny ossicles within the middle ear to the thigh bone. The skeleton consists of two main groups of bones:

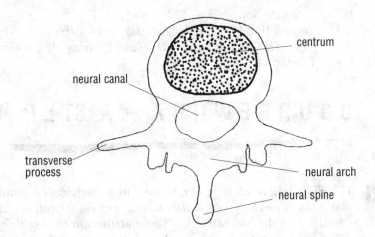

Fig.14.4 Typical Vertebra

(a) **the axial skeleton.** This is composed of the skull and backbone and encloses the central nervous system (Ch.13). The backbone, or vertebral column, is made up of numerous vertebrae (Fig.14.4); these provide a point of attachment for many other bones and also muscles. A central canal (neural tube) protects the spinal cord.

   (b) **the appendicular skeleton.** This consists of the limbs, the limb girdles and the ribs.

EXAMINATION QUESTION

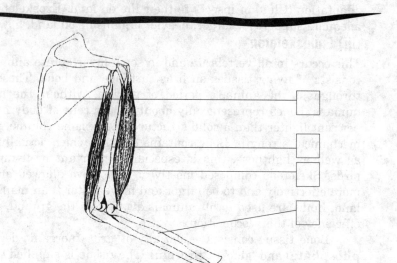

1. Ligament **2.**Shoulder Blade **3.**Biceps **4.**Tendon **5.**Ulna **6.**Triceps **7.**Humerus **8.**Radius

The diagram below shows certain bones and muscles in the arm.
(a)   Correctly label the structures shown, using names chosen from the following list. Write only the number of the name in the box provided. **2 marks**
(b)   Describe how the muscles of the arm are used to raise it. (2 lines) **2 marks**
(c)   Name the structure which attaches muscle to bone. (l line) **1 mark**
                                                          Total 5 marks (WJEC)

OUTLINE ANSWER

(a)   From the top: 2, 7, 6, 5.
(b)   Contraction of the biceps muscle raises the arm, which bends at the elbow joint. The triceps muscle is relaxed during this process.
(c)   Tendon.

COURSEWORK – A STEP FURTHER

1 ▷ SUPPORT IN PLANTS

The distribution of vascular tissues in a herbaceous plant can be studied using plants such as Busy Lizzie (*Impatiens*) or celery (*Apium*); the procedure for this is described at the end of Ch.12. The distribution of vascular tissue in sections from different parts of the plant should be compared, using large, clearly labelled diagrams.

2 ❯ SUPPORT IN ANIMALS

Obtain a fresh, suitably sized bone from a butcher. Observe and draw the the intact bone. Comment on any structures which apparently adapt the bone for support or movement (you need not identify the bone or any particular structure). If possible investigate the effect of removing certain components from the bone; dissolve away the salts from the bone by hydrochloric acid (CARE! this is corrosive). Using the same or a similar bone, remove the protein by soaking the bone in a 'biological' detergent containing a protein-digesting enzyme. In each case the bone may need to be soaked for 24–48 hours. Rinse the bone, then investigate any changes in the 'stiffness' of the bone. Write a brief account of your investigation, including a conclusion.

3 ❯ SUPPORT IN GENERAL

Some simple but very effective experiments on support can be conducted using drinking straws. The straws should be held together by elastic bands and supported at each end. Weights are gradually loaded onto the central part of the straws; the weights can be placed in a small container such as a yoghurt carton suspended from the straws using a wire hook. The effect on load-carrying capacity can be compared using (a) different straw number and (b) different straw length. Weights are loaded until the straws obviously bend. The experiment should be repeated at least three times, using new straws each time. The results can be presented as a line graph (Appendix 2), with straw *number* or *length* (horizontal axis) against *maximum mass supported* in each case.

STUDENT'S ANSWER – EXAMINER'S COMMENTS

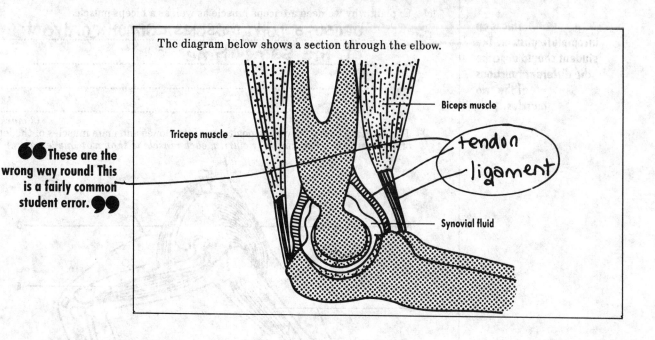

The diagram below shows a section through the elbow.

Triceps muscle

Biceps muscle

tendon
ligament

Synovial fluid

"These are the wrong way round! This is a fairly common student error."

"Correct."

"*Another* set of antagonistic muscles should also be stated."

"This *is* correct, though it does not answer the question. The student should refer to opposing muscles contracting *or* relaxing."

"This is correct; extending the foot often presses against the ground, resulting in forward movement."

(i) Explain the term "antagonistic muscles", illustrating your answer by reference to TWO sets of antagonistic muscles from the muscles labelled A to F on the diagram.

B and E are antagonistic muscles.
When B contracts, the leg is straightened.
When E contracts, the leg is bent.

(4 marks)

(i) Suggest why muscle C is more powerfully developed than muscle F.

because more power is needed to straighten the foot than bend the foot, eg while running.

(1 mark)
(Total 11 marks)

NEA

"Correct answer."

"This is an incomplete answer. The student should describe the different functions of the two muscles."

(a) ON THE DIAGRAM,

   (i) label a tendon with the letter X,   *(1 mark)*

   (ii) label a ligament with the letter Y.   *(1 mark)*

(b) Why does the joint have synovial fluid?

for lubrication

(1 mark)

(c) Explain why we need a triceps muscle as well as a biceps muscle.

because both muscles cannot contract at the same time

(3 marks)

(d) The diagram below shows the positions of the bones and main muscles of the legs of a human when running. (*For clarity, each muscle is shown on one leg only.*)

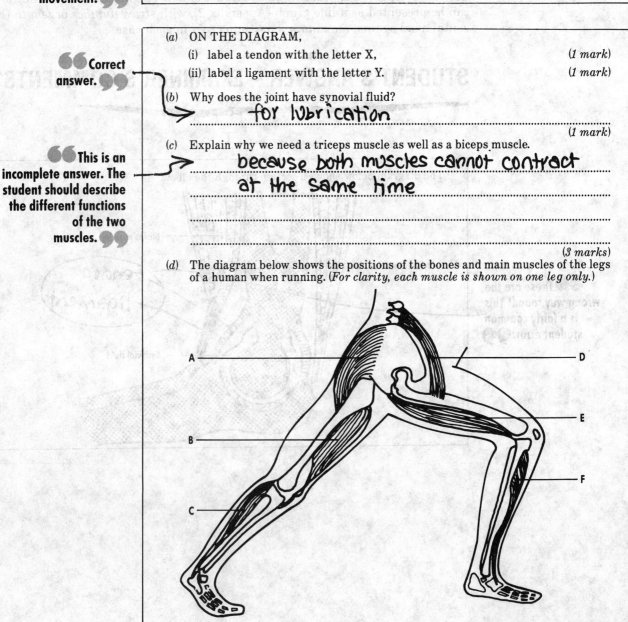

GETTING STARTED

Nutrition is the process by which organisms obtain materials from their environment for growth, development and the maintenance of life. Nutrition is a **characteristic of life**.

All forms of nutrition involve organisms obtaining both -*inorganic* and *organic* molecules. There are two main methods of obtaining essential molecules from the environment: autotrophic (holophytic) and heterotrophic nutrition:

1 **Autotrophic nutrition** (also called **holophytic nutrition**) is used by green plants. Inorganic molecules only are obtained from the environment. Organic molecules are formed within the tissues of such organisms from inorganic molecules. This process is called **photosynthesis** and requires light energy which is trapped by pigments, especially **chlorophyll**. **Autotrophs** (organisms using autotrophic nutrition) are also called **producers**, because they provide food, either directly or indirectly, for all other organisms via **food chains.**

2 **Heterotrophic nutrition** is used by animals and any other organisms not capable of photosynthesis. All organic and most inorganic molecules are obtained from living or decaying organisms. This process involves **ingestion (feeding)** and **digestion (chemical breakdown)** of food. **Heterotrophs** (organisms using heterotrophic nutrition) are called **consumers** because they consume other organisms, living or dead.

Nutrition is an important factor in the relationships between different organisms, including **competition** within and between species. The type of nutrition determines the **trophic** (feeding) **level** of a organism in a **food chain** (this is more fully explained in Ch.17).

AUTOTROPHIC
NUTRITION
HETEROTROPHIC
NUTRITION
HOLOZOIC NUTRITION
INGESTION (FEEDING)
MALNUTRITION
FOOD ADDITIVES
FOOD ANALYSIS
DIGESTION
SAPROPHYTIC
NUTRITION
PARASITIC NUTRITION

ESSENTIAL PRINCIPLES

1 ▷ AUTOTROPHIC NUTRITION

Autotrophic nutrition involves the incorporation of simple inorganic molecules into complex organic molecules, normally using light energy. This process, called **photosynthesis**, consists of a series of enzyme-controlled reactions. The light energy for photosynthesis is absorbed and converted to chemical energy by **chlorophyll** molecules, contained in **chloroplasts**. The possession of chlorophyll molecules is a characteristic of all organisms capable of photosynthesis. The overall process of photosynthesis can be summarised in the following word and chemical equation:

66 **You should make a point of learning this word formula. Do not, however, confuse this formula with that for aerobic respiration (Ch.10).** 99

$$\text{Carbon dioxide} + \text{water} + \text{energy} \xrightarrow{\text{chlorophyll}} \text{glucose} + \text{oxygen}$$
$$6CO_2 \qquad 6H_2O \qquad (\text{light}) \qquad\qquad C_6H_{12}O_6 \qquad 6O_2$$

The overall reaction is, in many respects, the reverse of that for **aerobic respiration** (Ch.10); aerobic respiration and photosynthesis are complementary processes.

Light energy absorbed by chlorophyll is used to 'split' water molecules into the separate elements (Appendix 1) of hydrogen and oxygen. This process is called **photolysis** ('light-splitting'). The **hydrogen** is combined with carbon dioxide to form the carbohydrate (Ch.4) glucose. This can then be converted into other molecules, including **sucrose** which can be transported (Ch.12) around the plant, and **starch**, which can be stored for future use. Starch is therefore regarded as evidence of photosynthesis and can be tested for (see below) to confirm that photosynthesis has taken place. **Minerals** are used to make other organic molecules from carbohydrates; for example, nitrogen can be used to make **proteins** (Ch.4). The **oxygen** produced by photolysis is a waste product of photosynthesis. Oxygen can be used in aerobic respiration (Ch.10) or released into the atmosphere, depending on the **rate** of photosynthesis (see below).

(a) THE SITE OF PHOTOSYNTHESIS

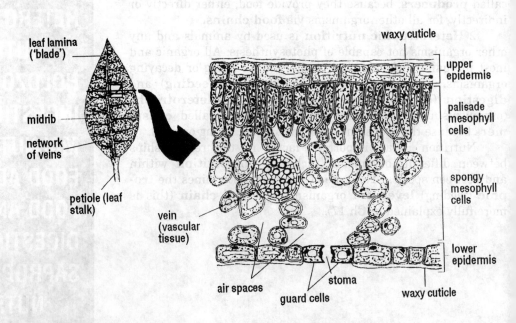

Fig.15.1 Structure of a typical leaf (vertical section; dicotyledonous leaf, see Ch.5).

Photosynthesis takes place within **chloroplasts**; these **organelles** (Ch.4) are particularly numerous in leaf cells. Leaves can be regarded as the main organs of photosynthesis. **Leaf structure** (Fig.15.1) is well adapted for this function. The role of the main components of the leaf in relation to photosynthesis is summarised in Fig.15.2.

Component	Description	Adaptation
Chloroplasts	Comparatively large membrane-bound organelles (Ch. 4) which contain pigments such as **chlorophyll**. These pigments absorb light energy and convert it to chemical energy.	Chloroplasts contain complex molecules, such as pigments and enzymes, necessary for photosynthesis. The relative number and distribution of chloroplasts corresponds with the amount of light available to the leaf.
Palisade mesophyll cells	Vertically arranged 'column' (palisade) shaped cells, containing many (up to about 100) chloroplasts; main site of photosynthesis in 'broad-leaved' *dicotyledonous* (Ch. 4) plants. Absent in 'narrow-leaved' *monocotyledonous* plants.	The vertical arrangement of cells reduces the number of cross-walls which would interfere with the passage of light.
Spongy mesophyll cells	Loosely packed rounded cells, surrounded by air spaces. Main site of gas exchange surrounded by **air spaces**. Main site of photosynthesis in monocotlyedonous plants.	Air spaces surrounding the cells are continuous, via the **stomata**, with the atmosphere around the leaf. Cells are surrounded by a film of water in which gases entering the cells dissolve.
Epidermis and waxy cuticle	Epidermis cells maintain shape of leaf and produce a waxy cuticle layer. This protects the leaf from excess water loss and the entry of disease-causing microbes.	The epidermis and waxy cuticle are well-adapted to preventing excess water leaving the plant and also to preventing the entry of microbes. Light is allowed to enter the leaf, however, as most epidermis cells do not contain chloroplasts.
Guard cells and stomata	A pair of guard cells surround each **stoma** (pore); leaves have many stomata (see Ch. 12). **Stomata** are the main route for the movement of gases into and out of the leaf. Each stoma can be opened or closed by changes in the shape of the guard cells.	Unlike other epidermis cells, guard cells contain chloroplasts and can photosynthesise. This is thought to be important in their opening and closing. These cells have *uneven thickening* of their walls (Ch. 12) which causes them to change shape when water is gained or lost by osmosis (Ch. 4).
Veins (vascular bundles)	Veins contain **vascular tissue** (Ch. 12) which conducts water and minerals to the leaf and removes products of photosynthesis to the rest of the plant. A network of veins supports the leaf (Ch. 14) and keeps it flat.	Leaf cells need a supply of water for photosynthesis. Minerals are necessary for the formation of certain molecules, such as proteins (Ch. 15). Many molecules made during photosynthesis will be needed by other parts of the plant so, are transported away through veins. Leaves of most plants are kept flat to maintain a sufficient surface area for the absorption of light and for the exchange of gases with the environment.

Fig.15.2 Summary of the main leaf components involved in photosynthesis

Leaf cells need a supply of water for photosynthesis. Minerals are necessary for the formation of certain molecules, such as proteins (Ch.4). Many molecules made during photosynthesis will be needed by other parts of the plant so are transported away through veins. Leaves of most plants are kept flat to maintain a sufficient surface area for the absorption of light and for the exchange of gases with the environment.

The **total surface area of leaves** of a particular plant is an important factor in deciding how much photosynthesis the plant can undertake. There are two main reasons for this. Firstly, leaves absorb light for photosynthesis. Secondly, leaves absorb carbon dioxide for photosynthesis and allow waste oxygen to escape. Leaves are thin enough for diffusion distances (Ch.4) to be relatively short.

Plants often turn their leaves towards the most intense source of light (see Ch.13). The leaves are normally positioned so that they do not shade each other. The total surface area available will normally allow the plant to make enough materials for growth and development (Ch.7). However, leaves are also the main region of water loss from the plant. The pores (stomata) through which water is lost from the plant (Ch.12) need to be opened for at least part of each day to allow oxygen and carbon dioxide to pass through for respiration and photosynthesis.

(b) FACTORS AFFECTING PHOTOSYNTHESIS

The **rate** of photosynthesis is controlled by various *internal* and *external* factors. If any one of these is in short supply it is known as a **limiting factor** since it will determine the overall rate of photosynthesis. Note that, although water is needed in photosynthesis, this is not likely to be a limiting factor since a wilted plant (see Ch.12) will not in any case be functioning normally.

The main factors affecting photosynthesis are chlorophyll, light, carbon dioxide and temperature. Relatively simple experimental methods are available for studying the effect of various factors on photosynthesis. The presence of starch is often used to show that photosynthesis has taken place since starch is formed quite rapidly from the glucose which results from this process. Before the experiment is conducted the plant is destarched. **Destarching** is the removal of starch contained in a plant by placing the plant in darkness for about 48 hours, for instance by covering it with black polythene. The plant uses up any starch that is present in its leaves during this time. The way in which leaves, for example, may be tested for starch is shown in Fig.15.3.

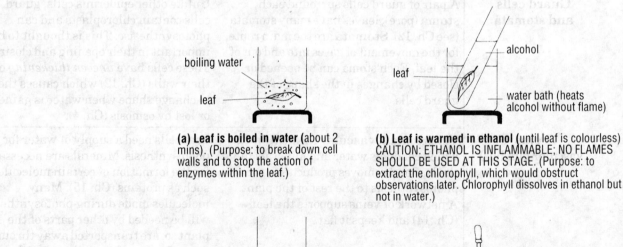

(a) **Leaf is boiled in water** (about 2 mins). (Purpose: to break down cell walls and to stop the action of enzymes within the leaf.)

(b) **Leaf is warmed in ethanol** (until leaf is colourless) CAUTION: ETHANOL IS INFLAMMABLE; NO FLAMES SHOULD BE USED AT THIS STAGE. (Purpose: to extract the chlorophyll, which would obstruct observations later. Chlorophyll dissolves in ethanol but not in water.)

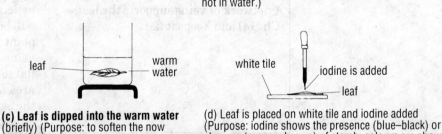

(c) **Leaf is dipped into the warm water** (briefly) (Purpose: to soften the now brittle leaf.)

(d) Leaf is placed on white tile and iodine added (Purpose: iodine shows the presence (blue–black) or absence (orange–brown) of starch; colours are shown against the white tile.)

Fig.15.3 Testing a leaf for starch

Chlorophyll

Chlorophyll is essential for photosynthesis; it is necessary for converting light energy into chemical energy for splitting water. Chlorophyll molecules are formed in the presence of light and are broken down in darkness. A plant kept in prolonged darkness (i.e. more than about ten days) will look yellow rather than green; this condition is known as **chlorosis**. An example of chlorosis occurs if insufficient light is available during germination, resulting in etiolated seedlings. Chlorosis also occurs if certain minerals, especially **magnesium**, are lacking.

Experiment to demonstrate the need for chlorophyll in photosynthesis

The experiment involves the use of *variegated* leaves. Such leaves have an uneven distribution of chlorophyll; some areas of the leaf may lack chlorophyll completely. Examples of plants which may have variegated leaves are privet (*Ligustrum*), ivy (*Hedera*), geranium (*Pelargonium*), laurel (*Laurus*). The presence of starch (Ch.4) is used to confirm that photosynthesis has taken place.

A variegated leaf is exposed to light whilst still attached to the rest of the plant. The leaf is then removed from the plant and tested for starch, as described above. The distribution of starch after testing is compared with that of chlorophyll before testing. If possible, the leaf should be sketched before testing and again afterwards. Possible results are shown in Fig.15.4. The distribution of starch is found to correspond very closely to that of chlorophyll. This suggests that chlorophyll is necessary for the formation of starch, during photosynthesis.

> **This common photosynthesis experiment sometimes causes confusion with exam candidates. In particular, you should understand the significance of the presence or absence of starch.**

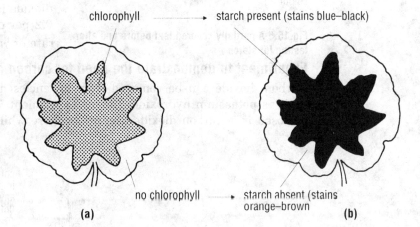

Fig.15.4 A variegated leaf before and after testing for starch (a) before testing (b) after testing

Light

Light provides the energy for splitting water, which provides hydrogen for photosynthesis. Light may be a limiting factor (see above) in dim light, for instance at dawn and dusk. Light is a highly variable factor in the environment (Ch.16), for instance depending on the time of day or, in many areas of the world, the time of year. Light varies in three main ways:

(i) **Intensity**. The amount of light available will depend on the time of day and seasons, weather and shading. Small plants may be shaded by other, taller plants. Some plants, e.g. bluebell (*Endymion non-scriptus*) growing in woodland complete most of their life cycle before the *deciduous* (see below) trees above them form leaves.

(ii) **Duration**. Photosynthesis can only occur when sufficient light is available. For instance in the UK, the light available during 24 hours will be about 17 hours during the summer but only 8 hours during the winter. For this reason, **deciduous** plants lose their leaves at those times of the year when the duration of light is short, and when temperatures are relatively low. **Evergreen** plants do not lose their leaves in this way.

(iii) **Wavelength**. The rate of photosynthesis depends also on the type of light available; for instance, blue and red light is more effective than green light, which is reflected from leaves. It is possible to show the effect of varying the intensity and wavelength of light on the rate of photosynthesis (see below) and also the effect of the absence of light.

Experiment to demonstrate the need for light in photosynthesis

The leaf used in this experiment remains attached to the rest of the plant until it is tested for starch. The leaf is destarched (see above) and is then partially covered with a 'mask' from material through which light cannot pass; aluminium foil or

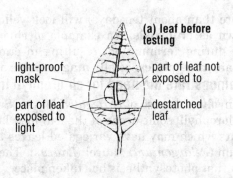

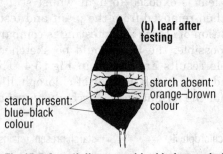

Fig.15.5 A partially covered leaf before and after testing for starch

card is suitable. A simple pattern (stencil) can be cut in the mask to make the experiment more interesting (Fig.15.5).

The leaf is exposed to light for several hours, then tested for starch (see above). Those parts of the leaf which were exposed to light are found to contain starch. Those parts that were covered are found to contain no starch.

Carbon dioxide

Carbon dioxide is present in low concentrations (normally about 0.04 per cent) in air. For this reason, carbon dioxide is often a limiting factor (see above) in photosynthesis; this can limit the rate of photosynthesis. In greenhouse crops the concentration of carbon dioxide is raised artificially up to about 0.2 per cent; this increases the growth rate or *yield* of the plant.

Experiment to demonstrate the need for carbon dioxide in photosynthesis

Carbon dioxide can be removed from an enclosed atmosphere by an absorbant such as potassium hydroxide. In this experiment, a leaf of a destarched plant is enclosed in a carbon dioxide-free atmosphere whilst still attached to the rest of

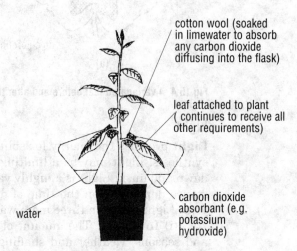

Fig.15.6 Apparatus to show that carbon dioxide is needed for photosynthesis

the plant (Fig.15.6). Another leaf is enclosed in a similar way, but without a carbon dioxide absorbant being present; this is for comparison and is called a control (Appendix 3).

The plant is then exposed to light for several hours, to allow photosynthesis to take place. Both leaves enclosed in the flasks are then tested for starch, as described above. The leaf which was kept in an atmosphere free of carbon dioxide is found not to contain starch; the control leaf does contain starch. This experiment indicates that carbon dioxide is necessary for photosynthesis.

Temperature

Temperature affects photosynthesis because the process is *enzyme*-controlled. There will therefore be an increase in the rate of photosynthesis as temperature increases. However, if the **optimum temperature** (Ch.4) is exceeded the enzymes may be destroyed and photosynthesis will cease. Sources of light, especially the sun, are also sources of heat so variations in light and temperature tend to occur together. Both are kept constant and relatively high within glasshouses, where economically-important plants are grown independently of fluctuations in climate.

The effect of this and of raising carbon dioxide concentrations (see above) is to raise the average yield of food plants.

(c) THE RATE OF PHOTOSYNTHESIS

The **rate of photosynthesis** an be determined for various conditions. This is most easily done by using an aquatic plant such as Canadian pondweed (*Elodea canadensis*); the plant produces from its cut stem oxygen bubbles which are clearly visible (Fig.15.7). The experiment can also be used to demonstrate that oxygen is produced during photosynthesis.

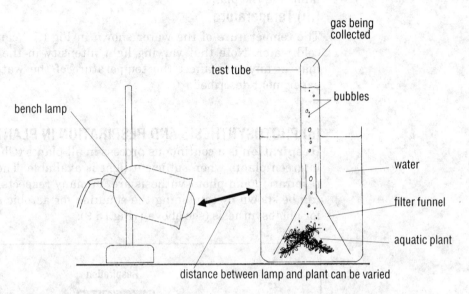

Fig.15.7 Experiment to demonstrate the effect of light intensity on the rate of photosynthesis

In this experiment, the intensity of light reaching the plant is varied by moving the lamp towards or away from the plant. The **number of bubbles per minute** is counted and noted. This is repeated twice more for each light intensity and an average (mean) value calculated (Appendix 1). Only the larger, slower moving bubbles should be counted. If they are too numerous, especially at higher light intensities, dots can be made with a pencil on paper and the dots counted afterwards. The results of this experiment can plotted as a line graph (Appendix 2); the average number of bubbles per minute is taken as the *rate of photosynthesis* (vertical scale), *decreasing* distance is taken as increasing *light intensity*. An example of such a graph is shown in Fig.15.8.

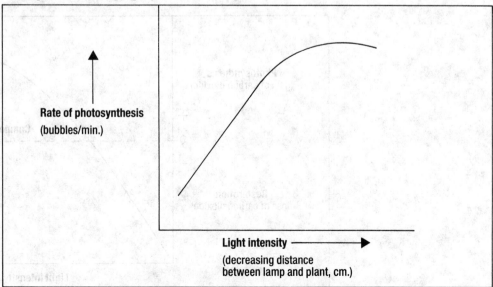

Fig.15.8 Graph to show the effect of light intensity on the rate of photosynthesis

If sufficient bubbles are collected they can be tested with a glowing splint which should be re-lit; this confirms that the gas collected is rich in oxygen. The amount of oxygen produced by the plant during a particular time can be measured by using a 10 cm^3 measuring cylinder instead of the test tube shown in Fig.15.7. Other variations include:

(i) Carbon dioxide concentration

Different amounts of **sodium hydrogen carbonate** (sodium bicarbonate) can be dissolved in the water shown in Fig.15.7. This releases carbon dioxide in solution.

(ii) Colour of light

Different wavelengths of light can be used by inserting coloured filters between the lamp and the plant

(iii) Temperature

The temperature of the water shown in Fig.15.7 can be varied by adding hot or cold water. Note that varying light intensity in the experiment described above may in any case affect the temperature of the water; this is a *criticism* of the experiment described.

(d) PHOTOSYNTHESIS AND RESPIRATION IN PLANTS

Respiration is a continuous process in all plants (Ch.10). **Photosynthesis** occurs in green plants when sufficient light is available. The overall processes of aerobic respiration and photosynthesis are, in many respects, opposite to each other. This can be shown by combining the equation for aerobic respiration (Ch.10) with that for photosynthesis (see above): (Fig.15.9):

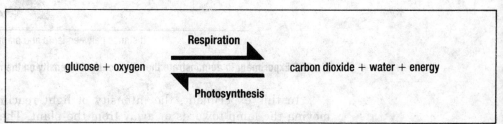

Fig.15.9 Respiration and photosynthesis as related processes

The energy is released from respiration in the form of heat and chemical energy (Ch.10). The energy used in photosynthesis is light energy which is converted by chlorophyll molecules into chemical energy. The source of light energy most commonly used by plants for photosynthesis is the **sun**. Photosynthesis is therefore very important in allowing the sun's energy to be temporarily 'trapped' by living things. This is further explained in Ch.17.

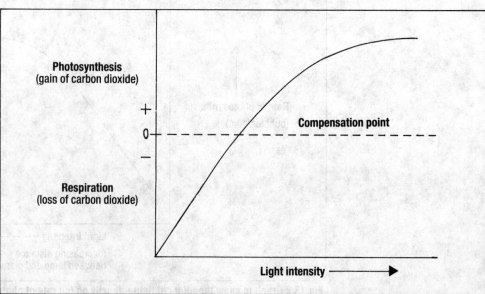

Fig.15.10 Graph to show compensation point

If the average rates of photosynthesis and respiration within a plant were the same there would be *no overall gain* in materials for **growth** (Ch.7); growth can only occur if new materials are made available through nutrition, such as photosynthesis. In relatively **bright light**, the rate of photosynthesis will be greater than the rate of respiration, so there will be an overall gain in organic molecules. These molecules can be used for growth, or to provide energy in respiration.

In **dim light**, the rates of respiration and photosynthesis may be very similar, so that there is no overall gain or loss of glucose, oxygen or carbon dioxide in the plant tissues. This is known as the **compensation point**. The compensation point can be shown on a graph; the relative rates of respiration and photosynthesis can be expressed in terms of gain or loss of oxygen or carbon dioxide (Fig.15.10).

Experiment to investigate the relative rates of respiration and photosynthesis in leaves

This experiment is based on the relative loss or gain of carbon dioxide from leaves in different light conditions. Changes in carbon dioxide concentration can be monitored by using **bicarbonate indicator**. This shows colour changes in the presence of different amounts of carbon dioxide. The gas dissolves in the indicator to form a weak acid (carbonic acid) which causes an alteration of acidity or alkalinity (Appendix 1) (Fig.15.11):

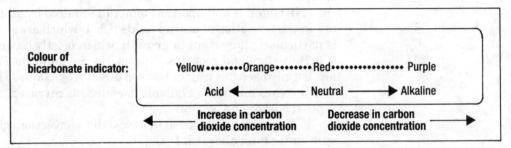

Fig.15.11 Colour changes of bicarbonate indicator

The bicarbonate indicator is **equilibrated** with normal atmospheric air before the experiment begins; air is bubbled through the solution, for instance by an aquarium pump. The solution should be *red* at the start of the experiment.

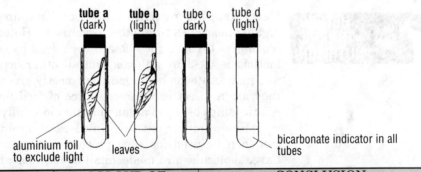

TUBE	COLOUR OF INDICATOR AT END OF EXPERIMENT	CONCLUSION
A	Yellow	Carbon dioxide concentration is high; produced by respiration.
B	Purple	Carbon dioxide concentration is low; used in photosynthesis.
C	Red	Carbon dioxide concentration remains constant; no respiration or photosynthesis is occurring because no living tissue is present.
D	Red	

Fig.15.12 Experiment to investigate respiration and photosynthesis in leaves

Leaves are placed in tubes containing bicarbonate indicator, as shown in Fig.15.12. The lower surfaces of the leaves should face inwards, so that gas exchange with pores (stomata) on the underside of the leaves can occur more easily. One tube is set up in darkness, the other in light. Two *control* tubes (Appendix 3) are set up without leaves, for comparison. All the tubes are left for about two hours.

Respiration occurs in *both* Tubes A and B, resulting in the production of carbon dioxide. However, in Tube B photosynthesis is *also* occurring and this process is more rapid than respiration in bright light; the carbon dioxide concentration is therefore lowered in Tube B.

(e) MINERAL NUTRITION IN PLANTS

Photosynthesis allows plants to make carbohydrates using the inorganic molecules carbon dioxide and water. Plants also need inorganic **minerals** to make other organic molecules such as proteins, lipids, nucleic acids (Ch.4) and vitamins (see below). Minerals are absorbed, with water, from the soil through the **roots** (Ch.12) by **diffusion** and also by **active transport**. Active transport allows minerals to be moved against a concentration gradient (Ch.4). It also allows plants to absorb required minerals **selectively**. The relative amounts of different types of minerals in the soil can be important in determining the distribution of different plant species (Ch.16).

Nitrogen is an important mineral, required by all plants. Nitrogen is important in the formation of **amino acids** (Ch.4) which are assembled into proteins; this is particularly important in **growth**, which mostly occurs in the **meristem tissue** (Ch.7) at stem and root tips. Nitrogen is a significant (79 per cent) component in air, but nitrogen gas cannot be used directly by plants. There are two main ways in which nitrogen is made available to plants, as **nitrate**:

(i) **Nitrogen fixation**

This *natural* process involves the conversion of nitrogen to nitrates by **symbiotic microbes** (Ch.16).

(ii) **Fertilisers**

This *artificial* process involves fertilisers being added to the soil. Fertilisers contain industrially produced nitrates, often with other minerals.

Heterotrophic nutrition involves obtaining a supply of both inorganic and organic molecules from other organisms. Heterotrophic organisms are also called *consumers* because they obtain their food by consuming other living things. This method is used by animals and all other organisms not capable of autotrophic nutrition. Autotrophic organisms, mostly green plants, are called **producers** and they are a direct or indirect source of food for consumers. The feeding (trophic) relationships between organisms are more fully described in Ch.17.

Heterotrophic nutrition involves absorbing relatively small molecules which can then be used for such processes as growth (Ch.7) and respiration (Ch.10). Large molecules are made small enough for absorption by being broken down by **enzymes** (Ch.4). This process of **digestion** in many heterotrophic organisms occurs within a specialised region called the **gut** or **alimentary canal**.

Heterotrophic organisms are adapted in many ways to the food that they normally consume and the method by which they obtain it. The adaptations include the structure and functioning of the gut and also many other aspects of the organism's mode of life; examples of this are given below. Heterotrophic organisms include:

(a) **Herbivores** ('plant eater') which feed directly on producers and are also called **primary consumers**;

(b) **Carnivores** ('meat eaters') which feed indirectly on producers by eating herbivores; they are also called **secondary consumers**; and

(c) **Omnivores** which feed on a mixed diet of plant and animal material. Organisms tend to be **adapted** in many ways to their type of nutrition; for instance, in their movement and support, sensitivity, growth and development, excretion and in their dentition and gut structure.

There are three main *types* of heterotrophic nutrition, namely **holozoic**, **saprophytic** and **parasitic**. Each of these is explained below:

3 ▷ HOLOZOIC NUTRITION

Holozoic nutrition is used by many organisms, and includes the *internal* digestion of food within a specialised gut which can produce particular enzymes. The process also involves taking food into the body by **ingestion** (feeding), **absorption** of the products of digestion and **egestion** of undigested materials. A summary of the process of holozoic nutrition is given in Fig.15.13.

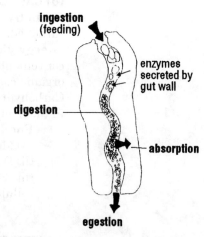

Fig.15.13 Summary of holozoic nutrition

4 ▷ INGESTION (FEEDING)

The **amount** and **type** of food consumed depends on **availability** and also the **organism's needs** at any one time. An individual's requirements are determined by **activity, size, growth rate, age** and **sex**. A relatively large proportion (about 65 per cent) of the energy eventually released from food (Ch.10) is used to maintain body temperature in endothermic ('warm blooded') animals (Ch.11); **environmental temperature** is therefore also important in determining how much food such organisms consume. Feeding behaviour is coordinated by the brain. **Carnivores** and **omnivores** tend to feed occasionally whilst **herbivores** feed almost continuously. If excess food is consumed it can often be **stored** for future use.

Animals use **senses** including **sight, smell** and, later, **taste** to obtain and to evaluate food before ingesting it; food may be harmful if not checked first. The quality and quantity of food consumed by an organism is called its **diet**. In humans, a **balanced diet** consists of food of an appropriate type and in suitable proportions to meet all of an individual's needs. The main components of a balanced diet are: **Organic:** protein, carbohydrate, lipids (fats), vitamins. **Inorganic:** minerals, water. Not absorbed: roughage (fibre).

TYPES OF NUTRIENT

The importance each of these nutrients is described below, together with examples of typical sources in the diet. Proteins, carbohydrates and lipids are sometimes called macronutrients ('macro-' = large) because they are required in relatively large amounts. Vitamins are called micronutrients ('micro-' = small) because they are needed in smaller amounts. Minerals can be macronutrients or micronutrients.

(a) PROTEINS

Proteins are absorbed as **amino acids** (Ch.4) which are then assembled according to the genetic instructions (Ch.8) within the organism. **First class** ('high biological value') **proteins** contain all or most of the eight **essential amino acids**; another twelve or so can be formed within human tissues. **Second class** ('low biological value') **proteins** contain fewer essential amino acids. There are two main functions of proteins:

(i) **growth and repair**, proteins make new protoplasm (Ch.4)

(ii) **metabolism**, proteins can acts as **enzymes** (p..) which control chemical processes. The digestion of proteins allows them to be absorbed (as amino acids). Proteins are not, under normal circumstances, used much (i.e. less than 10 per cent) for respiration; if they are used, the **energy yield = 17 kJ/g**. Excess proteins in the diet cannot be stored; they are broken down in the liver to carbohydrates and urea (Ch.11).

Food sources:
First class: milk, cheese (dairy products), eggs, meat
Second class: peas, beans (pulses).

(b) CARBOHYDRATES

Carbohydrates are absorbed as **monosaccharides** (Ch.4). The main function of carbohydrates is to provide **energy**, from **respiration** (see Ch.10); the average **energy yield** = 17 kJ/g. Carbohydrates are not essential in the diet, but they are a convenient source of energy because they are readily available; they are the main organic component of all plants. Also, carbohydrates are relatively easy to digest. Carbohydrates which are not required immediately are stored as **glycogen** (Ch.4) in the liver and muscles.

> **Food sources**:
> (i) Monosaccharides: fruit, honey
> (ii) Disaccharides: cane sugar, milk (lactose)
> (iii) Polysaccharides: starch – flour, potatoes.
> cellulose – important as roughage (see below).

(c) LIPIDS (FATS AND OILS)

Lipids are absorbed as **glycerol** and **fatty acids** (Ch.4). Lipids have three important functions:

(i) **respiration**, the energy yield = 39 kJ/g. This is more than twice that of carbohydrates (or proteins); however lipids are less readily available and are more difficult to digest.

(ii) **component of cell membranes**, lipids form part of the **phospholipid** molecule (Ch.4).

(iii) **insulation and protection**, lipids are stored under the skin for insulation (Ch.11) and around organs for protection.

> **Food sources**: butter, vegetable oil

(d) VITAMINS

Vitamins are required in small ('trace') amounts in the diet; they are micronutrients which are in many cases necessary for **enzymes** (Ch.4) to work properly. The exact way in which many vitamins function is not fully understood, however. Vitamins have no energy value and are not digested. Most vitamins are not formed in the tissues of the organism that needs them; instead, they are obtained from other organisms that can make them. A lack of sufficient vitamins in the diet results in deficiency diseases. There are two main groups of vitamin:

(i) Water-soluble (present in certain vegetables and fruits)

Examples:

Vitamin B complex (consists of several vitamins), important for **respiration enzymes** (Ch.10). **Food source**: yeast, unrefined cereal grain. **Deficiency**: **beri-beri** (paralysis).

Vitamin C (ascorbic acid), needed for formation/repair of tissue, including skin, teeth and bones. **Food source**: green vegetables, potatoes, citrus fruits (e.g. lemons). **Deficiency**: **scurvy** (tissue not formed/repaired).

(ii) Fat-soluble (present in animal and vegetable fats)

Examples:

Vitamin A (retinol), important in forming 'visual purple' pigment in light-sensitive cells in the eye (Ch.13). **Food source**: liver, cheese, milk. **Deficiency**: poor 'night vision'

Vitamin D (calciferol), essential for the absorption of calcium and phosphorus in the gut; also needed for the formation of teeth and bone. **Food source**: fish, egg (yolk), milk, liver. Also formed by the action of sunlight on skin. **Deficiency**: rickets (poor bone formation during development).

(e) MINERALS (SALTS)

Minerals are inorganic molecules which can be important in the formation of more complex organic molecules. Heterotrophic and autotrophic organisms (see above) share many requirements for minerals because minerals often perform similar functions in plants and animals. In animals, certain minerals may be available from protein, carbohydrate, and lipid molecules; these contain carbon, hydrogen, oxygen, nitrogen, phosphorus and sulphur (Ch.4). About ten additional minerals are needed in a balanced diet. Minerals can be divided into two main groups according to the amount in which they are required:

(i) Macronutrients (needed in relatively large amounts)
Examples:

Calcium and phosphorus, important in the formation of teeth and bones. Food source: milk, cheese, fruit. Deficiency: brittle teeth and bones

(ii) Micronutrients (trace elements) (needed in relatively small amounts)
Examples:

Iron, important as a component of the haemoglobin molecule (Ch.12). Food sources: Liver, egg (yolk), spinach. Deficiency: anaemia (insufficient haemoglobin in blood).

Iodine, forms part of the molecule growth of the hormone thyroxin. Food source: sea foods, table salt. Deficiency: goitre (adults), swelling of thyroid glands (Ch.13)

(f) WATER
Water is a major component (65–70 per cent) of the human body. It is essential in chemical reactions and as a means of carrying substances around the body (see Ch.12). About half of all water absorbed is present in food, the rest is consumed as a liquid. The amount of water taken into the body corresponds to the amount lost from the body and is under involuntary control (Ch.13).

(g) ROUGHAGE (FIBRE)
Roughage is an essential part of the diet, but it is not digested or absorbed. Roughage consists mainly of cellulose (Ch.4). Humans do not produce an enzyme to break this down, so it is egested (see below) without being significantly altered. However, roughage provides bulk which presses against the gut walls, especially in the large intestine. This stimulates the movement of food by peristalsis (see below). Food sources: vegetables (especially uncooked). Deficiency: constipation.

5 ▷ MALNUTRITION
Malnutrition occurs when a particular diet is not appropriate to an individual's needs. This may result from the person's food preferences or because a balanced diet (see above) is not available. There are two main types of malnutrition:

(a) UNDERNUTRITION
Many people, particularly in the Third World, are suffering from undernutrition. They do not obtain enough food, or they do not receive a suitable range of foods, to keep them healthy. Protein deficiency (kwashiorkor) is a serious problem in some parts of the world.

(b) OVERNUTRITION
People living in areas of the world where food is more readily available may consume more than they need. Excess food is stored, mainly as fat, leading to obesity. This may be cause health problems such as heart disease (Ch.12)

6 ▷ FOOD ADDITIVES
Food additives include preservatives and artificial colourings and flavourings. They are added to food to make it more acceptable and economical. The long-term effects of many additives are not fully understood, although they are included in most processed food. Some additives are known to cause allergic reactions. Additives may, in certain cases, increase the possibilities of disease such as cancer.

7 > FOOD ANALYSIS

There are fairly simple methods for analysing foods for some nutrients and also for energy content.

(a) EXPERIMENT TO INVESTIGATE THE COMPOSITION OF FOOD

The **food tests** summarised in Fig.15.14 (which can be conducted separately) are in most cases undertaken with food in a dissolved or suspended state. This allows food particles to come into more direct contact with the test chemical. Only a small amount of food is needed for each test. Most of the *positive results* (when food is present) involve a colour change.

Type of food	Food test	Positive result
Carbohydrate: starch	Add *iodine* to the solid or liquid food.	Colour change: orange/brown ♦ blue/black.
Glucose	Add *Benedict's solution* to liquid food in a test tube; solid food should be ground up in a little water. Heat the tube in a beaker of boiling water.	Colour changes: blue ♦ green ♦ yellow ♦ red
Protein	Add equal amounts (a few drops) of copper sulphate and dilute sodium hydroxide (CARE: avoid skin contact) to liquid food in a test tube; solid food should be ground up in a little water. This is called the Biuret test.	Colour changes: blue ♦ purple
Lipid (fat)	Make a solution of the food in a little *ethanol* (ethyl alcohol) (CARE: avoid flames). Filter this solution to obtain a clear solution; add this to a little *water*.	A milky (cloudy) mixture
Vitamin C	Add a small amount of liquid food to a solution of the dye *DCPIP* dichlorophenyl indophenol).	Colour change: blue ♦ colourless

Fig.15.14 Summary of common food tests

(b) EXPERIMENT TO INVESTIGATE THE ENERGY VALUE OF FOOD

Energy is released from food in the body during respiration (Ch.10). The amount of energy that is released depends on the **calorific value** of food. A **calorie** is the amount of heat energy that can raise the temperature of 1g (1 cm) of water through 1 C. The energy value of food is often given by food manufacturers in calories or kilocalories (= 1000 calories). In science, the unit used is the **joule** (J) (4.2 joules = 1 calorie) or **kilojoule** (kJ) (= 1000 joules).

In this experiment, food is burnt (combusted); the heat energy which is released is used to raise the temperature of a known amount of water and can be measured. A suitable food for this experiment is an unroasted peanut, which is first ignited in a bunsen flame and then quickly placed under a boiling tube of water (Fig.15.15).

The energy value of the peanut can be estimated using the formula:

$$\text{Energy value (kJ)} = \frac{\text{increase in temperature (°C)} \times \text{amount of water (cm}^3) \times 4.2}{\text{mass of food (g)} \times 1000}$$

For instance, if a 0.5g peanut raises the temperature of 20 cm^3 of water from 24°C to 60°C (an increase of 36°C), the energy value can be calculated as follows:

$$\text{Energy value} = \frac{36 \times 20 \times 4.2}{0.5 \times 1000} = 6.1 \text{ kJ/g}$$

This method of determining energy value is fairly approximate because of several inaccuracies in the experiment. More accurate measurements can be made using a much improved version of the apparatus called the **calorimeter** The energy value of food determined using a calorimeter will be higher and more reliable; for peanuts the energy value is about 24 kJ/g.

8 ▶ DIGESTION

The overall purpose of digestion is to prepare ingested food for absorption into the tissues of the organism. This is achieved by reducing the size of food particles and also by making food more soluble. In holozoic organisms, including humans, digestion takes place within the **gut** (**limentary canal** (see Fig.15.19). Digestion can be conveniently divided into two stages; **physical digestion** and **chemical digestion**.

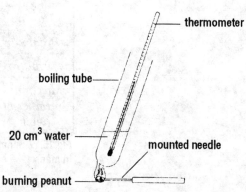

Fig.15.15 Determination of the energy value of a peanut

(a) PHYSICAL DIGESTION

Food is mechanically broken down by **teeth** and also by the **muscular activities of the gut**. These processes increase the surface area (Appendix 1) for **enzymes** to act upon (see below) and make the movement of food through the gut easier.

(i) Teeth

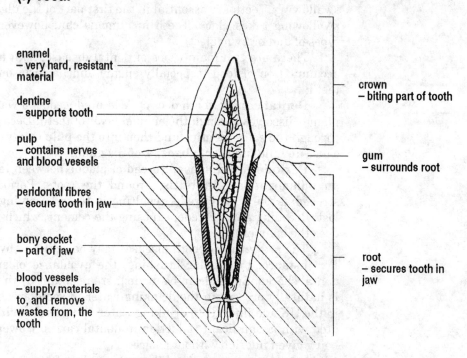

Fig.15.16 Structure of a 'typical' tooth (vertical section; canine)

Arrangement of teeth

The relative number, arrangement and types of teeth that an animal has, its **dentition**, is an **adaptation** to diet. Other variations include the action of the jaws in bringing teeth together. Teeth in animals other than mammals tend to be fairly uniform in structure and function; they are used for killing and holding food rather than for chewing. There are *four* main types of teeth in mammals; **incisors** (cutting), **canines** (piercing, grasping), **premolars** and **molars** (crushing, slicing). These teeth have the same basic structure (Fig.15.17) but they have different functions so are adapted by being different in shape and in position in the jaw. Some of these differences are included in the comparison of **herbivores** (vegetation eaters)

Type of tooth	Deciduous teeth	Permament teeth
Incisor	8	8
Canine	4	4
Premolar	8	8
Molar	0	12
Maximum number of teeth	20	32

Fig.15.17 Summary of teeth development in humans

and **carnivores** (meat eaters) (see below). In mammals, teeth develop in two stages: **deciduous** (temporary, 'milk') teeth and **permanent** (adult) teeth (Fig.15.17). Deciduous teeth appear first, when the young mammal is *weaned* onto solid food. Having two sets of teeth allows the older animals gradually to acquire larger and more numerous teeth as the jaws increase in size during growth.

The arrangement of teeth in mammals can be expressed in a **dental formula**. Only half of the teeth are shown for the upper and lower jaws because each **half-jaw** is symmetrical (a 'mirror image') with the other half. The total numbers of each type are represented with those for the upper half-jaw being written over numbers for the lower half-jaw. **The dental formula for an adult human would** be written:

$$\text{(upper half-jaw)} - \quad i\,\frac{2}{2} \quad c\,\frac{1}{1} \quad pm\,\frac{2}{2} \quad m\,\frac{3}{3} \quad \text{total for complete jaws} = 32$$

i = incisor, c = canine, pm = premolar, m = molar

Action of teeth

Teeth are brought against or past each by jaw movements; this action forms part of the process of **chewing (mastication)**. Chewing also includes movements of the cheeks and tongue, which position food between the teeth. Secretions contained in **saliva** help bind food into a bolus (lump of food) and lubricates it for swallowing. Teeth are essential in the first part of the digestion of solid food, before swallowing takes place. Teeth in humans can, however, be damaged by certain types of diet or by neglect.

There are two main types of dental disease; both are caused by **plaque**, an accumulation of food (especially sugar) and bacteria on the exposed surfaces of teeth:

Dental caries (tooth decay). Acid produced as a waste product by bacteria in plaque dissolves through the enamel layer of teeth. Decay can spread more rapidly through the softer dentine and then into the pulp cavity. Infection of the pulp may cause an inflammation, **abscess**, of the gum.

Periodontal disease. Spread of plaque between teeth and gums may cause an inflammation, **gingivitis**, around the roots. Periodontal fibres become destroyed as the gums recede, resulting in teeth becoming loose and possibly being lost. Receding gums recede, exposing the cement, which decays more rapidly than does the enamel.

The prevention of both diseases may be achieved by increased **oral hygiene**. For instance, by regular brushing, the avoidance of sugary foods and periodic dental checks. Enamel can be made more resistant by the presence of *fluoride*; this is naturally present in the drinking water in some areas. Many water authorities in the UK add fluoride to drinking water and this **fluoridation** seems to be associated with a significant reduction in dental caries. However, some people object to being given fluoride without choice.

(ii) Muscular movements of the gut

The gut is, in many respects, basically a muscular tube. The muscles are mostly under **involuntary control** (Ch.13). Muscular movements of the gut cause food to be physically broken down and also mixed with digestive enzymes, for chemical digestion (see below). Muscular movements also move food through the gut; this is achieved by peristalsis. **Peristalsis** is caused by the alternate contraction of the circular and longitudinal muscles contained in the gut wall (Fig.15.18).

Muscles are also used to control the movement of food through the gut. For instance the **epiglottis** is a muscular flap which closes during **swallowing** to prevent solid and liquid food from entering the trachea (Ch.10). **Sphincters** are circular muscles which, when contracted, prevent food moving in the wrong direction or at the wrong time; for example, at the entrance and exit of the stomach and at the anus.

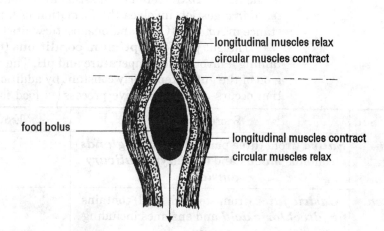

Fig.15.18 The action of peristalsis

(b) CHEMICAL DIGESTION

Chemical digestion involves the breakdown of food mainly by the action of enzymes (Ch.4). This breakdown results in large, insoluble molecules being made small and soluble so that the food can be absorbed (see below). Most foods consumed by holozoic animals consist of large molecules which are insoluble in water. The **gut (alimentary canal)** (Fig 15.19) is a specialized tube which has various glands associated with it. These glands secrete substances which are involved in digestion.

Enzymes involved in digestion are made in cells in the gut wall or in specialised glands which empty their contents directly into the gut through tubes, or *ducts*. Enzymes digest food in the **gut cavity**, or **lumen**. Digestion is *extra-cellular*; enzymes are secreted onto food outside living cells. The gut is essentially a hollow tube which is continuous with the environment at each end (see Fig.15.19) and food does not pass through a living membrane until it is ready for absorption

> It is worth becoming familiar with the layout of the gut so that you can recognise the relative position of different parts of the gut.

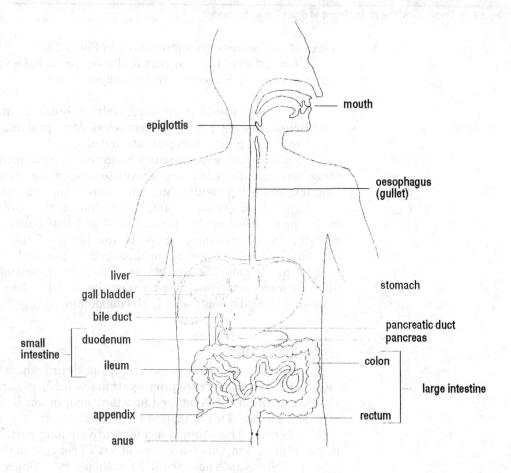

Fig.15.19 Structure of the human gut

in the ileum. Extra-cellular digestion also occurs in saprophytes (see below). *Intra-cellular* digestion involves the formation of a food vacuole within the cell, for instance in *Amoeba* (Ch.4) and phagocytic white blood cells (Ch.12).

The gut provides **optimum conditions** (Ch.12) for enzyme activity by maintaining a favourable temperature and pH. The pH (acidity or alkalinity) in each region of the gut is kept fairly constant by additions of acid or alkali. Chemical digestion occurs as a progressive process as food is moved through the gut; the main

Region of gut	Secretions	Examples of chemical digestion
Mouth	*Saliva* (from three pairs of *salivary glands*) contains *mucus* and the enzyme *salivary amylase*.	amylase Starch → maltose (pH 7)
Stomach	*Gastric juice* (from stomach wall) contains *hydrochloric acid* and enzymes including *pepsin*.	pepsin Protein → peptides (pH 2)
Duodenum	*Intestinal juice* (from duodenum wall) contains enzymes, including *maltase* and *amylase*.	maltase Maltose → glucose (pH 8.5) amylase Starch → maltose (pH 7)
	Pancreatic juice (from pancreas) contains alkaline secretions and also enzymes, including *amylase, trypsin, lipase*.	lipase Fats → fatty acids + glycerol (pH 7)
	Bile (from liver) contains *bile salts*.	Bile salts *emulsify* lipids; they reduce lipids into small droplets, increasing the surface area for digestion.

Fig.15.20 Summary of the main stages of digestion in humans

stages of this process are summarised in Fig.15.20.

Each region of the first part of the gut tends to be specialised for a particular chemical process. Enzymes can be grouped according to the type of food that they break down:

Carbohydrases, e.g. amylase, maltase, break down carbohydrates.

Proteases, e.g. pepsin, trypsin break down proteins.

Lipases, e.g. lipase, digest fats and oils.

Food is mixed with enzymes by muscular movements of the gut, which also cause physical digestion (see above) to take place. Food remains briefly in the mouth before being **swallowed**; conditions in the stomach are very acid (pH 2) and any digestion of starch by amylase is temporarily prevented. Food is held (by sphincter muscles) in the stomach for about four hours. This allows protein to be digested. A mucus lining prevents the lining of the stomach (which contains protein) from being digested, or damaged by the acid conditions. The acidic mixture in the stomach is called *chyme*. This is later neutralised in the duodenum by alkaline secretions from the pancreas; the mixture then becomes known as *chyle*. Digestion is mostly completed in the duodenum.

(c) ABSORPTION

Most absorption of nutrients occurs in the **ileum** which is adapted by having the blood and lymphatic **transport systems** (Ch.12) to carry absorbed materials to the rest of the body. Another important adaptation is the *large internal surface area* of the ileum. This is achieved in several ways:

(i) *Length*. The ileum is a comparatively long part of the gut. In humans the ileum is about 5 m; this represents about 45 per cent of the total length of the gut.

(ii) *Villi*. Numerous (about 30 million/mm^3.) 'finger-like' projections increase the surface area; each *villus* has further projections called *microvilli*, producing a total surface area within the ileum of about 10 m^2. Each villus contains a *capillary network* (Ch.12) and also a *lacteal*, a branch of the lymphatic system.

Nutrients are absorbed through the lining of the ileum by *diffusion* or *active transport* (Ch.4), depending on the size of molecules and concentration gradients. Digested lipids are absorbed into the lymphatic system; all other nutrients, which are now water soluble, enter the blood system. Water enters the blood mostly in the **colon** (large intestine). Nutrients are **assimilated** (**utilized**) within the body in various ways, according to needs.

(d) EGESTION

After most water has been absorbed, the contents of the gut are known as **faeces**. These consist of any undigested material, mainly **cellulose**, combined with microbes, mucus and dead cells from the lining of the gut. This is passed out of the body through the anus during the process of **egestion**, or **defecation**. This should not be confused with **excretion** (Ch.11) which involves getting rid of the waste products of metabolism. Faeces are temporarily stored in the **rectum** and then egested at intervals.

(e) COMPARISON OF HERBIVOROUS AND CARNIVOROUS DIGESTION

Herbivores, e.g. sheep, rabbits, are animals whose diet consists mainly of plant material. **Carnivores**, e.g. cats, foxes, are animals whose diet consists mainly of animal material. **Omnivores**, including humans, are animals whose diet is mixed. Animals belonging to one of these groups often exhibit characteristic **adaptations** of the gut; these are summarised for herbivores and carnivores in Fig.15.21. In particular, the **skulls** of herbivores and of carnivores are quite distinctive. Some

Adaptation	Herbivore: e.g. sheep *(Ovis aries)*	Carnivore: e.g. cat *(Felis* spp.)
Feeding frequency	**Continuous:** also includes re-chewing partially digested food (**cud**).	*Occasional.* Food is more 'concentrated'.
Teeth	Incisors and canines absent in upper jaw. Gap (*diastema*) between front and back (cheek) teeth allows grass to be manipulated by the tongue. Premolar and molar teeth are ridged, for grinding. Teeth continue growing in adult.	Large canines used for seizing and killing prey. Some (*carnassial*) premolar and molar teeth are shaped for slicing; others, nearer the jaw attachment, are used for grinding.
Jaw attachment	Loose jaw attachment, allowing sideways jaw movement.	Tight jaw attachment, preventing disloation.
Stomach	'Stomach' consists of several chambers, allowing digestion of cellulose by symbiotic microbes.	Simpler stomach arrangement.
Length of gut	Relatively long	Relatively short

Fig.15.21 Some adaptations of herbivores and carnivores to diet

other important adaptations, such as sight are described elsewhere. Omnivores tend to have intermediate characteristics.

Saprophytic nutrition is used by simpler organisms, such as bacteria and fungi. It involves **external digestion** of dead and decaying food, outside the tissues of the feeding organism. Enzymes are secreted onto the food (**substrate**) and the products of digestion are then absorbed, along with nutrients which do not require digestion. Saprophytic organisms do not need a specialised gut for digestion. However, this may mean that conditions for the enzymes are not ideal. Some saprophytic organisms, e.g. certain bacteria, may become parasitic (see below) if there is a host available. Saprophytes are very important in **re-cycling minerals** in nature.

Saprophytic nutrition can be demonstrated in fungi such as common bread mould (*Rhizopus stolonifer*). This can be grown on starch agar jelly. It can be shown, by using iodine, that starch is digested around the strands (**hyphae**) of the mould which are embedded in the agar jelly. Areas of digestion will be coloured orange/yellow; undigested starch will be blue/black.

10 ⟩ PARASITIC NUTRITION

Parasitic nutrition is used by organisms called **parasites** in a close relationship with other organisms called **hosts**. The relationship is likely to be harmful to the host; in many cases the host may eventually die as a result. There are many different examples of parasites including all viruses and many bacteria (which may also be saprophytes, see above). Parasites include higher plants, which may not possess chlorophyll (see 'Autotrophic Nutrition') and animals.

Parasites are typically smaller than their host. Some, the **exoparasites**, live *outside* their host. Others, the **endoparasites**, live *within* their host. Parasites absorb nutrients directly from their host and do not require a gut for digestion. They often lack many other complex structures, too; however, parasites characteristically have complex life cycles.

EXAMINATION QUESTIONS

QUESTION 1
A well-watered geranium plant had one of its leaves covered with tin foil as shown in Fig.15.22. After three days the leaf was removed, decolourised with ethanol and treated with iodine solution as shown.

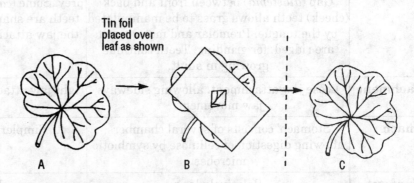

Tin foil placed over leaf as shown

A — Geranium leaf attached to plant well watered and kept in bright light

B

C — Three days later. Leaf is decolourised and treated with iodine solution

Fig.15.22

(a)   (i) What was the purpose of the tin foil in the experiment? (1 line) **1 mark**
(ii) Complete diagram C to show the areas stained black with iodine solution.
2 marks
(iii) Name the substance in the leaf which produces the black stain with iodine. (1 line) **1 mark**

(b)   Why should the tin foil in drawing B be fitted as shown to both sides of the leaf? (2 lines) **1 mark**

(c)   (i) Name the coloured substance removed by the ethanol. (1 line) **1 mark**
(ii) While the leaf is being decolourised, the tube containing ethanol is not heated directly over a Bunsen burner. Explain why. (2 lines) **1 mark**

Total 7 marks (LEAG)

QUESTION 2

A 22-year old woman kept a precise record of her food and drink intake for one day. The quantities of some major nutrients were calculated, and the totals compared with the average daily requirements of a woman of that age. The figures are summarised in the table (Fig. 15.23).

Meal	Item	Quantity	Energy (kJ)	Protein (g)	Fat (g)	Carbo-hydrate (g)	Calcium (mg)	Iron (mg)	Vitamin C (mg)
Breakfast	White bread	90 g	950	7	2	50	90	1	0
	Butter	15 g	450	0	12	0	2	0	0
	Jam	30 g	330	0	0	19	5	0	1
	Black coffee	1 cup	20	0	0	1	4	0	0
Lunch	Hamburger	150 g	1560	30	15	30	50	4	0
	Ice cream	100 g	800	4	12	20	130	0	1
	Fizzy drink	1 can	550	0	0	30	0	0	0
Evening meal	Sausages	75 g	1150	9	24	10	30	0.5	0
	Chips	200 g	2100	8	20	70	25	2	20
	Baked beans	220 g	600	10	1	20	100	2.5	4
	Apple pie	150 g	1800	5	25	60	60	1	1
	Cream	30 g	550	0.5	15	1	20	0	0
	Tea with milk	2 cups	200	2	4	6	100	0	0
Snacks	Chocolate	50 g	1200	5	20	25	1	1	0
	Peanuts	50 g	1200	15	25	5	30	1	0
TOTAL INTAKE FOR DAY			13460	95.5	175	347	766	13	27
AVERAGE DAILY REQUIREMENT			9400	58	*	*	600	14	30

Fig.15.23   *Amounts variable

(a) (i) By how much did the energy content of the day's diet exceed the average daily energy requirements of the 22-year old woman? **1 mark**

(ii) What would be the probable effect of this difference on an average woman of this age over a long time? **1 mark**

(iii) This woman could have a daily energy requirement much greater than average. Suggest *one* reason why this would be so. **2 marks**

(b) The recommended carbohydrate:fat ratio in a balanced diet is 5:1 by weight.

(i) Which individual meal in the day given in the table had a carbohydrate:fat ratio of exactly 5:1? **1 mark**

(ii) To the nearest whole number, what is the carbohydrate:fat ratio for the whole day's intake? **1 mark**

(iii) What effects may this proportion of fat in the daily diet have on the woman's circulatory system? **2 marks**

(c) *Excluding* coffee, tea and fizzy drinks, which of the items eaten during the day had the highest level of calcium per gram of food? Give the calcium content of this item in mg per g of food. **2 marks**

(d) Identify *one* nutrient in which the day's food intake is *deficient* and name a deficiency disease that may result if the woman's diet continues to provide too little of the nutrient. **1 mark**

(e) A sample of the woman's urine taken the morning *after* the day described above contained a high concentration of urea. How might this have been predicted from the information in the table? **1 mark**

Total 12 marks (LEAG)

QUESTION 3

A piece of knotted Visking tubing was filled with a mixture of starch solution and saliva. The open end was then sealed with a tight knot and the outside of the bag washed. The bag was then placed in a beaker of water kept at 37°C. This is shown in diagram A.

A control was set up in a similar way using starch solution and boiled saliva in a Visking tubing bag. This is shown in diagram B.

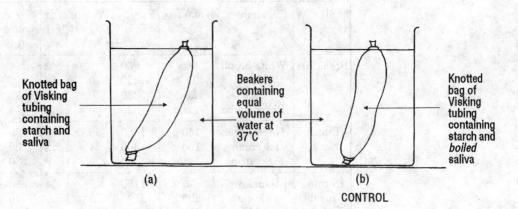

Knotted bag of Visking tubing containing starch and saliva

Beakers containing equal volume of water at 37°C

Knotted bag of Visking tubing containing starch and *boiled* saliva

(a)   (b)
CONTROL

After one hour the water in each beaker was tested for reducing sugar and starch.
In A the water contained reducing sugar but no starch. In B the water contained no reducing sugar and no starch.

(a)   Why was the bag washed before placing it in the beaker of water? (2 lines) **1 mark**
(b)   Why was a temperature of 37°C chosen for this experiment? (1 line) **1 mark**
(c)   From the observations made made in the experiment, what appears to be the action of saliva on starch? (3 lines) **2 marks**
(d)   Describe the test you would use to detect the presence of reducing sugar in the beaker of water. (3 lines) **2 marks**
(e)   Why was no reducing sugar found in the beaker of water in the control B? (1 line) **1 mark**
(f)   What does the experiment tell us about the properties of the Visking tubing? (2 lines) **2 marks**
(g)   Give *two* ways in which the Visking tubing used in this experiment is incomplete as a model of the human small intestine. (4 lines) **2 marks**
(h)   If the experiment was repeated at a lower temperature, it would take longer before reducing sugar appeared in the beaker. Give *two* reasons why this is so. (4 lines) **2 marks**

Total 13 marks (LEAG)

OUTLINE ANSWERS

ANSWER 1
(a)   (i) To exclude light.
       (ii)

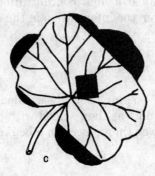

(iii) Starch
(b) To prevent light falling on either side of the leaf.
(c) (i) Chlorophyll
(ii) Ethanol is inflammable.

ANSWER 2
(a) (i) 4060 kJ (i.e. 13460 - 9400)
(ii) Gain weight (fat)
(iii) She may be pregnant, or be very active.
(b) (i) Breakfast (70:14)
(ii) 2:1 (347:175)
(iii) May cause blocked arteries, coronary thrombosis (heart attack).
(c) Chocolate; 2.4 mg/g (120÷50)
(d) Iron, anaemia; or vitamin C, scurvy
(e) Excess protein in the diet (presence of urea indicates that protein has been broken down).

ANSWER 3
(a) To remove any starch present on the outside of the bag
(b) This is the optimum temperature for the enzyme (amylase).
(c) It converts starch to a reducing sugar, which is a smaller molecule and can pass through the Visking tubing.
(d) Add Benedict's solution and boil; colour change blue→green→yellow→red.
(e) The enzyme contained in saliva was destroyed (denatured) by boiling, so starch is not converted to a reducing sugar.
(f) The Visking tubing is selectively permeable; small molecules (e.g. reducing sugar) can pass through, large molecules (e.g. starch) cannot pass through.
(g) (i) No active transport of molecules.
(ii) No transport system to remove molecules.
(h) (i) Enzyme activity would be slower.
(ii) Diffusion rate would be slower.

COURSEWORK – A STEP FURTHER

Below are suggestions for extending some experiments already described in this chapter. Experimental procedure should include controls (Appendix 3) and care must be taken to reduce possible inaccuracies as far as possible. Results should be suitably presented (Appendix 2).

EXPERIMENT 1

TO INVESTIGATE RESPIRATION AND PHOTOSYNTHESIS IN DIFFERENT FOODS

Two variations are suggested here; in each case, leaf discs are used. These can be most easily cut from leaves by using a large cork borer. Leaf discs of the same area allow experimental comparisons to be made more fairly. The leaf discs need to be supported on cotton wool within the test tubes.

(a) **Amount of chlorophyll**
Leaf discs from variegated leaves e.g. of ivy (*Hedera*) can be used to demonstrate the effect of different amounts of chlorophyll on the rate of photosynthesis. The resulting colour of the bicarbonate indicator can be noted.

(b) **Compensation point**
The rates of photosynthesis and respiration are very similar in dim light; this is the compensation point. Dim light conditions can be produced by wrapping layers of muslin around one of the test tubes.

> **EXPERIMENT 2**

TO INVESTIGATE THE VITAMIN C CONTENT IN DIFFERENT FOODS

Vitamin C (ascorbic acid) is tested for by the blue dye DCPIP, which is 'bleached' in the presence of the vitamin.

(a) **Comparison of the amounts of vitamin C in fruit juices**

The relative amounts of vitamin C in different fruit juices can be compared. Drops of fruit juice are carefully added to a certain amount of the dye until the blue colour disappears. The number of drops used in each case is noted.

(b) **The effect of cooking on vitamin C content**

It is estimated that about 75 per cent of any vitamin C present in a food is destroyed by cooking. This effect can be investigated with equivalent amounts of a fruit juice before and after boiling. The vitamin C content is estimated as above.

> **EXPERIMENT 3**

TO INVESTIGATE THE ENERGY CONTENT IN DIFFERENT FOODS

The experiment can involve:

(a) the use of different foods, e.g. raisins, currants

(b) improvement of the experimental technique, so that the energy value for the peanut is closer to the 'official' value of 24 kJ.

> **EXPERIMENT 4**

TO INVESTIGATE THE EFFECT OF TOOTHPASTE

If hard-boiled eggs are placed in dilute hydrochloric acid [CARE: acid is corrosive], the shell will dissolve. This is in some respects similar to dental decay, caused by acid from plaque. Eggs can be completely or partially coated with different brands of toothpaste. This may delay or prevent the effects of the acid.

> **EXPERIMENT 5**

TO INVESTIGATE THE ACTIVITY OF SALIVARY AMYLASE

Salivary amylase converts starch to the reducing sugar maltose; this should occur if 5 cm^3 of 2 per cent starch solution and 2 cm^3 saliva are mixed in a test tube. The progress of this reaction can be followed by using iodine and/or Benedict's solution. The time taken for the conversion to take place can be noted for various conditions, e.g. temperature, including boiling.

> **FURTHER INFORMATION**

The following addresses may be useful in finding out more about nutrition and food production.

British Nutrition Foundation:
15 Belgrave Square,
London SW1X 8PS
Tel. 01-235-4904

Butter Information Council:
Tubs Hill House
London Road
Sevenoaks
Kent TN13 1BL
Tel. 0732-460060

Colgate Hoyt Professional Dental
  Service
Dept DA
76 Oxford Street
London W1A 1EN
Tel. 01-580-2030

Flora Project for Heart Disease
  Prevention
24-28 Bloomsbury Way
London WC1A 2PX
Tel. 01-831-6262

Gibbs Oral Hygiene Service
Hesketh House
43/45 Portman Square
London W1A 1DY
Tel. 01-486-1200

STUDENT'S ANSWER – EXAMINER'S COMMENTS

The table below shows the food value of a school lunch eaten by a 16-year-old girl.

Food eaten	Protein in g	Carbohydrate in g	Fat in g	Iron in mg	Vitamin C in mg
Sausages	9	5	24	1	0
Chips	8	70	20	2	20
Baked beans	10	20	1	3	4
Apple pie	5	60	25	1	1
Ice cream	2	20	12	0	0
Fizzy drink	0	30	0	0	0

"Correct answers."

(a) (i) In this meal, which food gave the girl most protein?

baked beans

(1 mark)

"Incorrect answer; the main function of protein is for growth and repair."

(ii) Name *one* other food not eaten in this meal which is rich in protein.

cheese

(1 mark)

(iii) Why does the girl need protein?

for energy

(1 mark)

"Correct answer, though *units* should also be given."

(b) (i) The total energy value of this meal is 6600 kJ.
In one day the girl needs 9600 kJ.
If she ate this meal, how many *more* kJ would she need in that day?

3000

(1 mark)

"More precisely, excess food would be stored, resulting in obesity."

(ii) What would happen if she eats much more than 9600 kJ of food every day?

She would get fat

(1 mark)

"Correct answers."

(iii) A lot of energy comes from carbohydrate and fat.
Name the *two* foods in this meal which gave her most energy.

chips
apple pie

(2 marks)

(c) The girl needs 14mg of iron and 25mh of Vitamin C each day to keep healthy.
(i) How much of her daily iron needs did this meal give her?

"Correct."

7mg

(1 mark)

"Incorrect; the answer should be 25mg."

(ii) How much of her daily Vitamin C needs did this meal give her?

24 mg

(1 mark)

(iii) What will happen if she does not have enough iron and Vitamin C?

"Correct answers."

Not enough iron may cause ...... anaemia

Not enough Vitamin C may cause ...... scurvy

(2 marks)

(d) Why sould she eat fibre (roughage) every day?

to stop constipation

(1 mark)
(Total 12 marks)

LEAG

ENVIRONMENT: ABIOTIC FACTORS

ABIOTIC FACTORS
CLIMATIC FACTORS
EDAPHIC (SOIL) FACTORS
CLASSIFICATION OF SOIL TYPES
CIRCULATION OF MINERALS

GETTING STARTED

The **environment** consists of abiotic and biotic factors. **Abiotic** (non-living) **factors** are the *physical* and *chemical* components of the environment. **Biotic** (living) **factors** are the *biological* components of the environment. Both abiotic and biotic aspects of the environment affect the distribution and relative numbers of different types of organism.

The study of the environment is called **ecology**. The natural 'ecological unit' is the **ecosystem**, which is a relatively stable outcome of an interaction between abiotic and biotic factors. Each ecosystem therefore has fairly characteristic living and non-living components. Examples of ecosystems include ponds, woodlands and grasslands.

The main abiotic factors for a *terrestrial* (land) environment can be grouped in the following way:

(1) **Climatic factors**, including temperature, light, rainfall and wind. These can be quite variable.

(2) **Edaphic (soil) factors**. Soil is an important link between the abiotic and biotic parts of the terrestrial environment. The soil affects plant growth directly, for instance because of the amount of water and minerals that are made available.

(3) **Circulation of elements**. Many elements are necessary for life and are obtained directly from the abiotic environment by plants or from the biotic environment by animals. These nutrients are liberated again from living or dead tissue and become available in the abiotic environment again. This cycling of substances such as carbon, nitrogen and water is essential for the continuance of life.

ESSENTIAL PRINCIPLES

1 > **ABIOTIC FACTORS**

Abiotic (non-living, 'physical') **factors** provide the raw materials for life, including nutrients for plant growth and the release of energy, generally involving the absorption of oxygen. Substances are exchanged between organisms and their non-living environment; **nutrients** are constantly **recycled** and **energy** flows between organisms and their environment (Fig. 16.1). There is therefore a considerable amount of interaction between the biotic and abiotic components of the environment. Organisms are **adapted** (Ch.9) to their environment and both the **distribution** and **abundance** of species is affected by abiotic, as well as biotic,

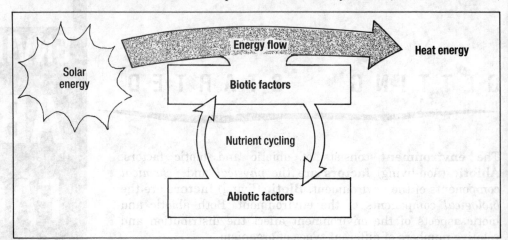

Fig.16.1 Interaction between abiotic and biotic factors

factors.

ECOLOGY

Ecology is the study of natural environments, and often includes a study of ecosystems. An **ecosystem** (Ch.17) is a natural 'unit' in ecology involving the interaction of abiotic and biotic components and consisting of a fairly distinct **community** of organisms.

THE TERRESTRIAL ENVIRONMENT

Most organisms live either in a *terrestrial* (land) or an *aquatic* (water) ecosystem; some organisms are adapted to living in both environments.

There is often more variation of abiotic factors in *terrestrial* (land) ecosystems than in aquatic ecosystems; this is because water provides fairly stable conditions. Variations in environmental conditions are significant because they result in an uneven distribution of different organisms; the study of this forms the basis of ecology (see Ch.17).

The main abiotic factors, particularly for terrestrial ecosystems are:
1 Climatic factors
2 Edaphic (soil) factors
3 Circulation of elements

2 > **CLIMATIC FACTORS**

Climatic factors include temperature, light, rainfall and wind; variations in these occur in different regions of the world.

(a) TEMPERATURE

The *climatic range* of temperature is about -60°C to 60°C. Very few organisms can tolerate extremes of temperature, however. Most organisms live within a *metabolic range* of about 0°C–45°C. Below this, enzymes are fairly inactive; above this range, proteins (including enzymes) are permanently changed (**denatured**, Ch.4). Organisms are generally more efficient when their temperature is about 40°C; mammals and birds maintain their body temperature at a relatively high *constant* value and this allows them to operate more successfully in colder environments. Plants are generally more tolerant than animals of extremes of temperature in the environment. However, temperature is important in affecting **transpiration** in plants.

Fluctuations in air/land temperature occur in most regions of the world. In *temperate* (cooler) regions these fluctuations tend to be *annual* (*seasonal* as well as *diurnal*). In *tropical* (hotter) regions temperature variations are more *diurnal* (*daily*). Organisms adapt to variations in temperature in different ways, for instance in their breeding cycles. Temperature tends to be fairly constant in many aquatic ecosystems, especially where there is a large volume of water, e.g. lakes, oceans; temperature decreases with depth in such water.

(b) LIGHT

Light and heat tend to vary together because both are part of **solar radiation** in natural ecosystems. Variations in light include **intensity**,**duration** and **quality** (wavelength). Light is essential for all life. Plants need light for **photosynthesis**; this is the means by which plants obtain their food. Photosynthesis also provides food directly or indirectly for all other organisms as well as releasing oxygen (which can be used for respiration) into the environment. Most plants grow towards the maximum available light and many animals are sensitive to the presence of light (see Ch.13) in their environment. In aquatic ecosystems, light decreases with depth.

(c) RAINFALL

Water is made available to land organisms from the atmosphere in various ways, particularly as rain; this is part of the **water cycle**. Water is essential for all life and is an important factor in determining the distribution of organisms in terrestrial ecosystems. The availability of water depends on various factors including rainfall, temperature and the drainage of soil.

(d) WIND

Air movements are caused by temperature differences in the environment. Wind is particularly important in plants, for instance in **pollination** and **seed dispersal** and in determining the rate of **transpiration**.

3 EDAPHIC (SOIL) FACTORS

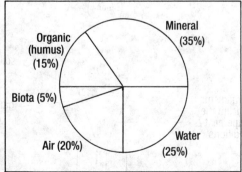

Fig.16.2 Components of soil (the appropriate proportion of each component is given)

Soil consists of particles of rock, organic material, air spaces and water. Soil is a **habitat** for various soil organisms and is very important for plant roots for anchorage and also for the absorption of water and minerals. Soil represents the result of complex interactions between physical, chemical and biological aspects of the environment. The main components of the non-living part of soil are rock particles and soluble **mineral ions**, **humus**, **air** and **water**. Soil also contains an important living component, sometimes known as

biota (Fig. 16.2). The relative proportion of each of these components varies considerably and results in different types of soils having characteristic properties (Fig. 16.6), mainly determined by the size of the rock particles.

(a) MINERAL COMPONENT

Soil minerals are derived from the parent rock by **weathering** (**erosion**); the rock fragments may be blown or washed away. The presence of plant roots may be very important in holding the soil together. The size of the mineral particles determines **physical properties**, such as air and water content and also drainage.

Experiment to investigate the drainage rate of a soil

The rate at which water drains through a moist soil can be determined by the method shown in Fig. 16.3. The amount of water which drains through the soil in a particular time is noted. This is the **permeability** (**porosity**) of the soil. The soil should be loosely placed in the filter funnel. Different types of soil can be

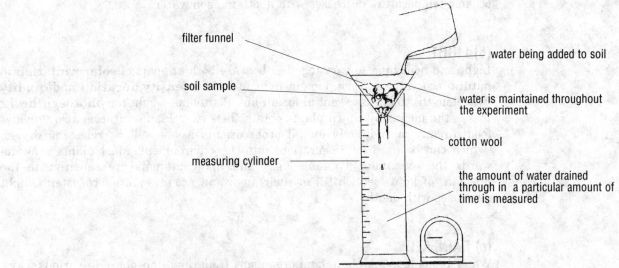

filter funnel

water being added to soil

soil sample

water is maintained throughout the experiment

cotton wool

measuring cylinder

the amount of water drained through in a particular amount of time is measured

Fig.16.3 Determination of the drainage rate of soil

compared by this method, provided similar volumes of each sample are used.

The rock parts of soil also affect the **chemical properties**; for instance in the availability of inorganic nutrients for plant growth and soil pH (acidity or alkalinity). The mineral component of a soil sample can be determined experimentally (see below).

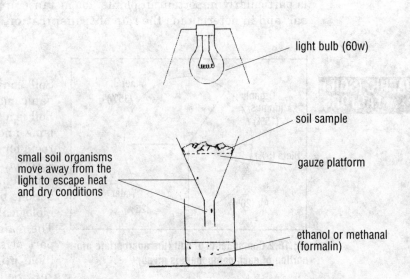

light bulb (60w)

soil sample

gauze platform

small soil organisms move away from the light to escape heat and dry conditions

ethanol or methanal (formalin)

Fig.16.4 The tullgren funnel

(b) ORGANIC (HUMUS) COMPONENT

The organic component of soil is derived from the **decomposition** of dead organisms. The organic component of a soil can be determined experimentally (see below). The process of humus formation is important because it allows minerals to be recycled, for example carbon and nitrogen (see below). Decomposition of organic material involves the activity of two main groups of soil organisms:

(i) **Detritus feeders**. Detritus ('debris') feeders are mostly invertebrates which break up organic matter and also add their own faeces to the soil. The activities of detritus feeders increases the surface area of the organic material which can then be further broken down by microbes. Examples: earthworm (*Lumbricus*), mites (*Trombicula*), centipede (*Lithobius forficatus*). These may be separated from the soil using a Tullgren funnel (Fig. 16.4).

(ii) **Saprophytic organisms**. Saprophytic organisms include fungi and many bacteria. They obtain their nutrients in solution from decaying organic material.

Saprophytes are essential in the recycling of nutrients (see below).

(c) AIR COMPONENT

Air is important in soil because it provides **oxygen** for respiring organisms such as soil organisms and also for plant roots. Spaces which are not occupied by air

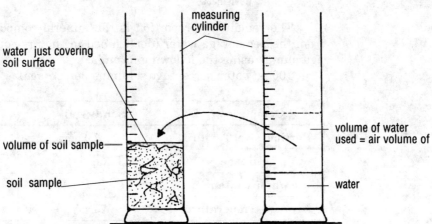

Fig.16.5 Determination of the proportion of air in a soil sample

may otherwise be filled with water, especially in poorly-drained soil. This can prevent the activity of **aerobic microbes** in the soil and limit the breakdown of organic materials in the soil. The result can be **peat** which contains undecayed organic matter. Conditions in peat soil are typically acid and with low amounts of calcium.

Experiment to determine the proportion of air in soil

Water is gradually added to a known volume of soil until it just covers the surface of the soil (Fig. 16.5); the water fills any air spaces and the volume of water used corresponds with the approximate air content of the soil. This can be calculated as a percentage of the total soil and water volume using the following formula:

$$\frac{\text{water volume} \quad \times \quad 100}{\text{water volume} \quad + \quad \text{soil}}$$

> rather than simply learning formulae such as this, it is worth understanding what the formula actually does

(d) WATER COMPONENT

The water content of soil is often quite variable, depending for instance on **rainfall** and the **drainage rate** of soil. Drainage itself depends on particle size (see below) and also such factors as **slope**. Water may remove soluble mineral ions by *leaching* as it drains. Drained water may rise by **capillarity**; water is attracted to soil particles. The availability of soil affects plant growth and also the type of plant present; plants have different adaptations for obtaining water from the soil and for conserving it, such as with the arrangement of root systems. The presence of water in soil may have a *cooling* effect; this may inhibit early germination or the activities of soil organisms.

Experiment to determine the proportion of water in soil

A sample of fresh soil is weighed (= **fresh mass**) and then gently heated in an oven at 100°C for about 48 hours. The soil is then reweighed (= **dry mass**). For added accuracy the sample should be reweighed repeatedly until a constant mass is reached. The percentage of water in the soil can be calculated using the following formula:

$$\frac{\text{fresh mass} - \text{dry mass}}{\text{fresh mass}} \times 100$$

Experiment to determine the proportion of organic and mineral components in soil

The **organic component** of a soil sample can be found by continuing to heat the soil from the previous experiment, using a much more intense heat. The humus will burn and there will be a further loss in mass; the remaining mass (= *ash mass*) consists only of the rock particle component of the soil. The percentage of organic material (humus) in the sample can be calculated from the following formula:

$$\frac{\text{dry mass} - \text{ash mass}}{\text{fresh mass}} \times 100$$

The remaining proportion is the mineral component and can be calculated from the percentage water (determined in the previous experiment) and percentage humus using the following formula:

100 – (water percentage + humus percentage)

Comparison	Sandy soil	Clay soil
Particle size; Texture	0.02–2.0 mm	Less than 0.002 mm
Drainage	Rapid	Slow
Water content	Low	High, easily waterlogged
Average temperature	Warm	Cold
Air content	High, good aeration	Low, poor aeration
Mineral content	Fairly low	Fairly high
Cultivation	'Light'	'Heavy'

Fig.16.6 Summary of the characteristics of sand and clay soils

(e) mineral ion component

Many soluble ions (Appendix 1) are very important in plants and, indirectly, to animals. Examples of such ions are nitrates, magnesium, sulphates and phosphates. The relative amounts of these ions varies according to the soil type. Also, some ions are easily leached from well-drained soils.

4 ▶ CLASSIFICATION OF SOIL TYPES

Soils are classified in terms of their *average particle size* or *texture*; this is because physical and chemical properties derive to a large extent from the size of mineral particles which they contain. The characteristics of two quite different soils are summarised in Fig. 16.6.

Both sand and clay are extreme examples of soils; each provides a combination of advantages and disadvantages for **cultivation**. **Silty soil** or **loam** ('garden soil') has an intermediate texture and therefore combines the properties of sandy and clay soils; loam provides generally suitable conditions for cultivation. Both sandy and clay soils can be improved by adding humus, for example as **manure**. Clay can be improved by the addition of **lime** (calcium oxide) which causes soil particles to stick together, or **flocculate**, forming a crumb structure.

A soil sample (about 25–30 g) can be shaken with some water (about 200 ml) in a 250 ml measuring cylinder. The soil is allowed to settle; the largest (heaviest) particles tend to settle first, followed by smaller particles. The process of **sedimentation** reveals the relative proportion of different particles in a particular type of soil (Fig. 16.7). The technique can be used to compare different types of soil.

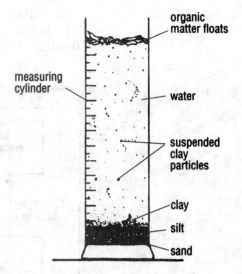

Fig.16.7 Sedimentation of soil particles

The circulation of minerals provides an important link between the abiotic and biotic environment. Minerals from the environment are required directly by plants and indirectly by all other organisms. Minerals are returned to the environment from organisms by **excretion**, **egestion** and by **death and decay** of tissues. The circulation of mineral elements, also called **biogeochemical cycling**, involves chemical, physical and biological processes. Examples include **carbon**, **nitrogen** and **water**.

(a) THE CARBON CYCLE

Carbon is a component of all organic molecules and is essential for all life. The

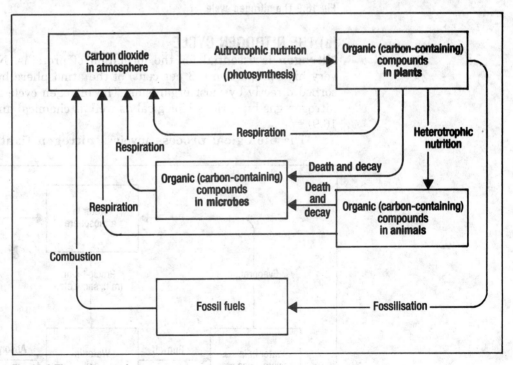

Fig.16.8 The carbon cycle

> make a particular effort to learn and understand the carbon, nitrogen and water cycles. You may be asked to identify particular processes occuring within them

carbon cycle mainly involves the conversion of the inorganic molecule carbon dioxide to or from organic molecules which are formed within the tissues of organisms. The carbon cycle is summarised in Fig. 16.8.

The concentration of carbon dioxide in air is fairly constant; however, there is a possibility of levels gradually increasing because of the increased burning of fossil fuels or because vegetation is being reduced, for instance by the clearing of tropical rain forests, which decreases **carbon fixation** by photosynthesis. An increase in atmospheric carbon dioxide would 'trap' retransmitted solar energy which might otherwise be lost into space. This is called the **greenhouse effect** and would raise the earth's average surface temperature. One possible outcome of this is the melting of polar ice caps and an increase in sea levels, resulting in flooding of low-lying land throughout the world.

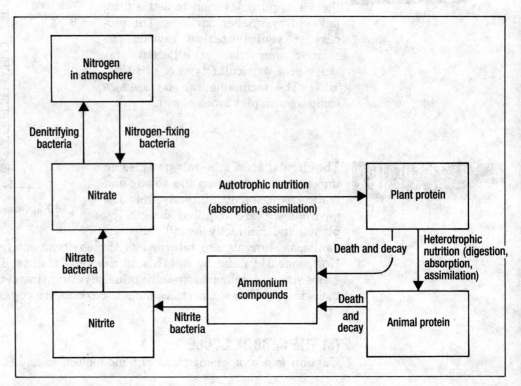

Fig.16.9 The nitrogen cycle

(b) THE NITROGEN CYCLE

Nitrogen is essential for the formation of proteins. Nitrogen gas represents a very high proportion (78 per cent) of the atmosphere but nitrogen cannot be absorbed directly by most organisms. The nitrogen cycle involves the conversion of nitrogen gas by various biological as well as chemical and physical processes (Fig. 16.9).

The **biological process** involves **nitrogen fixation**, either by free-living

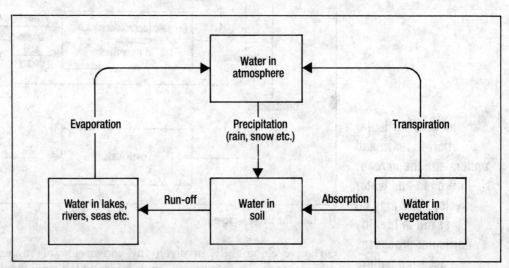

Fig.16.10 The water cycle

microbes or by microbes living in a *symbiotic* relationship with certain plants, especially **legumes**. Legumes, for example pea (*Pisum*) and clover (*Trifolium*), develop **root nodules** within which **nitrogen-fixing bacteria** live. The resulting **ammonia** and **nitrate** can be absorbed by plants which use them to make amino acids. This organic form of nitrogen is then available directly or indirectly for animals.

Nitrogen also enters the abiotic environment by the **decomposition** of organic material by fungi and bacteria in soil. Decomposition results in the release of ammonia (**ammonification**) which is converted to nitrate (**nitrification**) bacteria. Nitrate may then be absorbed by plants. Some nitrate is lost by **leaching** (see above) or by bacteria which convert it back to nitrogen gas (**denitrification**).

Chemical and physical processes which converts nitrogen gas into nitrate include the action of **lightning** and the production of **nitrate fertiliser**. The amount of nitrate added to the soil as fertilisr is about the same as that added by nitrogen fixation. The production of nitrate fertiliser is energy-intensive in production and application. Fertilisers dramatically increase crop yield, and this is important as a means of providing enough food for a growing population (see Ch.17). However, increased growth rates of crops remove more minerals from the soil and these may not all be replaced. Excess nitrate may be washed off agricultural land and result in an over-growth of aquatic plants (**eutrophication**).

(c) THE WATER CYCLE

Water is essential for all life. The water cycle involves mostly physical processes such as **evaporation** and **rainfall**. Transpiration from plants also contributes to the water cycle (Fig. 16.10). Rain dissolves some **pollutants** in the air and these are then deposited on the earth's surface onto soil and vegetation and into water. An example of this is **sulphur dioxide**, from burning fossil fuels; this is deposited as dilute sulphuric acid, in **acid rain**.

EXAMINATION QUESTIONS

QUESTION 1

The drawing below shows the layers in a woodland.

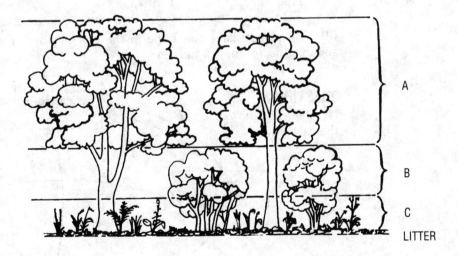

(a)   Name the layers shown by the letter A, B and C. (3 lines) **3 marks**

(b)   (i) State how the light intensity in layer C differs from the light intensity in layer A during daylight. (1 line) **1 mark**

(ii) How might this difference in light intensity affect the plants in layer C? (3 lines) **2 marks**

Total 6 marks (LEAG)

QUESTION 2

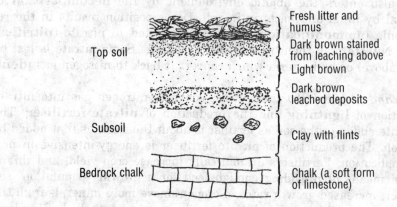

Top soil {
Fresh litter and humus
Dark brown stained from leaching above
Light brown

Subsoil {
Dark brown leached deposits
Clay with flints

Bedrock chalk {
Chalk (a soft form of limestone)

The diagram shows a section through the soil found in an area of forest growing on chalk. The forest contains oak, beech and sweet chestnut trees.

(a)   There is a deep layer of litter and humus at the surface of the soil.

(i) What does the litter come from? (2 lines) **1 mark**

(ii) What is humus? (1 line) **1 mark**

(iii) How is humus formed? (1 line) **1 mark**

(iv) Eventually the litter becomes a part of the topsoil. Name a group of organisms responsible for this. (1 line) **1 mark**

(b) **After a period of heavy rain, the soil** becomes very water logged. Using the information in the diagram above suggest why this happens. (2 lines) **1 mark**

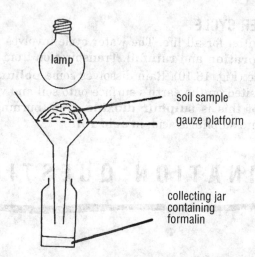

lamp

soil sample
gauze platform

collecting jar containing formalin

(c)   The apparatus shown was used in an experiment to investigate the numbers and variety of organisms found in topsoil and in subsoil.

(i) What is the apparatus called? (1 line) **1 mark**

(ii) Why is it important to use equal amounts of topsoil and subsoil in the experiment? (2 lines) **1 mark**

(iii) What is the purpose of the lamp? (2 lines) **2 marks**

(d)   More organisms are found in the top soil than in the subsoil. Give *two* reason for this. (4 lines) **2 marks**

Total 11 marks (LEAG)

QUESTION 3

The diagram shows the carbon cycle in nature.

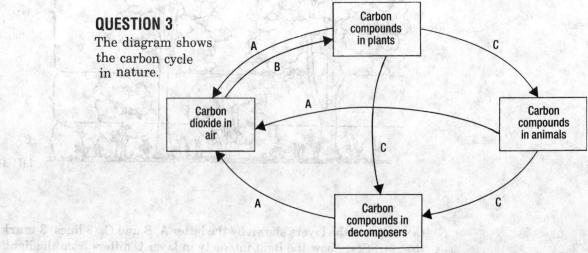

(a)   Name the process shown by the three arrows marked A. (1 line) **1 mark**

(b)   Name the process shown by the arrow marked B. (1 line) **1 mark**

(c)   Name the process shown by the three arrows marked C. (1 line) **1 mark**

Total 3 marks (SEG)

QUESTION 4

The diagram below shows part of the nitrogen cycle in a woodland. The labelled arrows represent different processes.

In the table, write the name of a process occurring at each labelled arrow. Two lines have been completed already.

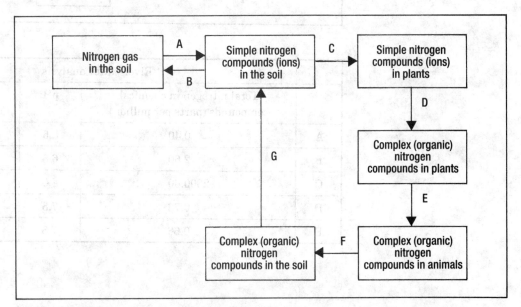

Arrow label	Process
A	
B	Denitrification
C	
D	Protein synthesis
E	
F	
G	

Total 5 marks (LEAG)

QUESTION 5

The map shows a river flowing through farms Y and Z.

Farmer Y changed from beef to dairy cattle. His herd no longer stayed all day in the fields but came twice a day to the farm buildings to be milked. Farmer Z had a fish farm and kept his fish in tanks filled with water from the river. His fish began to die. Scientists analysed the river water at A, B, C, D and E along the river. Their results are shown in the table.

(a) (i) What *three* factors shown by the table could have caused the death of Farmer Z's fish? **1 mark**

(ii) Which factor do you think the most likely to have caused the death of Farmer Z's fish? Why would this factor have caused the death of his fish? **2 marks**

(b) Suggest *one* explanation each for:

(i) The rise in nitrogen compounds between A and C. (**2 marks**)

(ii) The fall in nitrogen compounds between C and D. **2 marks**

(iii) The low pH at C? **2 marks**

(iv) The low oxygen content at D. **2 marks**

(c) Farmer Y's cows had polluted the river.

(i) What is pollution? **1 mark**

(ii) Suggest *one* way in which pollution by the cows could be reduced. **2 marks**

(iii) Instead of fish, Farmer Z wanted to grow watercress in his tanks, but the local health authority would not let him sell it. Why not? **1 mark**

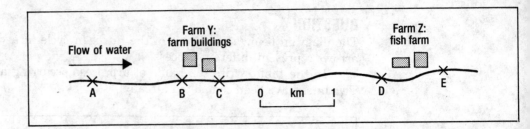

	River-water analysis		
	Total nitrogen in chemical compounds (parts per million)	pH	Dissolved oxygen (parts per million)
A	0.40	8.5	10.0
B	2.60	6.8	3.6
C	2300.00	4.0	10.0
D	0.76	7.8	1.2
E	0.66	7.8	4.0

Total 15 marks (SEG)

OUTLINE ANSWERS

ANSWER 1
(a)　A = tree (canopy); B = shrub; C = herb
(b)　(i) The intensity will be lower at C than at A.
(ii) A lower light intensity would reduce the rate of photosynthesis and therefore growth; also the need for early development in C-layer plants.

ANSWER 2
(a)　(i) Litter comes from fallen leaves and twigs, bark, etc.
(ii) Humus is organic material.
(iii) Humus is formed from the decomposition of plant and animal tissues by detritus feeders and saprophytic organisms in the soil.
(iv) Detritus feeders, e.g. earthworms.
(b)　The soil contains a layer of clay which prevents rapid drainage.
(c)　(i) Tullgren funnel
(ii) To allow a fair comparison.

(iii) To create conditions of light, heat, dry soil which the soil organisms move away from.

(d) There is more organic material in the topsoil; conditions such as warmth, oxygen and moisture are more favourable.

ANSWER 3

(a) Respiration
(b) Photosynthesis
(c) Nutrition.

ANSWER 4

A = nitrogen fixation, C = absorption, E = nutrition, F = excretion, egestion, death G = decomposition, decay.

ANSWER 5

(a) (i) Nitrogen, pH, dissolved oxygen
(ii) Low amounts of dissolved oxygen; oxygen is needed for respiration.
(b) (i) Excretion, egestion from cattle
(ii) Nitrogen is absorbed by various aquatic organisms.
(iii) Acids from excretion, decomposition
(iv) Oxygen is used by the increased activity of aquatic organisms, including bacteria.
(c) (i) Pollution is the addition of an unnatural and potentially harmful concentration of a substance in the environment.
(ii) Products of excretion and egestion could be diverted away from the river or collected, then perhaps used as organic fertiliser on the land.
(iii) Watercress could become contaminated with bacteria if grown in these conditions.

COURSEWORK – A STEP FURTHER

Two projects are suggested; each requires a suitable experimental design (Appendix 3) and, if the experiment is conducted, any results should be presented in an appropriate way (Appendix 2).

INVESTIGATION OF VARIATION IN PLANT GROWTH IN DIFFERENT LIGHT CONDITIONS

Plants may become adapted during their growth and development to different abiotic conditions, including light. Stinging nettle (*Urtica dioica*) plants growing in shade often have obvious differences compared with nettle plants growing in sunny conditions. Suitable plants for this comparison are those which are growing in conditions which are very similar other than with respect to light, for instance 'shade' plants growing in a wood and 'sun' plants growing outside the wood nearby. Plants should be chosen randomly (see Ch.17) for this investigation. Many of the differences between 'shade' and 'sun' plants can be measured. Here are some suggestions:

– average plant height
– average leaf area
– average number of leaves per plant
– average distance between leaves along stem (internodal distance)

1 ▷ PROJECT 1

Write a complete account of the investigation, including references to any difficulties encountered or any criticisms of the techniques used.

COMPARISON OF SOILS FROM TWO DIFFERENT HABITATS

There are many features of soils which can be compared experimentally. Any combination of the following could be attempted, using small soil samples and without doing obvious damage to the environment:

> drainage rates
> – soil organisms
> – air content
> – water content
> – humus content
> – mineral content
> – texture (by sedimentation)

2 ▷ PROJECT 2

Further analysis could include:

> – soil temperature (different depths)
> – capillarity of soils, using open glass columns filled with soil; water can be observed 'climbing' up the soil
> – chemical analysis of pH and the more common minerals, using a soil testing kit (obtainable for instance from garden centres).

A complete account of the investigation should be written, including a summary of results and conclusions.

The following publications may be useful for an increased understanding of the abiotic environment:

> '*Ecology of Soil Organisms*', Alison Leadley Brown (Heinemann, 1978)
> '*A Field Approach to Biology*', (Pupils' Guide), R. W. Wilson and D. F. Wright (Heinemann, 1972)
> '*Fieldwork Projects in Biology*', Marjorie Hingley, (Blandford, 1979)
> '*School Grounds: Some Ecological Enquiries*' P. F. Jenkins (Heinemann, 1973)
> '*Techniques and Fieldwork in Ecology*', (Bell and Hyman, 1987)

3 ▷ FURTHER INFORMATION

STUDENT'S ANSWER – EXAMINER'S COMMENTS

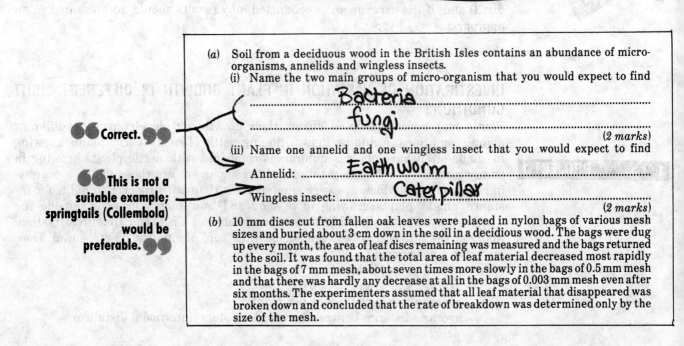

66 Correct. 99

66 This is not a suitable example; springtails (Collembola) would be preferable. 99

(a) Soil from a deciduous wood in the British Isles contains an abundance of micro-organisms, annelids and wingless insects.
(i) Name the two main groups of micro-organism that you would expect to find

Bacteria
fungi

(2 marks)

(ii) Name one annelid and one wingless insect that you would expect to find

Annelid: Earthworm

Wingless insect: Caterpillar

(2 marks)

(b) 10 mm discs cut from fallen oak leaves were placed in nylon bags of various mesh sizes and buried about 3 cm down in the soil in a deciduous wood. The bags were dug up every month, the area of leaf discs remaining was measured and the bags returned to the soil. It was found that the total area of leaf material decreased most rapidly in the bags of 7 mm mesh, about seven times more slowly in the bags of 0.5 mm mesh and that there was hardly any decrease at all in the bags of 0.003 mm mesh even after six months. The experimenters assumed that all leaf material that disappeared was broken down and concluded that the rate of breakdown was determined only by the size of the mesh.

(i) List the organisms named in your answer to (a) in the appropriate part of the following table.

Size of mesh	Organisims which could NOT pass through the mesh
7 mm	Caterpillar (if big and fat)
0.5 mm	Earthworm. Caterpillar
0.0003 mm	earthworm. caterpillar

(4 marks)

> **66** This is a very muddled answer. An improved answer would be: 7mm – earthworms; 0.5mm – springtails; 0.003mm – fungi. **99**

(ii) Comment on the assumption and conclusion of the experimenters stating clearly what criticisms may be made of them.

The rate of breakdown was determined by the amount of animals small enough to enter. Not all the leaf material will have been broken down. It will have been (eaten) washed away (soluble bits) by water. The rate of breakdown will also be determined by the season and the temperature and other food levels to determine the number of micro-organisms.

(4 marks)

> **66** This would be part of the breakdown process. **99**

> **66** This is a good, complete answer, showing a fairly thorough understanding. **99**

(c) Examination of the faeces of millipedes (small herbivorous arthropods) feeding on fallen oak leaves revealed that their faeces were very similar to the leaf litter except that the oak leaves were now in very small fragments. In view of this finding an investigation was carried out on the rate of carbon dioxide release from entire oak leaf litter, ground up oak leaf litter and millipede faeces. The following results were obtained.

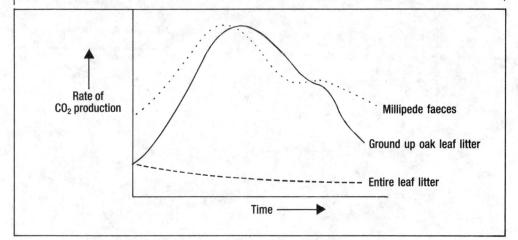

(i) The rate of carbon dioxide release was taken as a measure of the extent of microbial activity. Explain the reasoning behind this.

Respiration provides the energy for the microbial activity and it produces Carbon dioxide.

> **66** Correct. **99**

(ii) In view of the information provided in this and in earlier sections of the question, put forward a hypothesis to explain the part played by soil invertebrates in the breakdown of leaf litter. State clearly what support your hypothesis is given by the results described earlier.

Soil organisms break down ~~leafs~~ leaves and the bigger the organisms allowed to enter the faster the material is broken down as shown by the mesh experiment.

(5 marks)

> **66** This answer *is* correct, though the hypothesis is rather limited, and insufficient reference is made to the available information. **99**

NISEC

(Total 16 marks)

ENVIRONMENT: BIOTIC FACTORS

GETTING STARTED

The study of the relationships between living organisms with their environment is called **ecology**. The environment consists of non-living (inorganic, physical) or **abiotic factors** and living (organic), **biotic factors**. Abiotic and biotic factors are components of **ecosystems**, which are 'ecological units' within the environment; ecosystems have characteristic abiotic and biotic features.

Biotic factors consist of all the organisms living within a **community**, i.e. within a *particular* ecosystem. Each organism is part of another organism's environment and they **interact** in various ways. For instance, interactions may involve - **competition** for resources such as food and space. Interactions between organisms are important in determining the relative **distribution** and **abundance** (numbers) of each type of organism.

Feeding relationships are very important within the communities of ecosystems. Plants use energy from the sun to make food; this is then available directly or indirectly for animals in a **food chain**. Different types of organism occupy a different position, or **trophic level**, within the food chain. Food chains and also food webs allow energy to *flow* from one trophic level to the next, whilst minerals are *recycled* within the eco-system. Energy is lost from organisms to the surrounding environment; energy is *not all* transferred from one trophic level to another. This results in a steady decrease in the numbers of organisms down a food chain.

Humans are a particularly significant biotic factor in many ecosystems because they often have a powerful effect on eco-systems. Humans affect the environment through **agriculture**, **land clearance**, and by various forms of **pollution**. An increased awareness of the direct or indirect impact of humans on their environment has resulted in a greater emphasis on **conservation**. Conservation involves activities designed to maintain the natural environment in a relatively intact state.

ESSENTIAL PRINCIPLES

Biotic factors represent the living component of the environment. Organisms exist within ecosystems (see below) and they interact with each other in various complex ways. These **interactions** determine the relative **distribution** and **populations** of particular species. The continuing rise in **human populations** has resulted in an increased human impact on the environment.

1 > ECOSYSTEMS

An **ecosystem** is an 'ecological unit' which has characteristic features, determined by **abiotic** (non-living, Ch.16) and **biotic** factors. Ecosystems often have fairly obvious limits which separate them from neighbouring ecosystems. Examples of ecosystems include grassland, woodland, ponds, sand dunes, heathland, rocky shorelines, dry stone walls and compost heaps. Ecosystems show variations in size. However, generally they are fairly convenient to study because they are often associated with particular physical conditions and characteristic types of organisms.

Organisms exist on a global scale within a continuous **biosphere**, consisting of *terrestrial* (land) and *aquatic* (water) environments, together with the atmosphere. However, organisms tend to be *adapted* (Ch.9) to particular ecosystems within the biosphere, and therefore relatively little movement occurs from one type of ecosystem to another.

There are two main components of all ecosystems:

(i) Habitat. The abiotic (physical) environment (Ch.16) within which organisms live; that is, their 'address'.

(ii) Community. The collection of organisms within a *particular ecosystem*. The collection of organisms within a *particular species* (see Ch.4) is called a **population**. Organisms within a species often need a particular range of resources because they have a specific role, or niche, within the community.

Organisms are adapted through **evolution** to perform a particular range of activities within a certain type of ecosystem. This **niche** or 'occupation' of organisms means that, in general, they can exist in the same community with other organisms having a different niche. This is because organisms from different niches do not require exactly the same range of resources from the environment (Fig. 17.1).

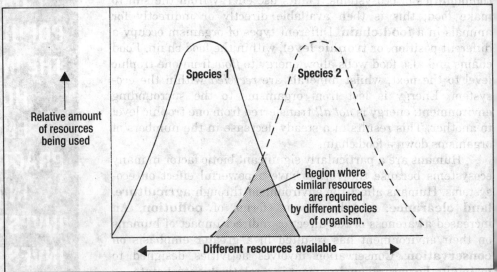

Fig.17.1 The niche concept

Communities become established within a habitat by a gradual process called **succession**. Succession occurs when different species enter and occupy a potential habitat; many organisms have a means of **dispersal** (Ch.14) which allows them to move into a new habitat. For example, newly cleared land tends to be **colonized** by certain plants, for example, rosebay willowherb (*Epilobium*), which have very good powers of dispersal and whose seeds can rapidly germinate on newly available land. These plants stabilise the soil, release nutrients through nutrient cycling (Ch.16) and provide food and shelter for small animals. Each organism in some way modifies its environment, resulting in a gradually changing habitat; species which are adapted to the changed conditions can then occupy vacant niches.

Succession results in a gradual increase in the numbers of organisms and also in the number of different species; this adds to the **diversity** of the ecosystem. A *maximum* diversity is reached when all available niches are occupied. This is called a **climax community** (Fig. 17.2) and is likely to be quite a stable ecosystem.

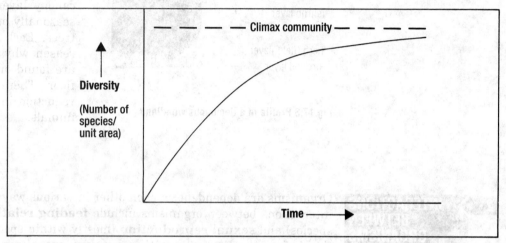

Fig.17.2 The effect of succession on species diversity

For *terrestrial* (land) ecosystems the climax community is forest or woodland. This sort of ecosystem can often support more species (several thousands) than any other. The climax community can only develop if abiotic and biotic conditions are suitable. For example, lack of sufficient water (an abiotic condition) is an important factor in preventing a desert gradually becoming a rainforest. Grazing (a biotic condition) may prevent grassland eventually becoming a deciduous woodland.

EXAMPLE OF AN ECOSYSTEM: A DECIDUOUS WOODLAND

The dominant species in a deciduous ('broad-leaved') woodland are trees such as oak (*Quercus*) and sycamore (*Acer*). They provide food and shelter for many other organisms, and they also have a significant effect on the abiotic environment (see Ch.16).

Plants in a deciduous woodland occupy distinct zones or **layers**, revealed in a **profile** ('cross section') of the wood (Fig. 17.3); this vertical arrangement of layers is called **stratification**.

There are *four* main plant components within the stratification:

(i) Tree layer (average height = 15 m)

The tree layer consists of large trees such as oak (*Quercus*), ash (*Fraxinus*) and beech (*Fagus*). The tree layer incudes a **canopy** of leaves which intercept a proportion of available light.

(ii) Shrub layer (average height = 5 m)

The shrub layer consists of bushes such as hazel (*Corylus*) and hawthorn (*Crataegus*), and also young trees.

(iii) Herb layer (field layer) (average height = 1 m)

The herb layer contains seedlings and straggling, non-woody (p..) plants such as bracken (*Pteridium*), bramble (*Rubus*), bluebell (*Endymion*).

(iv) Ground layer (average height = 0.02m)

This consists of low-lying plants such as moss and grass species. Each type of plant is adapted to its position within the woodland. The intensity and also the quality of light entering the woodland is changed as it passes through different layers (see

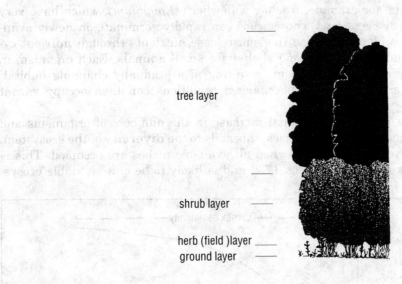

tree layer

shrub layer

herb (field) layer
ground layer

Fig.17.3 Profile of a deciduous woodland

Ch.16). This may affect **photosynthesis** and will prevent certain species growing under the canopy, whilst those that do grow are likely to be shade tolerant. Deciduous trees lose their leaves during autumn and this allows more light to penetrate into the woodland. Leaf fall also adds to the litter layer, which provides a source of nutrients in the soil. Coniferous (evergreen) trees form a relatively dense canopy layer and leaves are not lost seasonally as they are from deciduous trees. Lack of sufficient light is one reason why comparatively few plants are found on the coniferous woodland floor. There will be a corresponding reduction in the numbers and type of animals.

2 ▶ INTERACTIONS BETWEEN ORGANISMS

Organisms are dependent on each other in various ways for survival. Examples of interactions between organisms include **feeding relationships** (mostly between species) and **sexual reproduction** (mostly within species) (Ch.6). These interactions often involve **competition** between organisms living in the same community.

(a) FOOD CHAINS

Feeding relationships incorporate a transfer of **energy** and **nutrients** from one organism to another through a **food chain**. Each organism occupies a particular **trophic** (feeding) **level** within a food chain. The main trophic levels are:

(i) Producers

Producers are green plants. These can produce their own nutrients using the sun's energy, by photosynthesis. Photosynthesis basically involves the conversion by the green pigment **chlorophyll** of light energy from the sun into chemical energy. All organisms depend, directly or indirectly, on this process by which solar energy is made available. The sun is the ultimate source of energy for all food chains.

(ii) Primary (first level) consumers

Primary consumers are *herbivores*. These can eat plants directly. Plants are not a particularly concentrated source of protein and they contain a large proportion of cellulose (Ch.4), which is difficult to digest. For these reasons herbivores may spend a relatively large proportion of their time eating. Some other adaptations to herbivorous feeding are described in Ch.15.

(iii) Secondary (second level) consumers

Secondary consumers are *carnivores which mostly eat herbivores*. Meat is a fairly concentrated source of protein, so carnivores may eat fairly infrequently. Other adaptations to carnivorous feeding are described in below.

(iv) Tertiary (third level) consumers

Tertiary consumers are *carnivores* (sometimes called 'top carnivores') *which mostly eat other carnivores*.

An additional **quarternary** (fourth level) consumer group may be present in some food chains.

Omnivores consume a mixed diet of plants and animals and so are both primary and secondary consumers; in other words, they occupy more than one trophic level. **Parasites** (see below) may be primary, secondary or tertiary consumers, depending on the sort of host that they derive their nutrition from.

Producer	Primary consumer	Secondary consumer	Tertiary consumer
Oak (leaves)	→ Caterpillar	→ Shrew	→ Owl
(*Quercus*)	(*Pieris*)	(*Sorex*)	(*Strix*)

Fig.17.4 Example of a food chain (arrows represent the direction of energy and nutrient flow)

Organisms from different trophic groups are linked together in **food chains** (Fig. 17.4). When one organism is consumed by another, there is a transfer of energy; energy '*flows*' down a food chain. The only energy which can be transferred from an organism is chemical energy contained within the organism's tissues. This is always a small proportion (perhaps 10 per cent) of the energy originally consumed by the organism. Energy is lost from organisms by processes such as **respiration** , **excretion** , **egestion** and **heat loss**. This energy loss occurs at each trophic level (Fig 17.5) and is the reason why food chains do not usually contain more than five trophic levels.

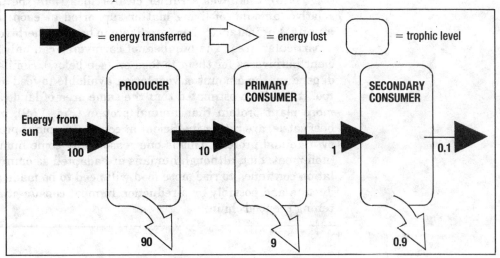

Fig.17.5 Energy flow in a food chain (The figures indicate the relative amounts of energy at each stage in the food chain)

(b) ECOLOGICAL PYRAMIDS

The loss of energy from a food chain means that there is progressively *less energy* available for organisms further 'down' the food chain. For this reason, there is often a *decrease* in numbers of organisms at each successive trophic level. This can be shown in a **pyramid of numbers** (Fig. 17.6), which shows the relative number of organisms in each trophic group. There is often an increase in *size* of organisms in each successive trophic level. However, pyramids of numbers can be misleading in some cases, for instance, where one relatively large organism supports many other organisms. For example, one oak tree is likely to provide food for many thousands of caterpillars; this sort of situation causes a 'partial inversion' of the pyramid of numbers (Fig. 17.7).

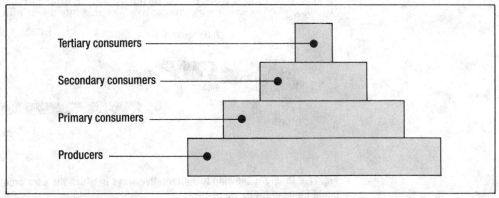

Fig.17.6 Pyramid of numbers

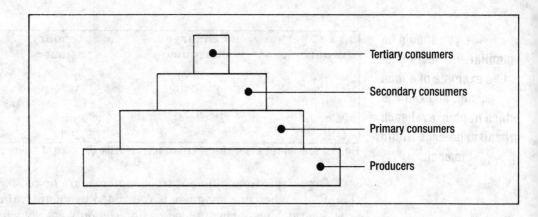

Fig.17.7 Example of a pyramid of numbers

The **biomass**, or total mass of organisms in a population, decreases in a progressive way 'down' the food chain. This can be shown in a **pyramid of biomass** (Fig. 17.8); this gives a rather clearer idea than the pyramid of numbers of the relative 'amount' of living matter supported at each trophic level within a community. For instance, there are likely to be more herbivores than carnivores within a particular area. The numbers of carnivores can only increase if there are sufficient herbivores for them to feed on (see below). Similarly, herbivore populations depend on the amount of vegetation available to feed on. This applies to humans, too. It has been estimated that the same area of land can provide about ten times more plant protein than animal protein (Fig. 17.9); many herbivores, including beef cattle, are rather inefficient at converting plant protein in their diet into their own animal protein. This is one reason why some humans consume a vegetarian (non-meat) diet, although humans are adapted as omnivores. As the human population continues to rise more food will need to be made available by increased production and possibly by a reduction in meat consumption, in other words by shortening the food chain.

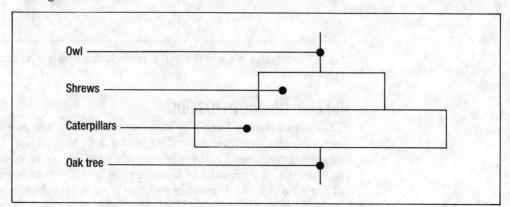

Fig.17.8 Pyramid of a biomass

The original examination question to which Fig.17.9 relates asked:
(a) Name *two* food substances in the corn which could be used by man.
(b) alternative *2* supports more people than alternative *1*.
(i) How much more efficient is alternative *2* than alternative *1*?
(ii) suggest *one* reason why alternative *1* represents a less efficient use of the cornfields.

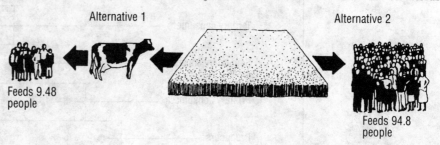

Fig.17.9 Diagram showing two alternative ways in which the corn produced by one hectare of land could be used (AEB, 1985)

Many individual food chains can be identified within the communities in an ecosystem. However, most consumers obtain their food from more than one type of organism, and many (such as the omnivores) obtain their food from more than one trophic level. For this reason, feeding relationships within communities can be quite complex, consisting of many interlinking food chains, making **food webs** (Fig. 17.10).

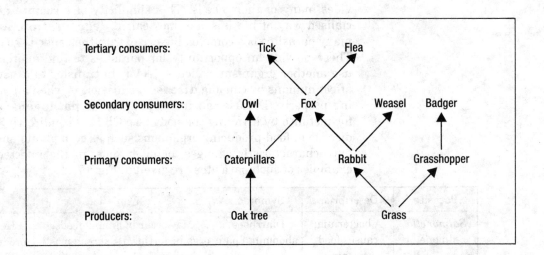

Fig.17.10 Example of a food web

(c) FOOD WEBS AND CYCLES

Energy passes from the sun and through food chains and webs in one direction (shown by the arrows in Fig. 17.4 and Fig. 17.10). Nutrients, unlike energy, can be *cycled* between organisms as **excreta** (urine, Ch.11) and **egesta** (faeces, Ch.15) and when organisms **die** and **decay**. Organic molecules (Ch.4) are broken down by **decomposers** into inorganic molecules, such as carbon dioxide and various minerals. These are then available to green plants which can use them to form organic molecules (see p..). The organic molecules may then provide nutrients for consumers to use directly or to re-form into their own organic molecules. Decomposers, which are **saprophytes** (see below), are essential to this cycling of nutrients, resulting in **food cycles**. Examples of food cycles include those involving carbon and nitrogen (Ch.16); these elements alternate between organic and inorganic forms.

(d) TYPES OF FEEDING RELATIONSHIPS

Feeding interactions between organisms within a community can be quite specific, involving various adaptations (Ch.9) of one or both participants. Organisms which are highly adapted to a particular feeding relationship can generally obtain their food more efficiently than those which are not. However, a specialised method of feeding depends on particular types of organism being available for food. Examples of feeding interactions include **predator/prey**, **parasite/host**, **saprophytes**, and **symbionts**.

(i) Predators

Predators are adapted in various ways (see Ch.13) to hunt prey animals. Predators organise their activities around those of their prey, for instance by having similar breeding cycles and distribution. Predator and prey species may have a direct effect on each other's populations (see below).

(ii) Parasites

Parasites are organisms which obtain their nutrients and sometimes also protection from a close, often harmful relationship with their *host* organism. Parasites may be harmful because they deprive their host of food, or because they produce poisonous (toxic) wastes. There are various examples of both plant and animal parasites and also simpler organisms such as microbes. Parasites and their hosts are normally different species; parasites are often adapted to a single species of host. Parasites are usually smaller than their hosts. Some parasites, called **endoparasites**, live within their host, for example viruses, some bacteria, tapeworm (*Taenia*). Others, called **ectoparasites**, live on their host, for example aphid (*Aphis*), flea (*Spilopsyllus*). Some parasites, the **facultative parasites**, adopt a saprophytic type of feeding (see below) in the absence of a suitable host. Others, the **obligate parasites**, depend entirely on finding a suitable host.

Parasites typically have a relatively simple structure because their host provides many of their needs. This simplicity of structure arising from a very specialised way of life is sometimes called **degeneration**. Another characteristic of many parasites is a complex life cycle, with the capacity to produce many offspring. These provide an opportunity for parasites to find another host. Some parasites use another organism, called a vector, to transfer to a new host. Many parasites affect humans by causing **diseases**; a disease is when an organism is not functioning properly. Disease-causing organisms, or **pathogens**, affect humans directly, for instance by invading the body (see Ch.12) or indirectly, for example by causing disease in food-producing organisms such as crop plants and cattle. Pathogens produce characteristic changes, or symptoms, in the infected host organism. Some examples of such parasites are given in Fig. 17.11.

Parasite	Description	Symptoms	Transmission	Control
Salmonella Salmonella	A bacterium; causes food poisoning.	Diarrhoea, abdominal pain	May occur in animal feeds, organic fertilizers; spread mostly in uncooked or undercooked meats.	Health checks during food production; suitable storage of food; thorough cooking of food.
Vibrio cholerae: cholera	A bacterium living within the gut; produces toxins.	Severe diarrhoea	Carried from contaminated faeces directly by contact with food or water or by vectors such as flies.	Vaccination; antibodies, e.g. chloramphenicol
Herpes simplex	A virus living under the skin	Blisters; 'cold sore'	Direct contact with open blister	Drugs, e.g. idoxuridine
Phytophthora infestans: potato blight	A fungus which colonises potato plants.	Potato tubers are made 'mushy' and inedible.	Spores carried by wind from infected plants.	Destruction of diseased plants; use of fungicides; use of resistant varieties.

Fig.17.11 Examples of parasites affecting humans

> **you may need to revise the functions of the body's defence system at this stage**

Humans have a natural defence system which resists the entry of pathogens into the body and which can destroy many invading parasites. The defence system includes the skin (Ch.11) and white cells in the blood (Ch.12). Disease from pathogens can be be further reduced by the use of **drugs**, which destroy the parasites and relieve symptoms. Disease can also be controlled by various **hygiene** measures, including **vaccination** and the use of **antibiotics** (see Ch.12).

(iii) Saprophytes

Saprophytes obtain their food from dead and decaying organisms. They digest the food *externally* (Ch.15) by secreting enzymes; the soluble products of digestion can then be absorbed and used within the saprophyte tissues. Examples of saprophytes include fungi and bacteria. Saprophytes are very important as **decomposers** (Ch.16) in cycling nutrients within the ecosystem.

(iv) Symbionts

Symbionts are organisms which live in a close symbiotic relationship with other symbionts of a different species. The symbiotic relationship, or **symbiosis**, is beneficial for *both* participants; for this reason it is also called **mutualism**. Examples of symbiosis include lichens (fungi and algae symbionts), nitrogen-fixing bacteria with legume plants (Ch.16), gut bacteria and humans (Ch.15).

Relationships between organisms of different species range from symbiosis, where both benefit, to **parasitism**, where *one* benefits and the other may be harmed. 'Intermediate' relationships exist, sometimes called **commensalism**, where one organism derives some benefit and the other is not directly affected. In fact, the distinctions between symbiosis, parasitism and commensalism are sometimes difficult to make.

**POPULATIONS**   A **population** is a group of organisms of the *same species* in the *same place* at the *same time*. Populations change owing to the relative rates of **birth**, **death** and **migration**:

(a) BIRTH RATE (NATALITY)

This depends on the rate at which new individuals are added to a population by **reproduction** (Ch.6). The rate of reproduction within a species depends on various abiotic (Ch.16) and biotic factors. For instance, reproduction may be limited by a decrease in space or temperature (abiotic factors), or a decrease in food or the numbers of sexually mature individuals (biotic factors).

(b) DEATH RATE (MORTALITY)

This depends on the rate at which individuals are removed from the population by death. Death occurs in most organisms (see Ch.4), and may take place before or after an individual has been able to reproduce.

(c) MIGRATION

This is the movement of individuals from one population to another. Such movement, or **dispersion** (see Ch.14) may involve all of the organism (e.g. a migrating bird) or part of an organism (e.g. a seed, Ch.6). Migration may be temporary or permanent. There are two types of migration, **emigration** and **immigration**. Emigration is the *departure* of individuals from a population. Immigration is the *entry* of individuals into a population. Migration can be a rapid means of increasing or decreasing populations, for instance when there is a fairly sudden change in conditions within the environment.

A population may be established by immigration from a relatively small number of individuals (see Ch.6) and, if conditions are suitable and the organisms are adapted (Ch.9), there will be an increase in numbers. This process of **colonisation** may be very important in the early stages of **succession** (see above). The increase might be quite rapid initially and in most species then slows down and possibly decreases as conditions become less favourable. For instance, resources such as food and space will become limiting. This increase and subsequent decrease in numbers can be shown in a graph (Fig. 17.12). The shape of this graph is characteristic for most species.

> ❝this graph fror population growth is very similar to that for individual growth in many organisms (see Ch.7)❞

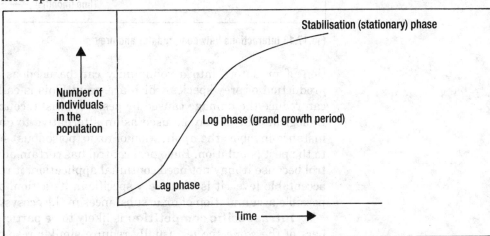

Fig.17.12 Typical population graph

The shape of the graph is known as *sigmoid* ('S'– shaped) and consists of three phases:

(i) Lag phase

This occurs when individuals may be emerging from dormancy (Ch.6) or adjusting to their new environment.

(ii) Log phase

This is a period of very rapid increase in numbers. The log (logarithmic, exponential) phase continues until resources become limiting.

(iii) Stabilisation

This takes place when the **limits** of the environment are reached; the population is maintained at a level which can just be supported by the environment. This may continue indefinitely in some populations; in others, there may be a decline in numbers if the log phase has exceeded the **carrying capacity** of the environment, or if conditions deteriorate.

Factors which are particularly significant in determining population growth are biotic factors such as **food supply**, **predation** and **disease**. In most species, population increase is self-regulated by density-dependent factors, caused by the individuals themselves. These factors may determine the relative rates of birth, death and migration.

(d) COMPETITION

Competition occurs between organisms when resources are limiting. There are two main types of competition; **interspecific competition**, between species, - **intraspecific competition**, within species.

Interspecific competition may result in populations affecting each other directly. This is particularly apparent in cases where there is a close feeding relationship, such as occurs between predator and prey animals. An example of this involves two species of mite; one pest species (*Eotetranychus*) is the prey to another species (*Typhlodromus*) which is its predator, and which can be used as a biological control. A graph (Fig. 17.13) showing the relative numbers of the two mite species strongly suggests that each population regulates the other. The artificial introduc-

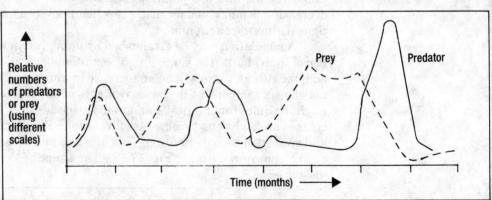

Fig.17.13 Interactions between predator and prey

tion of predators into a community can be used as a means of regulating the production of prey species which are pests. This is called **biological control** and can reduce the damage caused by pests, for instance to crops, to acceptable levels. Biological control may be used as an alternative to **chemical control**, which for instance involves the application of toxic (poisonous) substances, called pesticides, to the pest population. Biological control has certain advantages over chemical control because it may not need continual application, it regulates prey numbers at an acceptable level, it is often very specific in its action, and it does not result in the possible accumulation of toxic substances in the ecosystem.

Intraspecific competition is likely to be particularly intense because members of the *same species* usually require similar resources from the environment. Competition *within* a population can be an important process in evolution by natural selection (Ch.9).

(e) HUMAN POPULATIONS

Although there are national and regional differences, the world's population of humans continues to rise; it is currently in the log phase of very rapid increase (see Fig. 17.12). A stabilisation of global populations is not occurring, even though some vital resources may soon be limiting. About two-thirds of all humans do not receive sufficient food, and many die annually from starvation. Though this may currently be due to a poor distribution of the world's food, yet more food will need to be produced to meet future needs.

The continuing rise in human populations is a result of birth rate exceeding death rate. The distribution of age within a group of humans (Fig. 17.14) is significant for various reasons; for instance in determining what proportion of the population is likely to require additional social or medical support. The **life expectancy** of individuals in general has increased because improved standards of hygiene, diet, sanitation and medical facilities have reduced the death rate. However, in many areas of the world there has been no corresponding reduction in birth rates. One reason for this is that methods of **birth control** or contraception (Ch.6) are either not familiar or not acceptable in many cultures.

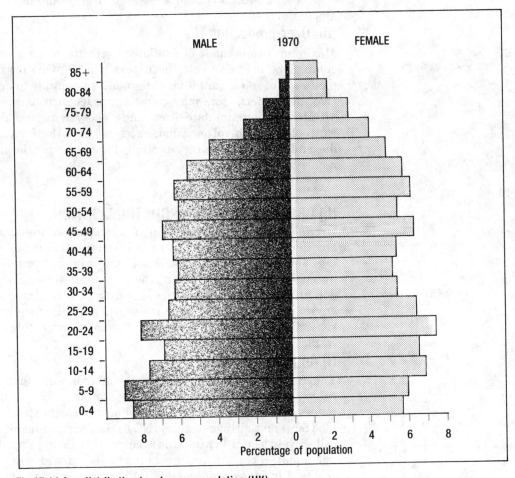

Fig.17.14 Age distribution in a human population (UK)

4 ▶ THE IMPACT OF HUMANS ON THE ENVIRONMENT

Humans can and do have a quite dramatic effect on their environment because of the increasing demands of a rapidly growing population (see above), and because of industrial and technological progress. There are three areas of activity where humans have had a significant effect on the environment; namely, agriculture, industrialisation and conservation.

❝this topic is given much emphasis in GCSE Biology ❞

(a) AGRICULTURE

A major purpose of agriculture is to produce food for human consumption. Both the efficiency and the intensity of food production are being continually increased to meet the demands of the human population. There are several environmental implications of this:

(i) Land clearance

Land is cleared for cultivation and for grazing; this reduces the number of potential habitats available. Tropical forests are cleared for timber and land use on a massive scale; this destroys important habitats and makes the soil unstable. In countries such as Britain, hedgerows are removed to allow an easier and more economic use of large farm machinery. This decreases the diversity of species and makes land more exposed and vulnerable to wind, which can blow away topsoil; this is called **erosion**.

(ii) Monoculture

Monoculture is the cultivation of a single species of crop on a particular area of land, for instance wheat (*Triticum*), barley (*Hordeum*). Monoculture is an 'artificial' situation because there will normally be a **succession** (see above) leading to a greater diversity of species. This is resisted in monoculture by the use of selective **herbicides** to prevent the growth of weeds, and **pesticides**, to remove insect and other pests. Mechanical processes such as ploughing often require a substantial amount of fuel.

(iii) Over-production

Maximum use is made of available agricultural land by intensive cultivation, including the use of nitrate **fertilisers** (Ch.16). One possible effect of this over-exploitation of soil is that it becomes more susceptible to **erosion** by wind and water. Over-use of fertilisers may cause minerals such as nitrates to be leached away; nitrates can accumulate in aquatic ecosystems, resulting in **eutrophication**. Eutrophication involves rapid, excessive growth of aquatic organisms which then die and decay; their decomposition lowers oxygen levels in the aquatic environment.

(b) URBANISATION AND INDUSTRIALISATION

Urban and industrial development often have a profound influence on the natural environment. Urbanisation and industrialisation include the construction of buildings and rail and road links. This requires land clearance and may be accompanied by an increase in **pollution**; the release of substances into the environment in potentially harmful quantities. Pollution can be described as the presence in the environment of substances in the wrong amount at the wrong place or at the wrong time. Pollution occurs in each of the three main types of habitat; air, land and water.

(i) Air pollution

This results from the burning (combustion) of fossil fuels such as coal, oil and natural gas. Combustion occurs in power stations, heavy industrial plants, vehicle engines and in domestic use. The products of combustion include lead, sulphur dioxide (SO_2) and nitrogen oxides (NO_x); sulphur and nitrogen oxides are often known collectively as **acid rain**. This is currently causing serious damage to crops, forests and aquatic ecosystems. One indirect effect of acid rain is to cause aluminium to be released in increased amounts into the environment and this is affecting various organisms, such as birds and fish. Air pollution also includes smoke particles, which may reduce photosynthesis in plants, and nuclear fallout, which may cause mutations (Ch.8) in organisms.

(ii) Land pollution

This results from the accumulation of industrial and urban waste, such as scrap metal and plastics.

(iii) Water pollution

This is caused by the addition of **effluents** (wastes) from three main sources; domestic, industrial and agricultural. Domestic pollution includes sewage; although this is often treated (by being filtered and oxidised), organic pollutants may be released in significant amounts. Industrial pollution includes toxic wastes which have not been adequately treated before release. Agricultural wastes include excess inorganic or organic fertilisers and pesticides. These may be washed off the land by leaching (Ch.16) and irrigation. Pesticides accumulate in the tissues of organisms, especially those towards the 'top' of food chains.

(b) CONSERVATION

Conservation involves active measures taken to offset the harmful effects of humans on their environment. Some conservation measures arise from political decisions taken at national or local levels, others result from the initiative of individuals or organisations who have a particular concern for the environment. Conservation measures include restrictions on the destruction of habitats, replanting of trees (**reafforestation**), limits on the release of pollutants. There has been an increased emphasis on recycling and, where possible, the use of - **renewable resources**. Conservation measures have also included the preservation of **sites of special scientific interest** and the development of nature reserves; this has been important in the improving the survival prospects of endangered species.

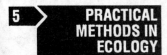

There are two main practical approaches in ecology, and they are often used together. **Qualitative methods** are a means of determining the presence or absence of particular abiotic and biotic factors in the environment. For instance, the composition of the habitat or community within a particular ecosystem can be fairly quickly assessed by **observation**. Also, organisms can be identified by using **identification keys** (Ch.5). **Quantitative methods** involve the **measurement** of abiotic and biotic factors and obtaining numerical information, or data. Since many ecosystems are too large and complex to make detailed measurements of, **random sampling** is used. The data obtained from random samples is likely to be fairly representative of the ecosystem, provided sufficient samples are taken.

METHODS OF SAMPLING

There are numerous methods of sampling the biotic environment, including **quadrats**, **transects** and **collecting**.

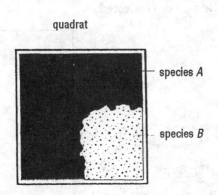

quadrat

species *A*

species *B*

Fig.17.15 Estimation of percentage cover

(i) Quadrats

Quadrats are square frames of a particular size which are placed on the surface being investigated, for example on a piece of grassland. Quadrats can be used, for instance, for percentage cover estimations; the area occupied by different species of vegetation can be estimated as a proportion of the total area (100 per cent) of the quadrat. In Fig. 17.15, species A occupies about 80 per cent, whilst species B occupies the remaining 20 per cent. This technique can be used to determine the relative amounts of species in different areas.

(ii) Transects

A transect is a line, for instance of string, between two poles, along which samples are taken at regular intervals. Sampling might involve taking a quadrat, a soil sample, or the relative height of ground or vegetation. The information obtained can be used to produce a **profile**; that is, an impression of changing abiotic or biotic conditions. A profile can be made of the changing distribution of plant and animal species at the boundaries of two ecosystems. For example, a rocky shore, the edge of a woodland or pond. In such situations, organisms frequently show **zonation**, a progressive change from one type to another. The profile can be represented using various graphs (Appendix 2).

(iii) Collecting

Animals are clearly more mobile than plants but their abundance and distribution can be estimated by collecting samples. Aquatic animals can be collected by using nets; land animals can be collected by using various traps, such as the pitfall trap (Fig. 17.16) (ground-living invertebrates) and the Tullgren funnel (soil organisms, Ch.16). Collecting of animals should be done, if at all, with great care to avoid disturbing communities and harming the animals. Animals can be collected, if possible counted and identified, and then released at the point of capture. With all organisms, particular care must be taken not to collect or disturb **endangered species**.

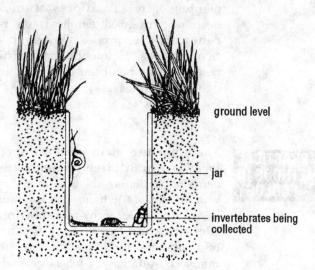

ground level

jar

invertebrates being collected

Fig.17.16 Pitfall trap

EXAMINATION QUESTIONS

QUESTION 1

The diagram below shows a section through a wood where two samples of animals, sample A and sample B, were collected.

Site of sample B

Site of sample A

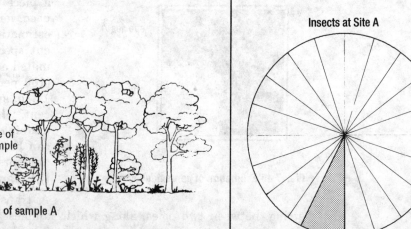

Insects at Site A

Ants

(a)   (i) Which animal was present in the largest number at site A? (1 line) **1 mark**

(ii) Which animal was present in the largest number in the combined samples, A and B? (1 line) **1 mark**

(b)   Complete the circle to form a pie-chart of the insects at site A. The circle has been divided into 20 equal parts. The sector for the ants has been completed on the pie-chart to help you. **3 marks**

(c)   From the numbers given in the table, which animal is likely to be a secondary consumer? (1 line) **1 mark**

(d)   Suggest *two* reasons why there are more snails in sample A than in sample B. (4 lines) **2 marks**
              Total 8 marks (LEAG)

	*Number of animals	
Animal	Sample A	Sample B
Snails	40	3
Mites	150	30
Spiders	10	40
True worms	10	0
Centipedes	5	1
Insects – Ants	30	5
– Springtails	140	65
– Aphids	70	100
– Midges	110	20
– Beetles	50	10

QUESTION 2

The diagram below shows a food web for a wood.

(a)   (i) What kind of organisms would be in box A? (1 line) **1 mark**

*Numbers simplified from actual data

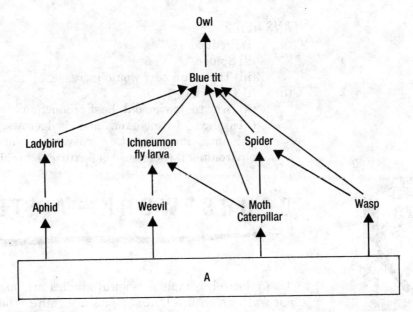

(ii) Name *one* secondary consumer shown in this food web. (1 line) **1 mark**

(iii) If all the ladybirds died, explain what might happen to the number of aphids. (3 lines) **2 marks**

(b)   Energy comes into the food web at A.

(i) Where does this energy come from? (1 line) **1 mark**

(ii) How do the animals in this food web use this energy? (2 lines) **2 marks**

(c)   Give examples of ways in which the activities of people damage or destroy natural habitats. (7 lines) **5 marks**

              Total 12 marks (LEAG)

OUTLINE ANSWERS

ANSWER 1

(a)   (i) Mites

(ii) Springtails

(b)

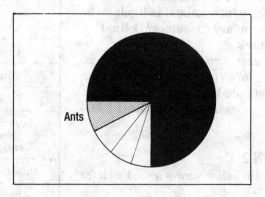

Ants

(c)   Centipede
(d)   More food, less predators

ANSWER 2

(a)   (i) Producers
       (ii) Spider,
       (iii) Their numbers would increase.
(b)   (i) The sun
       (ii) Growth, movement, heat production
(c)   Clearance of woodland and hedgerows, drainage of ponds, release of
       effluents into aquatic ecosystems, accumulation of wastes in the
       environment, excess use of fertilizers, herbicides and pesticides.

COURSEWORK – A STEP FURTHER

Two relatively simple ecological studies are suggested. Care should be taken in
each case to ensure that samples are both random and sufficient in number. The
investigation should be concisely and clearly written up and any data should be
suitably presented (Appendix 2).

1 ⟩ INVESTIGATION 1

THE EFFECT OF TRAMPLING ON VEGETATION

The percentage cover of vegetation across a footpath can be estimated using a
quadrat; quadrats can be easily made by bending wire (e.g. from a coathanger) into
a square of 20 x 20 cm.). The quadrat should be placed randomly on one side of the
path; a suitable way of doing this should be decided. Once the first estimates are
made and the results are recorded, the quadrat can be turned over on its edge
twice, towards the other side of the path; the cover is again estimated. This procedure is repeated until the other side of the path is reached. Common species of
vegetation in the UK, depending on the time of year, might be clover (*Trifolium*),
yarrow (*Achillea*), plantain (*Plantago*), buttercup (*Ranunculus*) and various grass
species. There may also be bare ground. A kite diagram (Appendix 2) can be drawn
of the results. The profile may reveal that certain plant species are more resistant
to trampling than others.

2 ▸ **INVESTIGATION 2**

THE DISTRIBUTION OF GROUND INVERTEBRATES IN DIFFERENT HABITATS

Certain ground-living invertebrate animals can be studied by setting up pitfall traps in different habitats, such as on grassland and in woodland. The pitfall trap consists of a jam jar or similar sunk into the ground (see Fig. 17.16) so that insects fall into the trap. Insects can be prevented from escaping by placing a small amount of detergent in the jar, though this is likely to kill them. Pitfall traps can be placed in different locations; care should be taken to avoid damaging any habitat however. The relative number of different types of invertebrates (Ch.5) can be determined over a certain time period, for *each location*. The results could be displayed as a frequency graph or pie diagram (see Appendix 2).

3 ▸ **SOURCES OF INFORMATION**

For further information on biotic factors in the environment, see for example those titles listed at the end of Ch.16.

Further information concerning the effects of humans on their environment can be obtained from:

Department of the Environment
Room P1/003
2 Marsham Street
London WC1P 3EP
Tel: 01-212-3434

National Society for Clean Air
136 North Street
Brighton BN1 1RG
Tel: 0273-26313

Greenpeace Environmental Trust
30-31 Islington Green
London N1 8XE
Tel.: 01-354 5100

Friends of the Earth
26-28 Underwood Street
London N1 7JQ
Tel.: 01-490 1555

STUDENT'S ANSWER – EXAMINER'S COMMENTS

(a) Describe how energy enters, passes through and is lost from a woodland ecosystem
(10 marks)

Energy enters a wood in the form of solar energy. It is converted to chemical energy by producers (green plants) during photosynthesis, and is then stored as the organic molecules that make up the structure of the plant. When a producer is eaten by a primary consumer (a herbivore eg rabbit), this energy is passed on again, in this case it will mostly be stored a glycogen. The chain continues as a secondary consumer (a carnivore eg stoat) eats the primary consumer. The secondary consumer might then have to give up this energy as it eaten by a tertiary consumer (eg fox) In this way energy passes through a woodland ecosystem;

> 66 **This is an excellent description of energy flow.** 99

> 66 **This is just one of many ways in which energy is available to a consumer; fats and even proteins are important, too.** 99

Flow diagrams like this can be a very effective part of an answer.

solar energy → producer eg grass → primary consumer eg rabbit → secondary consumer eg stoat → tertiary consumer eg fox

Good; this is a very important point.

Other processes such as excretion, egestion, death and decomposition should also be referred to.

Some energy however is lost as heat through respiration (ie for bodily processes eg digestion, movement ~~is~~ in obtaining more food). Because of this there can never be more energy passed on as there was gained and so energy is slowly lost.

(*b*) Why are woodland ecosystems being lost? What measures can be taken to conserve them?

(*4 marks*)

Air pollution is a factor in the decline of some woodlands.

It is important to refer to clearance of trees for *urban development*.

Woodland ecosystems are being lost through damage caused by pollution, erosion and by too many trees being cut down for things like paper and fuel.

In order to conserve them we must try to rearrange our lives in a more thoughtful way to the world we live in. By using unleaded petrol, by trying to clean the gases produced as waste industrially and by using water as power (eg for generating electricity). We can cut down drastically on the poisons we allow to fill the atmosphere. Simple things like recycling paper or by using methane as a fuel for Third World countries. We can stop the number of trees that are unnecessarily being cut down. As well as doing these things it would help if we replaced what we take away by planting more trees and also by using biological methods of controlling pests (eg by introducing predators) instead of using chemicals that are hard to breakdown and produce poisonous oxides that kill off many other things as well as the pests.

Conservation *does* require an understanding and awareness of ecosystems.

There are some good general points here, but the answer seems to refer more to large rain forests than woodlands.

This is a good point to make.

The student has not explained the particular effect of this on *woodland* ecosystems.

LEAG

(*Total 14 marks*)

PRACTICE EXAMINATION QUESTIONS

QUESTION 1 (see Ch.4)

(a)   Compare, by means of concise statements, the following terms:
(i) diffusion
(ii) osmosis
(iii) active uptake **9 marks**

(b)   It is biologically important that certain substances enter or leave organisms through the following structures. Explain what the substances are, why they enter or leave and how the structures are adapted to the purposes they fulfil:
(i) root hairs
(ii) leaves
(iii) villi **11 marks**

Total 20 marks (MEG)

QUESTION 2 (see Ch.4)

Fig. 18.1 below shows an animal cell, such as a cheek cell.

(a)   (i) Name the part labelled Q. (1 line) **1 mark**
(ii) Name the part labelled R which is the site of genetic material. (1 line) **1 mark**

(b)   On Fig. 18.1, draw in and label three extra structures that would change this animal cell into a diagram of a typical, green, plant cell. **3 marks**

(c)   (i) Name the process by which green plant cells produce a store of energy. (1 line) **1 mark**
(ii) Where does the energy come from? (1 line) **1 mark**
(iii) In what form is the energy stored? (1 line) **1 mark**

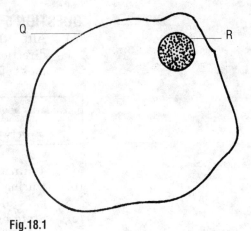

Fig.18.1

Total 8 marks (MEG)

QUESTION 3 (see Ch.5)

Fig. 18.2 shows three vertebrate animals. For each of the animals shown, answer the following questions.

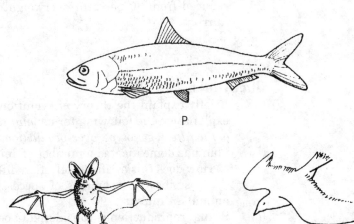

Fig.18.2

Total 8 marks (MEG)

QUESTION 3 (see Ch.5)

Fig. 18.2 shows three vertebrate animals. For each of the animals shown, answer the following questions.

(a) Name the main group to which each animal belongs. (3 lines) **3 marks**

(b) State *two* features, which can be seen in the diagram, which are characteristic of each group. (6 lines) **3 marks**

Total 6 marks (MEG)

Age in years	1	4	8	12	16
Mass (kg) Boys	10.0	16.5	27.5	38.0	69.0
Mass (kg) Girls	9.5	16.5	25.5	40.0	53.5

QUESTION 4 (see Ch.7)

Write a clear account of the mechanisms by which growth and development occurs in plants and animals.

Total 30 marks (MEG)

QUESTION 5 (see Ch.7)

(a) After the age of four years the masses of the two sexes take different directions. State TWO factors (other than sex) which could determine the mass of an individual. For each factor explain how it exerts its influence.

% deaths above normal	9	13	21	25	30	42
% overweight	10% W	10% M	20% W	20% M	30% W	30% M

4 marks

(b) During which period of four years does the greatest mass increase occur for boys and girls? (2 lines) **1 mark**

(c) State briefly the cause of this large increase in mass during this period of time. (4 lines) **2 marks**

(d) The following results were obtained when the relationship between human body weight and death rate was studied (W = woman; M = man).
What do these results indicate about the effect of overeating by
(i) both men and women? (1 line) **1 mark**
(ii) men compared with women? (1 line) **1 mark**
(iii) What is the decrease in the risk of dying from being overweight if a man reduced from 30 per cent overweight to 20 per cent overweight? (1 line) **1 mark**

Total 10 marks (MEG Human)

QUESTION 6 (see Ch.9)

(a) Briefly explain the theory of evolution by natural selection. Include in your explanation the following terms: *mutation, competition, inheritance, survival of the fittest, genotype, over-production.* **10 marks**

(b) Man has domesticated a number of animals and cultivated many plants.
(i) How does this artificial selection differ from natural selection? **2 marks**
(ii) Describe two examples of successful artificial selection in plants and animals. **4 marks**

(c) Sexual reproduction is considered to be essential if evolution is to take place, yet many higher plants reproduce asexually much of the time. Comment on this situation. **4 marks**

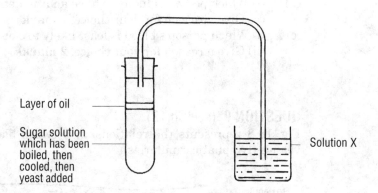

Fig.18.5

(a) Name the gas that would be given off by the yeast. (1 line) **1 mark**
(b) To confirm your answer to (a), what is solution X? (1 line) **1 mark**
(c) The experiment was repeated at 5°C intervals from 25°C to 65°C. The rate of respiration was measured by counting the number of bubbles of gas given off per minute. Using the axis provided, draw a graph to show the results you would expect. **2 marks**

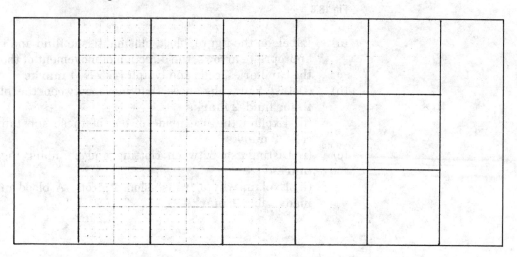

(d) Explain why your graph has this particular shape. **2 marks**
(e) (i) How would the amount of ATP produced by the respiration of the yeast compare under aerobic and anaerobic conditions? **2 marks**
(ii) How will this difference in ATP production affect the growth of the yeast? **3 marks**
(f) (i) Why are a yeast and a mould such as *Penicillium* both classified as fungi? **2 marks**
(ii) What is the principal difference between a yeast and a species of Penicillium? **1 mark**

Total 13 marks (MEG)

QUESTION 8 (see Ch.12)
Fig. 18.7 shows the composition of the blood of three people.

	Person A	Person B	Person C
Red cells/mm³	7 500 000	5 000 000	2 000 000
White cells/mm³	500	6000	5000
Platelets/mm³	250 000	255 000	500

Fig.18.7

(a) (i) Which person is most likely to live at high altitude? **1 mark**
(ii) Give a reason for your choice. **2 marks**

(b)   (i) Which person is likely to have an iron deficiency in their diet? **1 mark**
       (ii) Give a reason for your choice. **1 mark**
(c)   (i) Which person's blood is least likely to clot efficiently? **1 mark**
       (ii) Give a reason for your choice. **2 marks**

Total 9 marks (MEG)

QUESTION 9 (see Ch.12)

Fig. 18.8 represents the relationship between blood capillaries, cells and lymph vessels (lymphatic capillaries).

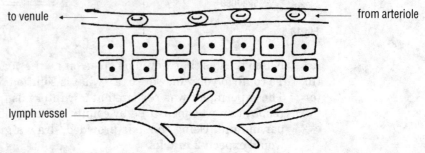

to venule   from arteriole

lymph vessel

Fig.18.8

(a)   Label, on the figure, blood plasma, tissue fluid and lymph and indicate, with appropriate arrows, the direction of movement of these fluids in and between the capillaries, cells and lymph vessels. **4 marks**
(b)   (i) List four substances that move between the blood capillaries and the tissue fluid. **2 marks**
       (ii) Explain the use made of *one* of these substances by the surrounding cells. **2 marks**
(c)   (i) Distinguish between clotting and clumping (agglutination) of blood. **2 marks**
       (ii) Explain why a transfusion of group A blood into a group B patient is inadvisable. **1 mark**

Total 11 marks (MEG)

QUESTION 10 (see Ch.13)

Fig. 18.9 is a diagram of a horizontal section through the eye. Suppose that a girl is looking at a fly on a book that she is reading.

(a)   Label in Fig. 18.9 with the letter X, the part of the eye containing muscles that focus light from the fly. **1 mark**
(b)   By means of an arrow, indicate on Fig. 18.9 indicate the position of the image of the fly. **1 mark**
(c)   Assume that the fly now flew off and landed on a wall and that the girl continued to watch it.
       (i) Draw on the diagram the shape of the lens focused on the fly on the wall. **1 mark**
       (ii) What brings about the change in the shape of the lens in (i)? (2 lines) **2 marks**

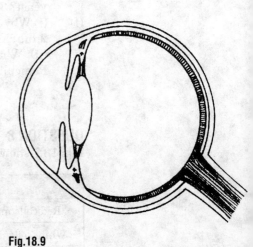

Fig.18.9

(d)   (i) Label with the letter Y the iris on the diagram above. **1 mark**
       (ii) Explain the effect of bright light on the iris of the eye. (4 lines) **2 marks**

Total 8 marks (MEG)

QUESTION 11

A pot of oat seedlings was treated as shown in Fig. 18.10 and then left in complete darkness for two hours. The result is shown in Fig. 18.10(b)

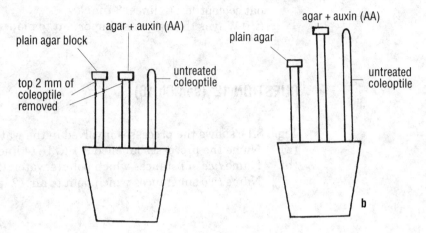

Fig.18.10

(a)   From the results in Fig. 18.10(b), what can you conclude about the effect of auxin (IAA) on the coleoptile? (3 lines) **1 mark**

(b)   Why did one decapitated coleoptile have a plain agar block added to it? (2 lines) **1 mark**

(c)   Where is auxin (IAA) made in the untreated coleoptile? (2 lines) **1 mark**

(d)   Suggest two reasons why the seedlings were left in complete darkness in this experiment. (2 lines) **2 marks**

(e)   A coleoptile tip was placed on two agar blocks, which were separated by a razor blade. It was illuminated from one side for two hours.

(i) Which agar block, *nearest to* or *furthest from*, the light source, would you expect to contain most auxin at the end of this two hour period? (1 line) **1mark**

(ii) Explain how this response to light brings about positive phototropism in oat coleoptiles. (3 lines) **3 marks**

(iii) Why is this response important to plants generally? (2 lines) **1 mark**

Total 10 marks (MEG)

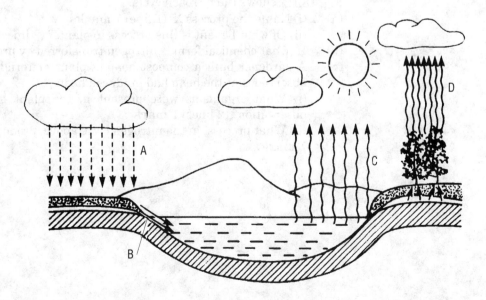

Fig.18.11

(i) Which agar block, *nearest to* or *furthest from*, the light source, would you expect to contain most auxin at the end of this two hour period? (1 line) **1 mark**

(ii) Explain how this response to light brings about positive phototropism in oat coleoptiles. (3 lines) **3 marks**

(iii) Why is this response important to plants generally? (2 lines) **1 mark**

Total 10 marks (MEG)

QUESTION 12 (see Ch.16)

Fig. 18.11 shows the processes involved in the water cycle.

(a)   Name the processes labelled A,B,C,D. (4 lines) **4 marks**

(b)   Name *two* substances which pollute water. (2 lines) **2 marks**

(c)   Name *two* substances which pollute air. (2 lines) **2 marks**

Total 8 marks (MEG)

QUESTION 13

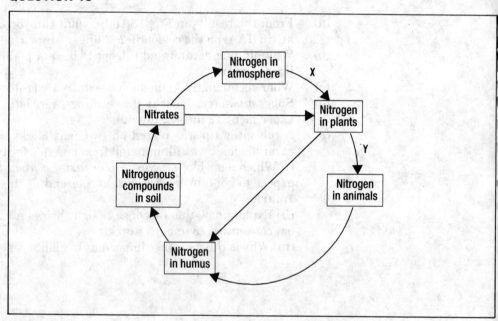

Fig.18.12

Fig. 18.12 shows the nitrogen cycle.

(a)   (i) Name the process X. (1 line) **1 marks**

(ii) Of what benefit is this process to plants? (2 lines) **1 mark**

(b)   In what chemical form is nitrogen transferred by process Y? (1 line) **1 mark**

(c)   A gardener built a compost heap of plant material. After several weeks he observed that the heap had produced heat.

(i) What organisms were present in the plant heap to account for this observation? (2 lines) **1 mark**

(ii) What process, in the nitrogen cycle above, produced the heat? (1 line) **1 mark.**

APPENDIX 1: SCIENTIFIC PRINCIPLES

Biology is not an isolated science. Many of the important ideas in this book can only be completely understood with an adequate background in chemistry, physics and mathematics; GCSE biology syllabuses (see Ch.3) specify what background understanding will be expected. The student is recommended to consult the books relating to these subject areas in the Revise Guides series. Presented below are some scientific principles which have been referred to in this book.

1 ⟩ CHEMISTRY

ATOMS, ELEMENTS, COMPOUNDS, MOLECULES AND IONS

Atoms are the components of all materials; they exist in nature as different elements. **Elements** are pure substances which cannot be further divided by chemical reaction. The biologically important elements are given in Fig.4.1 Different elements can often combine with each other to form compounds. **Compounds** are often chemically and physically very different from the elements that form them. A **molecule** is the smallest unit of a substance (element or compound) which retains the chemical and physical characteristics of the substance. The biologically-important molecules are describe in Ch.4. There are two main types of molecules. **Organic molecules** are relatively large and contain carbon. **Inorganic molecules** are relatively small and do not (except carbon dioxide) contain carbon.

Ions are electrically charged atoms or groups of atoms. All atoms include negatively charged electrons as part of their structure. If atoms lose electrons they become positively charged ions, or **cations**. Atoms which gain extra electrons become negatively charged ions, or **anions**. Though ions are very important in biology, an awareness of them only is required for GCSE biology.

SOLUTIONS

Many molecules can **dissolve** in various liquids to form solutions. The extent to which a substance dissolves in a particular liquid is known as its **solubility**. The substance which dissolves is known as a **solute**, and the liquid is known as the **solvent**. **Water** is effectively the only solvent found within organisms (Ch.4). When a substance dissolves it may **dissociate** to form ions, which can then take part in chemical reactions.

MOLES

A mole is really a unit of concentration of substances contained in gases and liquids. A mole of a particular substance is its 'molecular weight' in a given volume of gas or liquid, often expressed in terms of grammes per litre.

pH

pH is a measure of **hydrogen ion concentration** in solution. The pH scale operates from 0 to 14. Solutions which have a low pH (less than pH7) are more **acidic**. Solutions which have a high pH (more than pH7) are more **alkaline. Neutral** (pH7) solutions have an intermediate pH. The pH of a solution can be very important in biology, for instance in the functioning of **enzymes** (Ch.4).

CHEMICAL REACTIONS

Chemical reactions involve a chemical change occurring between different molecules. Chemical reactions within organisms take place in an *aqueous* (watery) solution; the reactant molecules are in solution. Many reactions within organisms are, at least in theory, reversible. Most biological reactions are controlled by enzymes

(Ch.4), which convert **substrate** molecules into **product** molecules. Enzymes are responsible for determining both the rate and the 'direction' of a particular reaction.

The general name for all chemical reactions within an organism is **metabolism.** . There are two types of metabolism; **catabolism** and **anabolism.** Catabolic reactions involve a breakdown of molecules, often releasing energy: $A{\rightarrow}B{+}C{+}energy$. Anabolic reactions involve building up, or synthesis, of molecules, often requiring energy: $energy{+}X{+}Y{\rightarrow}Z$.

2 ▷ PHYSICS

DIFFUSION

Diffusion is a *physical* process (Ch.4) which is essential for life. Molecules in a fluid (gas or liquid) which are free to move will tend to become distributed evenly throughout the available space. This movement is *random* and will occur most rapidly (i) at higher temperatures and (ii) down a 'steep' **concentration gradient** (Ch.4). The supply of materials by diffusion is, however, too slow for organisms over distances greater than 1 mm.

ENERGY

Energy is the capacity to do useful work. Organisms rely on a *flow* of energy to maintain their characteristics of life. Energy is mostly made available to organisms directly or indirectly from the sun. **Solar energy** is absorbed either as **light** or **heat**, depending on the wavelength. Organisms mostly use energy in a *chemical* form (Ch.10); when energy is converted from one form to another, some is always 'lost', often as **heat** energy. The units of energy are **joules (J)** and **kilojoules (kJ)**.

3 ▷ MATHEMATICS

Biology is becoming an increasingly mathematical science. An important use of mathematics is to deal with **data** (numbers) obtained from **quantitative** (measuring and counting) experiments.

EXPONENTIAL NUMBERS

An exponential increase in cells (Ch.4) and organisms (Ch.6) occurs when a repeated doubling takes place. This results in a very rapid increase in numbers. The sequence begins:

$1{\rightarrow}2{\rightarrow}4{\rightarrow}8{\rightarrow}16{\rightarrow}32{\rightarrow}64{\rightarrow}128..$

Note that each number after 2 is double the previous one and not simply the previous number multiplied by 2.

PERCENTAGES

A percentage is a proportion out of 100. One value is expressed as the percentage of another value by multiplying by 100 and dividing it by the other value. For example, finding the value 14 as a percentage of 52:

$$\frac{14 \times 100}{52} = 25 \text{ per cent}$$

AVERAGES

An average is simply a convenient means of summarising, in a single value, the **'central tendency'** of a group of values. There are different types of average; one of them, the **mean**, is often used in biology. The mean is determined by adding up all the values in the sample and then dividing the total by the number of values in the sample. For example, for the heights (in cm) of ten seedlings of the same age: 40, 54, 51, 38, 42, 47, 45, 50, 46, 47.

The total of these values = 460; the mean = 460÷10 = 46.

SURFACE AREA TO VOLUME RATIO

The relationship between surface area and size of cells and organisms is very important in biology. The *relative* size of a cell or organism surface area is an important factor in determining the rate of exchange of substances between the internal and external environment (for instance Ch.11). Surface area and volume can be compared as a ratio, called the **surface area/volume** (or **s.a./vol.**) **ratio**:

$$\frac{\text{surface area}}{\text{volume}}$$

The s.a./vol. ratio can most easily be compared in cube-type shapes (Fig. 19.1):

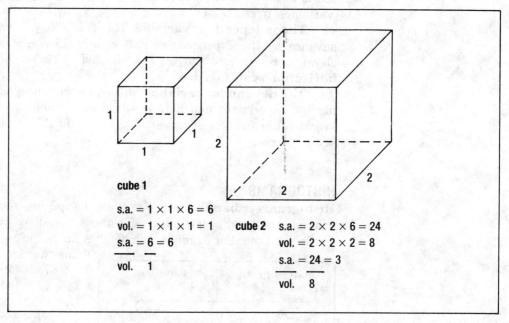

cube 1

s.a. = 1 × 1 × 6 = 6

vol. = 1 × 1 × 1 = 1

$$\frac{\text{s.a.}}{\text{vol.}} = \frac{6}{1} = 6$$

cube 2   s.a. = 2 × 2 × 6 = 24

vol. = 2 × 2 × 2 = 8

$$\frac{\text{s.a.}}{\text{vol.}} = \frac{24}{8} = 3$$

Fig.19.1

(a) **the effect of size on the s.a./vol. ratio** (the units for all dimensions are the same)

Cube 1 has a relatively large s.a./vol. ratio (= 6) compared with that of cube 2 (= 3). This means that substances would be exchanged more readily to and from cube 1, than from cube 2. For example, cube 1 would tend to gain or lose heat more rapidly than cube 2.

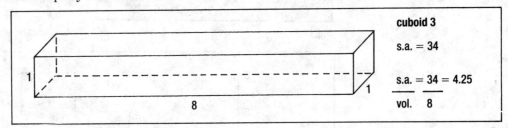

cuboid 3

s.a. = 34

$$\frac{\text{s.a.}}{\text{vol.}} = \frac{34}{8} = 4.25$$

(b) **the effect of shape on the s.a./vol. ratio**

Although cuboid 3 has the same volume as cube 2, its surface area is greater because of the 'flattened' shape.

APPENDIX 2: PRESENTATION OF DATA

Data, or groups of numbers, may not reveal an overall **pattern** or **tendency** unless they are suitably presented. Data can be **organised** into tables (this is sometimes called **tabulation**) and **displayed** in various types of **graph** or **diagram**.

Students are required both to be able to draw graphs from data and also to interpret information already displayed in this form. The main graphs used in biology at GCSE are the **line graph** and the **histogram**. **Pie diagrams** and **kite diagrams** are also used.

LINE GRAPHS

Line graphs are used for *continuous*, directly related data, for example (a) the increase in height of an individual (Ch.7) and (b) the average rate of photosynthesis in an aquatic plant (Ch.15). In these examples there are two sets of data (variables) in each case:

The independent variable. This is the 'known' variable. It is determined in advance by the experimenter and usually increases steadily. In the examples above, it is (a) *time* and (b) *light intensity*. These should be plotted along the **horizontal scale** (x-axis).

The dependent variable. This is the 'unknown' variable. It is produced during the experiment and may be quite changeable. In the examples above, it is *height* (a) or *bubbles of oxygen* (b). These should be plotted along the **vertical scale** (y-axis).

HISTOGRAMS

Histograms or **bar charts** are used for *discontinuous*, indirectly related data, for example the height distribution of different students within a certain class, at a particular time. For example, the heights (in cm) of twenty students in the same class were:

133, 122, 148, 126, 134, 125, 132, 146, 137, 141, 136, 130, 138, 140, 133, 137, 138, 143, 135, 142

These data can be arranged into height groups of suitable size; the number of values in each group is known as the **frequency**. The total frequency in this example should be 20 (see fig.19.3).

These data can now be arranged as a frequency histogram (Fig. 19.4), showing *frequency* (vertical scale) against *height groups*.

Height group (cm)	Frequency
120–124	1
125–129	2
130–134	5
135–139	6
140–144	4
145–149	2
	Total = 20

Fig.19.3

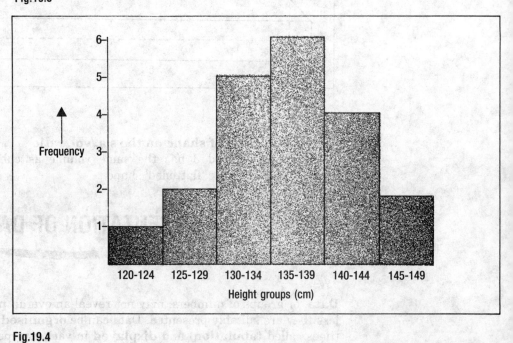

Fig.19.4

PIE DIAGRAMS

Pie diagrams consist of a circle divided into sectors representing a proportion of the total of 360 degrees (see Ch.16 for an example of this). The degrees in each sector are determined by the formula:

$$\frac{\text{quantity} \times 360}{\text{total quantity}}$$

KITE DIAGRAMS

A kite diagram is a suitable way of showing continuously varying values, for instance of the percentage cover of a plant species along a **profile** (Ch.17). The kite diagram is drawn using a 0 to 50 per cent scale on either side of a base line. Each percentage value is really represented in two halves, resulting in a **symmetrical pattern** (Fig. 19.5).

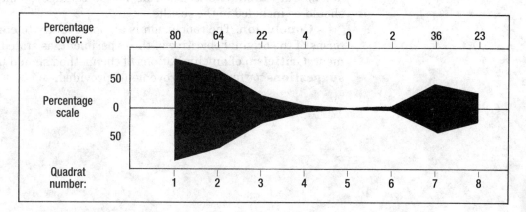

Fig.19.5 Kite diagram showing the distribution of clover (*Trifolium*) across a path

APPENDIX 3: EXPERIMENTAL DESIGN

1 ▷ PRINCIPLES OF DESIGN

One important feature of any experimental design is **clarity**. The purpose of the experiment must be clear. The most effective experiments are often those with quite limited and relatively simple objectives. Experiments in biology are commonly designed to investigate the *effect of one factor on another*; during the experiment, it is important that all other factors be kept as constant as possible. It is worth noting that organisms show enormous variation (Ch.8), and the behaviour of any living material in an experiment should be regarded with suspicion! This unreliability can be avoided if enough care is taken. For example, if the effect of water loss from different leaf surfaces was being investigated (see Ch.12), leaves of the same size and species should be used; care should be taken that other conditions, such as temperature, light and air movements are the same for each part of the experiment. It is still possible that results obtained from the experiment are caused by factors other than those being investigated. For this reason, **controls** are often used in biology. A control is a duplicate experiment in every respect except for that being investigated. A suitable control for the experiment above might be a leaf whose petiole is coated with petroleum jelly. A further precaution is the use of **repeat experiments**, perhaps using **sampling** techniques (Ch.17). Repeat experiments should produce similar results; in any case, **averages** (Appendix 1) can be calculated.

2 ▷ WRITING UP AN EXPERIMENT

It is important that a written account of an experiment be well-organised. A common format is **introduction**, **method**, **results**, **conclusion**, though there are several variations of this. The written account should be written in the past tense, in an impersonal style; i.e. 'the leaf was then cut' rather than 'next I cut the leaf' or 'you then cut the leaf'. This style of **scientific writing** may require practice. An account of an experiment might include the following components:

Title. The title should be clearly stated; for instance, 'Experiment to investigate the relative loss of water from upper and lower leaf surfaces'.

Introduction. The introduction is an opportunity briefly to expand on the **objective** of the experiment as stated in the title. It may be worth referring to any **theoretical assumptions** being made during the experiment, e.g. that loss in mass of leaves is caused by loss of water.

Method. The method should be briefly explained, emphasising any important techniques being used. A large, clearly labelled **diagram** is often preferable to much writing.

Results. The outcome of the experiment should be summarised in the results. This might include **observations** as well as **data**. The data should be organised into **tables**, and presented if possible as **graphs** or **diagrams** (Appendix 2). All **calculations**, such as for percentage or mean values (Appendix 1) should be included in the results.

Conclusion. The conclusion is an opportunity to **comment** on the results in terms of the original objective of the experiment, as stated in the title of the experiment. **Criticism** of any limitations of the method should be made if necessary, and **suggestions** for further improvements provided.

INDEX

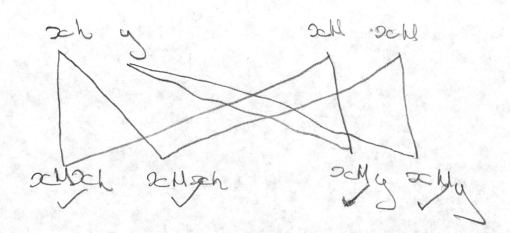

xy   x=H
      x=h

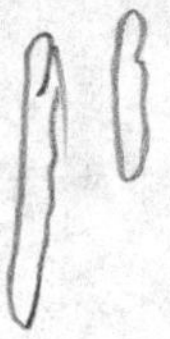

xx   x=HH
      x=Hh
      x=hH   haamophilia
      x=hh

      x=
      y

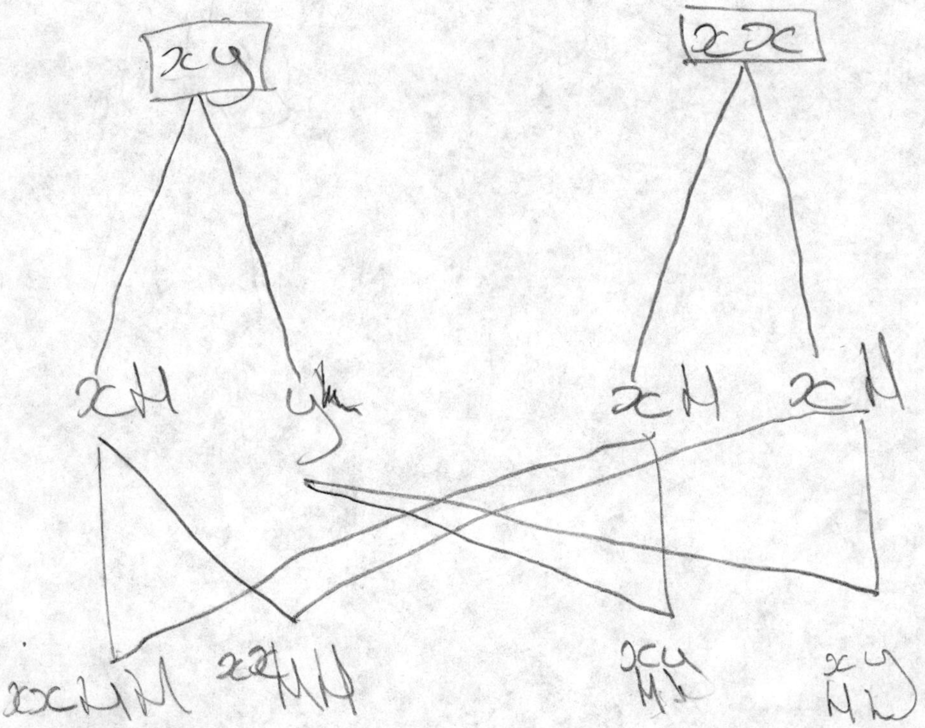

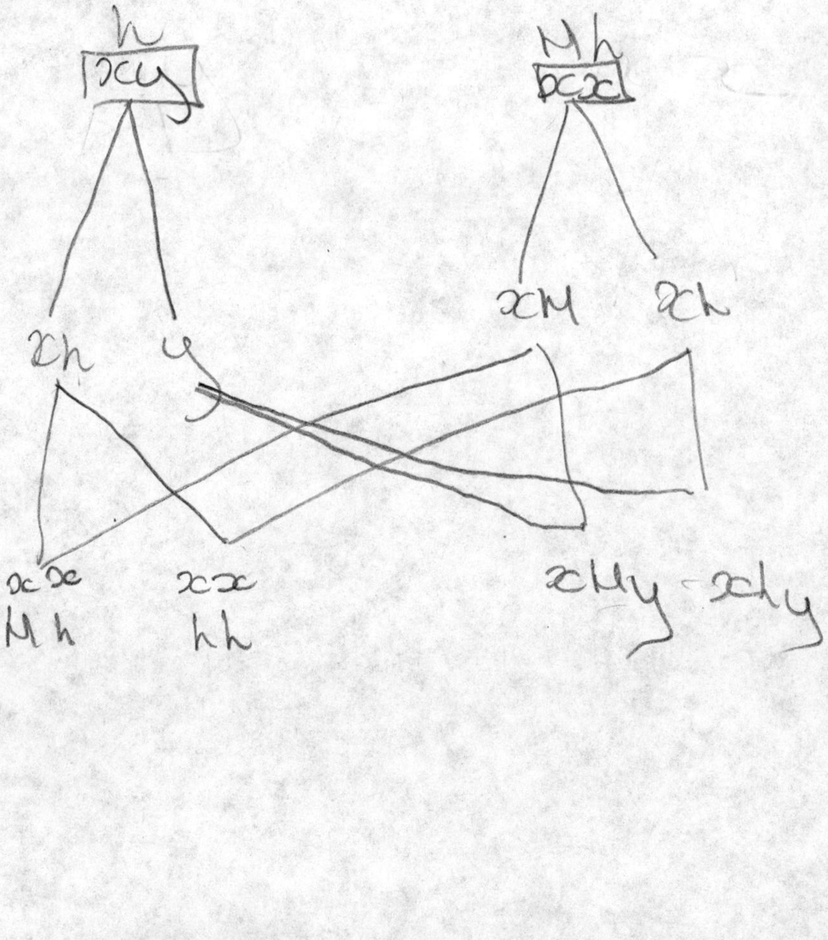

| xy |

xH   yh

xxHM   xxHH

| xx |

xH   xH

xy   xy
MM   Mh

h
| xy |

xh   y

xx   xx
Mh   hh

Mh
| xx |

xM   xh

xh   y

xMy   xhy